T0127731

footprints

michelle mercer

footprints

The Life and Work of Wayne Shorter

Jeremy P. Tarcher/Penguin
a member of Penguin Group (USA) Inc.
New York

JEREMY P. TARCHER/PENGUIN
Published by the Penguin Group
Penguin Group (USA) Inc., 375 Hudson Street, New York, New York 10014, USA ∘
Penguin Group (Canada), 90 Eglinton Avenue East, Suite 700, Toronto, Ontario M4P 2Y3,
Canada (a division of Pearson Penguin Canada Inc.) ∘ Penguin Books Ltd, 80 Strand, London
WC2R 0RL, England ∘ Penguin Ireland, 25 St Stephen's Green, Dublin 2, Ireland (a division
of Penguin Books Ltd) ∘ Penguin Group (Australia), 250 Camberwell Road, Camberwell,
Victoria 3124, Australia (a division of Pearson Australia Group Pty Ltd) ∘ Penguin Books
India Pvt Ltd, 11 Community Centre, Panchsheel Park, New Delhi–110 017, India ∘ Penguin
Group (NZ), 67 Apollo Drive, Mairangi Bay, Auckland 1311, New Zealand (a division of
Pearson New Zealand Ltd) ∘ Penguin Books (South Africa) (Pty) Ltd, 24 Sturdee Avenue,
Rosebank, Johannesburg 2196, South Africa

Penguin Books Ltd, Registered Offices: 80 Strand, London WC2R 0RL, England

First trade paperback edition 2007

The Library of Congress catalogued the hardcover edition as follows:

Mercer, Michelle, date.
   Footprints: the life and work of Wayne Shorter / Michelle Mercer.
      p.   cm.
   Includes bibliographical references (p.   ) and index.
   ISBN 1-58542-353-X
      1. Shorter, Wayne.   2. Saxophonists—Biography.   3. Jazz musicians—Biography.   I. Title.
   ML419.S55M47   2004   2004058845
   788.7'165'092—dc22
   [B]

ISBN 978-1-58542-468-9 (paperback edition)

BOOK DESIGN BY AMANDA DEWEY

While the author has made every effort to provide accurate telephone numbers and
Internet addresses at the time of publication, neither the publisher nor the author assumes
any responsibility for errors, or for changes that occur after publication. Further, the
publisher does not have any control over and does not assume any responsibility for
author or third-party websites or their content.

This book is dedicated to everyone who reads it.

FOOTPRINTS WAYNE SHORTER

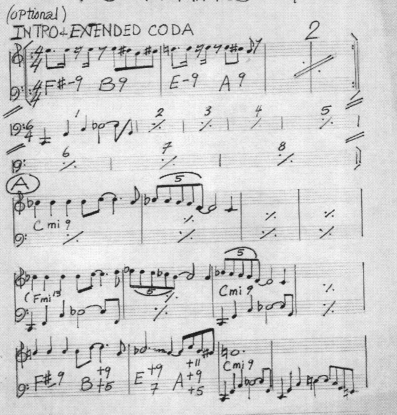

Contents

Foreword

A FEW MONTHS AGO, Wayne Shorter and I were being interviewed after performing in a quartet at the Newport Jazz Festival. Before any questions were asked, the interviewer remarked that in previous interviews, responses from Wayne "tripped him out" so much that he would be discovering new meanings in Wayne's words for several days. He said it wasn't just what Wayne said but how he said it that did the trick and that he was looking forward to another mind-blowing experience.

Even though I was the other interviewee, I was also looking forward to Wayne's profoundly creative and thought-provoking reactions to the questions. Reactions, not just answers, that are chock-full of wisdom. In his jovial way, and with an innately uncanny sense, Wayne says what a person needs to hear in order to expand himself. No, it's even better than that. It's more like, you feel that Wayne has gleaned deeper meaning from a question by using it as a springboard for an answer that will knock your socks off and perhaps change your life for the better. As a matter of fact, you might start to think, *Wow, I didn't know my question had so much in it.*

Wayne is a transformer. He exudes such honesty, purity, trust, and respect for others that he can transform, elevate, and awaken your life while you're both having fun. Wayne transforms people, all right, and he gets better and better at it. It's as though he's aware that it's safe to be honest, pure, and trusting. It's a source of light. He sees that inside everyone, and wants to let that light reveal itself in others. He takes you outside the box and into expanded possibilities.

You wonder why Wayne looks and acts so much younger than his years? Well, he feels joy in that world of infinite possibilities. According to Wayne, obstacles are opportunities, and believe me, he has experienced many tragic ones. Shouldn't we all develop the courage to transform our viewpoint in this way?

I'd bet that he has transformed Michelle Mercer, the author of this biography. What has she been transformed into, you ask? Perhaps she has become more herself through her encounters with Wayne. You see, it's not just his music, it's his life force that comes shining through in this book and everything about him, which *includes* his music.

I listen to what Wayne says now like I used to listen to the great Miles Davis. None of their words is wasted; none of their notes is wasted, either. It's up to me, and up to you, to discover the hidden gems inside them. Read on, and embrace the opportunity to know more about this great human being whom I've had the honor to know for more than forty years and whom I consider my best friend. I think you'll be transformed, too.

Herbie Hancock
September 2004

In response to an aspiring young actor's comment that his profession was just another job, actress Beah Richards, who played the part of Sidney Poitier's mother in the movie *Guess Who's Coming to Dinner,* gave the young novice something to ponder. She said something to this effect: "Acting is not just a job, because the whole world is waiting to hear your story!"

Personal stories—with many kinds of circumstances—are being recounted all the time to reveal who we are in the face of obstacles and challenges. With this in mind, Michelle Mercer has captured the essence of my story unedited. She did not attempt to dramatize my life based on professional achievements and fame; instead, she did the kind of research that would be true to the realities we all encounter in life's endeavor (a baseball player's baseball story alone does not sufficiently constitute his *life* story).

Music happens to be one of many vehicles commandeered through the journey of life, which suggests that it is merely a limited segment of *my* life that music occupies. Noble human behavior may remain dormant unless "awakened" due to trials and tribulations.

Ms. Mercer deftly accomplished the act of not reducing this biographical treatment to a type of classroom text on the dos and don'ts of a musical career. Moreover, she made a point of connecting seemingly divergent facets of my life to the "eternal journey" of the human condition.

Wayne Shorter
August 2004

Introduction:
Face of the Deep

ON AUGUST 25, 1991, Wayne Shorter's fifty-eighth birthday, he went to see his former bandleader Miles Davis perform at the Hollywood Bowl in Los Angeles. When Wayne went backstage to say hello to Miles, the trumpeter asked everyone else to leave his dressing room. Miles went over and stood directly in front of Wayne, placed his hands on Wayne's shoulders, and talked about something he almost never did: music. At the end of the conversation, he gave Wayne a mission. "You know, you need to be more exposed," the trumpet legend said emphatically, looking deeply into Wayne's eyes. These were his final words to Wayne; Miles died a few weeks later.

Miles knew that Wayne's genius was underestimated. For so many years he was a sideman who had a subtle, almost subversive influence on music. Wayne took Miles's advice to heart, and after emerging as the leader of the dynamic Wayne Shorter Quartet in 2001, he did finally gain some recognition for his musical gifts. By 2003, *The New York Times* was naming him "jazz's all-around genius, matchless in his field as a composer, utterly original as an improviser." But Wayne's obscurity was also the product of his self-effacing and strange personality. He says his lifelong challenge has been learning how to "speak up." When he does discuss his music in interviews, he usually frustrates expectations for direct answers and makes mind-boggling leaps of imagination. In the same breath he'll connect his work to an Arnold Schwarzenegger film and to the Buddhist philosophy that he's practiced for thirty years. As his friend and former bandmate Chick Corea says, "Wayne may be the one who invented the idea of thinking outside the box, 'cause I don't think he ever found the box."

Some people find Wayne's oblique and mystical comments in interviews to be precious, so it can be surprising to discover his basic friendliness. After a friend of mine met him, he said, "Wayne's really just a fun guy," as if he'd gotten past the moon-man posturing of his public persona. Wayne *is* fun and funny. His wit and wordplay are refined from forty years of road humor. On a recent tour, the subject of the Brazilian fascination for the *bunda,* or "backside," came up. Quick as a whip, Wayne joked, "They got what you call the two-car garage down there. Stacked out in back"—it was the beginning of an off-color riff that had the band tearing up with laughter.

But Wayne's jokes and cartoonlike imagery often serve more cosmic ruminations. Humor is a saving grace for him. In Seattle in October 2002, some music students had a brief Q&A with Wayne and his quartet. One student ingenuously asked him where he likes to play most: in auditoriums or clubs, in America or abroad? "It doesn't make any difference where we play," Wayne replied. "If you get fooled by those things, you'll have things controlled by your environment. You'll end up running away from your husband, trying to go to another place. And if you think you can ever really get to another place, you should know there's a little cat sitting on your suitcase swinging his tail, who's already got your trip planned out, and that cat's name is Karma."

In almost every interview with one of Wayne's close friends, I'd hear a story about a time when the cosmic cartoonist said something confounding that later turned out to be helpful in a trying time. The people who know him best and should be inured to his metaphysical gravity are the ones who remain most impressed by his depth. "We're living in an age of decadence," Joni Mitchell told me. "But Wayne's not. He's still soaring." Carlos Santana said he can think of Wayne only as an "entity." Herbie Hancock spoke to how Wayne's wisdom affects his music: "Wayne Shorter has evolved as a human being to a point where he can synthesize all the history of jazz into a very special, very alive musical expression. Nobody else can do that now."

My own first meeting with Wayne was an exercise in frustration and enlightenment. Sent to cover the start of his new band's tour in 2001, I asked him how he'd chosen the repertoire for the tour. "What's your earliest recurring memory?" he asked, by way of response. "'Cause *that's Occam's razor*!" Uh-oh, I thought. While Wayne's theorizing about the simplest known solution to the ontological dilemma, how would I get the information I needed for my article? But later that night, as I was falling asleep, I remembered my earliest moment of consciousness. It was of not being able to take the world for granted and having to narrate its events in my head: "Here I am with my sister. She's walking up the steps, one foot after the other, with her shoes untied." According to Wayne's logic, I guess that means I'm supposed to be a writer. Late in 2002, when I asked Wayne if he'd be willing to cooperate on this biography, he agreed, and said he'd convince any tentative friends or colleagues to talk to me with this testimonial: "Michelle's originally from Kansas, but she clicked her heels three times and ended up in Oz with me." Cooperation with Wayne the Wizard would clearly involve some uncharted territory.

One morning I went over to see him at his home in Miami, ostensibly to spend the day gathering material for the biography, as we'd agreed. I walked in the front door, past a closet where fifty flat, black music-score boxes were stacked, filled with his life's work as a composer. Wayne was in the multipurpose space he calls his "fun room," a studio, office, and rec room. He was wearing his favorite shirt, a royal-blue Superman muscle T-shirt, and he sat at his desk meticulously revising a composition, with a pen in one hand and a bottle of white-out in the other. He'd been up composing since 6 a.m., which is typical. He works in the morning hours and sometimes wakes up as early as 3 a.m. to start his workday. And it is a workday. He often talks about seeing the multiple rough drafts of Beethoven's symphonies, and on this day, as usual, he was practicing Beethoven's perseverance as a composer. Wayne also seemed to share the man's deafness: the TV was on at red-alert volume, blaring out an MSNBC report on Iraq.

I was ready to go to work. Wayne had other ideas. "Hey, what if we didn't do anything we think we're *supposed* to do today?" he asked, with a twinkle in his eye. The almost seventy-year-old man struck me as a precocious child trying to talk his way out of going to kindergarten. But I was game. So we spent hours watching movies, reading passages from his favorite books, and talking. In essence, he was showing me his creative process. His wife, Carolina, flitted in and out like an angel of hospitality, cool and graceful in loose white linen, a little flushed from work at the Buddhist Florida Nature and Culture Center near their home. She brought us snacks of fruit and diet Brazilian guarana soda. No milk and cookies, because Wayne is on an epic but often lapsing diet.

Wayne's encyclopedic knowledge of film is well-known, and his large video, DVD, and laser-disc collection fills his fun room. His book collection can't be contained there—it spills over into a bookcase in the living room and several cases in his bedroom. His library includes fiction, philosophy, science, science fiction, and five editions of *The Water Babies,* the first book he read, one that stimulated his curiosity about "netherworlds." He especially likes books with sumptuous, colorful metaphors and ambitious plots, the literary equivalents of his music. "I never put the fantasy aside," he says. "When I finish composing in my fun room, I'm thinking about the next book I'm going to read. I look at a cover and get started

reading the first page, start on that road of reading ten books at a time."
Wayne is constantly in dialogue with movies and books, always looking to
inhabit alternate realms. Alone, he'll improvise games for himself, like
holding up his hand with its palm facing him and pretending it's Wolf
Man come to get him. Other times he'll poke himself in the stomach, like
his finger is the mighty little attacker of a big, ugly monster. He deliberately bumps into walls, sliding along them like a kid who never gave up on
make-believe.

So when it comes to conversation, Wayne doesn't have much patience
for anything superficial or dull. Part of this comes from spending so much
time around jazz musicians, who tend not to think or speak in a linear
way. Among bebop musicians, Wayne's childhood idols, there was impatience for all things trite. "Somebody would bring Miles a record," Wayne
remembered, "thinking they'd show him something new: 'Miles, have you
heard this?' And Miles would say, 'Don't get cute, now.' Before he even
played it! Sometimes someone new would come to his house and see the
piano open. Miles would be cookin', he'd be talkin' about steak. And somebody would ease over to the piano and start tinkling, 'cause they're thinking Miles is a musician, right? And Miles would ease around out of the
kitchen—he had dim lighting so that you couldn't see him coming—and
he'd come up behind the person and reach around his shoulders and playfully put his hands on top of theirs to stop them, and he'd say, 'Don't play.'"

Wayne absorbed that attitude: Don't show me what I've already seen or
heard before. And don't talk about stuff we both already know. "Most time
is spent in judgmental, dead-zone talk," Wayne explains. "In throwaway
conversation, scratching each other's backs with illusions, a conversation
of appeasement going to and fro, backslapping that is unearned. Six hours
of 'I dub thee Sir James, or Sir Wayne.' Things that are governed by lower
life conditions." Wayne is, however, always ready to generously engage
in dialogue that trips merrily down one of the four noble paths of his
Buddhist practice: Learning, Absorption or Realization, Helping, and
Awakening.

One day we were sitting in companionable silence at his kitchen table, which had a bowl of fruit at its center. I was noticing to myself how the oranges had a particularly strong and heady scent. Wayne's mind was operating in a whole other dimension. "How do you think the oranges smell to the bananas?" he asked. No matter how silly his thought might be, it's bound to be different, an innovation. And he wants you to be creative, too. He conducts conversation as he leads his bands, always looking at you with a calm, amused gaze that says, *Who are you going to be now? And what are you realizing now? And now?* After a promotional interview we conducted for his record label, he implied we'd only scratched the surface of things: "Now let's see what's *under* the rug," he said, lifting up the corner of a tablecloth. On another occasion, backstage with a small group of people, he burst forth with this: "This is all safe stuff we're talking here! We can go deeper whenever you're ready." Once, in a crowded movie theater, he called out, "Everything is good about this movie except for the music!" Then he whispered, "Sometimes you have to be the one to shake things up."

There were times when I didn't feel up to the challenge of dealing with the Taskmaster of Depth. Once, Wayne told me a long story involving a scene from a movie, and I lost the thread of his anecdote. When he finished, he waited for my reply. I didn't have anything to say. He said, as if to explain his story, "The thing is, sometimes familiarity *can* breed contempt." I still didn't get the story, but I did take Wayne's comment as a sign that it was time for me to leave—his former bandleader Art Blakey often quoted Shakespeare's famous line to get rid of meddlesome people. If a conversation really gets stale, Wayne goes silent and looks down at his chest, pretending to pick lint off his shirt. And he can be downright arrogant about music. One time we were standing in an airport waiting for the band's equipment to clear baggage check. Wayne was off in his own world, looking across the airport with a thousand-mile stare. He jerked himself back to reality and volunteered, "I'm thinking about this piece I'm writing, conducting the horn and string traffic in my head." I asked, "Oh, you're thinking about the orchestration?" Wayne's answer was, "Dorchestration," which was both a commentary on my dorky question and an indication that he didn't care to answer it. This arrogance struck me as the defensive stance of a man whose musical gifts have too often been beyond the reach of words. After we got to know each other better, he said as much: "Genius to me means a lot of struggle. When you're out of reach, out of the many cages of interpretation of what genius is, when you're out of those cages, that genius takes on a terrific struggle."

"The long way is the short way," Wayne often says. With him, the long way is the *only* way. He will relax enough to stay on solid ground in conversation, but only after you've demonstrated a willingness to go off into the stratosphere with him. This made it difficult to prod him for basic details of his career during the first few months of our discussions. In March 2003, I met up with Wayne's quartet on tour in Amsterdam, where the group played the Concertgebouw. The next day, I went over to see Wayne at his hotel room, where he greeted me in his robe—"It's casual Wednesday here"—looking very relaxed, with the room's balcony doors open to a pond formed by a widened canal next to the hotel. I wanted to discuss the music he made in Weather Report, an entire fourteen-year period of his career that he always managed to avoid. This seemed like a good time, when there was nothing but the ducks on the pond outside to distract him. Wayne tried to be cooperative and did talk about some of the group's history. His spirit urged him on to another topic: his struggle to gain a deeper appreciation of life during his Weather Report years.

"And what is the root of appreciation?" he asked. "It probably could be compassion."

I forgot all about Weather Report. I said that appreciation was similar to enthusiasm, a word that comes from the Greek *entheos,* so "enthusiasm" literally means being "full of God." Then I free-associated on my favorite Rilke poem, "As Once the Winged Energy of Delight." In the poem, Rilke writes about building character and enthusiasm and seems to justify it with a stern German work ethic. But he gives the poem the ultimate cosmic twist in the final line, when he reveals the true incentive for self-improvement: "because inside human beings is where God learns."

Wayne thought about it. "You're still putting God in a place that's separate," he said. "The separation is ever so subtle, but if God doesn't learn, you're in trouble! You know what I mean?"

I admitted it was kind of disciplinary.

"If you learn, it's your responsibility," he went on. "You can't attribute anything to anyone other than yourself, and you can't blame anyone else for any tragedies. I'm thinking of the ultimate law of causality, and that even God is subject to this law."

The phone rang. Wayne had to give an interview about his forthcoming record, *Alegría.* During the call, I flipped through Michael Chabon's *Summerland,* one of several paperbacks Wayne had lying around. But I couldn't help eavesdropping on the phone interview. From what I could pick up on Wayne's end, he was trying to go mystical, and the interviewer persisted in asking him questions about music. Finally, Wayne relented and discussed his music in some detail. When the call was finished, he turned to me and asked, "You don't want me to talk to you like that, do you?"

Well, I did and I didn't. A "just the facts" interview would certainly have made my information-gathering process easier, but even so, I knew that eventually we'd get around to discussing all the periods of his career, and we did. And there was a more meaningful process enacted through our Socratic dialogues. That became clear a year later, when I had a trivial conflict with a friend and was laying some trifling stuff on him. I suddenly thought: *I'd never bug Wayne with this kind of stuff. Why wouldn't I try to treat everyone with as much respect?* As a biographer, you're almost guaranteed to overidentify with your subject. I got a lot more than I bargained for when I signed up to write a book about Mr. Shorter. I had to go through my own kind of awakening before I could appreciate what makes him great.

It's not just his legacy in music, though he is a living link to the last fifty years of jazz history, and as *The New York Times* said, he's beyond compare as a composer and improviser. What makes Wayne truly extraordinary is his ability to find hilarity or profundity in almost every moment, often both at the same time. He didn't become this happy jazz Buddha overnight. He's had a long struggle with plenty of personal loss along the way. Today, like my friend said, it's fun to be with Wayne, but it's a deep kind of fun, and he inspires the people around him to find the same thing in their own lives. Sometimes he does this through the sound of his music. That's why one of Miles Davis's final acts was passing the baton to him. Wayne Shorter deserves to be more exposed, as both a musician and a man.

1

Water Babies

WAYNE SHORTER'S earliest memory is the first time he saw a lake so large that he couldn't find the end of it. He doesn't remember the lake's name, or exactly how old he was—maybe two or three?—or why his parents took him there. But Wayne still recalls the image of the water and the sky joining together up on the horizon, that faraway place where they met and misquoted each other. His imagination stretched out across the lake to find the water's beginning or the sky's end. Where did they become the same thing? When Wayne got home, he had his first thought about the nature of life: *We were always here.* "The feeling was one of always being here, always existing," he said. "And when I realized I was thinking, I thought, *I always thought.*" Wayne wouldn't realize the full resonance of these big ideas until he discovered Buddhism at age forty.

An earliest memory is often some image or event that departs from the everyday scenery of life, and the open horizon of a lake was certainly a departure from the circumscribed neighborhood where Wayne was born and raised, the Ironbound District in Newark, New Jersey. It was a thoroughly and starkly composed world of bricks and mortar, sharp angles, and literal iron boundaries. The Ironbound District was named for the Pennsylvania Railroad tracks that enclosed it to the west, north, and southeast. The area was reinforced by McCarter Highway, which bounded it to the south. The Shorters lived on the neighborhood's southern edge, at 106 South Street, just a few blocks from McCarter Highway. The highway took Newark's residents the full twenty miles to New York City and brought some of the big city back to them, for better or worse. In 1935, just two years after Wayne was born, the gangster and one-time public enemy number one Dutch Schultz was gunned down in the restroom of the Palace Chop House on McCarter. And the Ironbound District's far northern boundary of Ferry Street could be just as forbidding—Wayne would learn that it was the wrong way to walk home.

Portuguese and blacks began arriving in the Ironbound in the 1920s to join a population that was largely Polish, Italian, Irish, and German. The growth of the black community increased significantly when the Newark Chamber of Commerce advertised on billboards throughout the southern and northeastern U.S., and Wayne's parents, Louise and Joseph, were part of that influx. Louise was born in Philadelphia to Sidney and Eleanor Paige, and she migrated to Newark when her mother divorced her father. Joseph was the son of William and Daisy Shorter and found his way up to Newark from Alabama, where his family ran a small farm with the help of Joseph and his eleven siblings.

At a dance in Newark, a friend of Joseph's introduced him to Louise. "My mother liked the way my father dressed—he was so well built that he could wear suits straight off the rack, with no alterations," Wayne said. "He had a very erect carriage when he walked." Joseph and Louise were married in 1929. They had their first son, Alan, on May 29, 1932, and then a second son, Wayne, on August 25, 1933. "A lady in Finland once told me that my father's orange-brown reddish glow from beneath the skin meant he had some Indian blood," Wayne said. Wayne also speculated that his father had some Caribbean blood, as New York cab drivers would later ask him if he was of Caribbean descent. No matter what his ancestry, Wayne looked up to his father: "I wish I had that physique. He was so much taller than me."

Joseph kept in shape working as a welder at the Singer sewing-machine factory in Elizabeth, New Jersey. Louise worked for a local furrier and took in tailoring jobs for supplemental income. "Wayne's family was economically lower class, but attitudinally they were middle class," remembered Nat Phipps, an early friend of Wayne's. The Shorters rented the second floor of a house that "had a slight lean to it," Wayne said. "We didn't have nothing. I mean, the house was clean, well scrubbed, Lysoled, but the important thing is that I had a lot of dreams in that house."

Louise didn't get past the freshman year of high school in her own education, but like Duke Ellington's mother, she indulged Wayne's every creative whim. She cultivated Wayne and Alan like hothouse flowers, nourishing them on the art of play, and initiating them into an aesthetic world of texture, tone, color, harmony, form, and design. Louise would often come home from work with some tools of invention: clay and X-Acto knives, or watercolor paints and brushes. And she protected them from the slings and arrows of outrageous mediocrity. When Wayne's father would come home and ask the boys to take out the trash or perform some chore, his mother would object. "But they're busy playing," she'd say, and then see to the duty herself. Playtime wasn't just amusement, it was a time for creative industry, and their state of inventive absorption was sacred.

In the inner sanctum of the Shorter household, Wayne's imagination flourished until it took on flamboyant forms and an almost absurd magnitude. By the time Wayne was seven, he and Alan presumed they could conjure up the entire planet with their bare hands. "One time we had a whole bunch of clay on the kitchen table," Wayne said. "We said, 'Let's make the whole world!' So we started making landmasses, and then we tried to make people, little tiny people out of clay, and we made about one hundred people. It was the beginning of World War Two, so we figured we'd start with the soldiers and we made about one hundred Japanese soldiers out of yellow clay; then Russia was the red and blue armies, we heard that Communism was coming. We made American soldiers out of that green-brown. We made submarines, and inside the submarines we put seats and whatever we could remember. And then let the thing sink. Then we made all the characters we read about in comic books. We made Frankenstein monsters and Captain America, and Superman, Batman; we had the gray clay, that darker purple-blue clay for the hood, all those characters. And we'd take them and move them around like they were doing things."

Wayne made some of his first trips out into the world on Sundays, when the Shorters attended services at Mount Zion Baptist Church. The outstanding Mount Zion choir sometimes featured the silky, fluid voice of a teenage singer named Sarah Vaughan, a Newark native nine years Wayne's senior. For the younger members of the congregation, singers were the highlight of the service, as Wayne remembered: "Walking home from church service, some adult would ask us kids, 'Did you hear what the preacher said?' Everybody would say, 'Well, the choir was happening.'" Wayne kept his opinions to himself. He didn't care much for church music, which seemed to strive too hard to believe in itself. "Sacred music, the holy rolling of the Baptists, that music turned me off," he said. "The sanctified gospel that had people jumpin' up and down and having fits—it felt negative and gloomy to me. I'd sit there suffocating, thinking, *Open the door and let me get some air!*"

At home Wayne heard popular music with his father. Like most Americans in the pretelevision era of the thirties and forties, Joseph routinely came home from work, turned on the radio, and settled down into his armchair to listen while he waited for supper. "My father liked country and western music," Wayne said in May 1996. "Also, he liked a show called *Music à la Mood*, which was like film music and soundtracks, like

Spellbound and *South Pacific.* There was one song he liked, 'Bali Ha'i,' and when that would come on, I knew he was going in his dreams to Tahiti. He had that on Saturday and Sunday and then week nights, 7:30 at night, it was WNEW, the *Make Believe Ballroom* with Martin Block."

Wayne listened to these radio programs with one ear, mostly just to please his father. His attention was more fully captured by the music he heard at the cinema, by the sounds that enhanced the emotional impact of scenes. "Film scores—what we called 'soundtracks' or 'background'—are the earliest recollections of music staying inside of me," Wayne said. "Films I saw at the Capitol theater in Newark like *Captive Wild Woman,* or the music behind Bela Lugosi when he played Igor in *Son of Frankenstein.* Or *The Wolf Man,* that music behind Lon Chaney when he changed into the werewolf . . . that stuff got me curious about sound." After seeing a film, Wayne and Alan reenacted favorite scenes and tested each other on how much of the *entire* soundtrack they could recall, humming and singing through the night. "We called it 'Say About,'" Wayne said. "Alan would wake me up in the middle of the night and say, 'Want to Say About?' Then we'd remember dialogue, sound effects, and the music. All with our voices and fingers."

For Alan and Wayne, this ability to remember and re-create major segments of soundtracks wasn't anything exceptional. It was just another pastime, as commonplace an activity as enacting scenarios with neighborhood kids in a vacant lot next to their house. "In the empty lot beside our house, there was a broken-down old milk wagon with a brake handle, a seat, and some pedals," Wayne said. "It was there defunct, and we'd convert it into a spaceship, or Mars itself, or the ocean, or sometimes it became a B-17 bomber. 'Thirty seconds over Tokyo!' we'd yell. It became all those things we saw in movies. Also, we dug trenches in this lot. Getting ready for the enemy. We'd have the girls be like frontier women, and we'd be like, 'Get the women in the trenches!' We'd make suits like Royal Mounted and carry wooden knives. That vacant lot became like whatever drama we were getting into."

Wayne played with an enthusiasm natural to most children, but by the time he was six, he already had a tendency toward self-effacement that would haunt him for much of his life. "My mom always said to speak up," Wayne said. "I heard that all the time. When I was younger, my big battle was knowing when to speak up about something. For example, I was told that I was too small to play on the baseball team, but I didn't step up and say, *Wait a minute, I'm a good pitcher.* What I did was, I pitched off to the side of the game, until the other kids saw me and found out I could pitch good. I thought not speaking up was part of being humble, modest, not being a show-off."

At the same time, Wayne and Alan's parents taught them to be critical of social norms. "In the evening my parents would sit around and analyze the day, like they were having a deposition of their daily events and encounters. And my mother was always reading the newspaper, scrutinizing the motives of candidates. She'd talk about things like zoning laws. Things that would move people into a place of being easy prey to the power players of the city that they lived in. They'd talk about landlords, and they'd question the educational system from time to time. So there was a social consciousness, not the know-nothing, do-nothing silence in the home."

Wayne's older brother went to grammar school on Oliver Street near their home, where his questioning, rebellious stance complicated his adjustment to the educational system. "My mother knew what Alan was talking about when he dissected things, and she knew that they didn't understand him in school," Wayne said. "A lot of that has to do with not believing that a little Negro boy in the forties would question the lesson plan, the daily teaching methods." When Wayne began school two years later, he quickly gained a healthy suspicion of socialization himself: "Mostly what I learned in school was how to avoid jumping out there and letting them mold my character." When he sensed that school's social conditioning compelled students to simply mimic what they were told, his hesitancy to speak up was compounded by a fear of conformity. "I thought speaking up made you into a standard-issue *take-charge* person," Wayne said. "I remember those group exercises in grammar school, where they would sit us all down and pose a dilemma or problem, then ask, 'What should we do about this?' All the take-charge hands would come up, saying, 'I think, I think, I think, I think.' Well, 'think' my ass. They wanted to give us hands-on, on-the-job experience of being Mr. Take Charge, Mr. Fix-it, Mr. Ever-ready-you-can-lean-on-me, 'cause if it's broke, I'll fix it. If it's not broke, I'll still fix it. And if it doesn't exist, well, I'll fix that, too."

Like many boys in the early forties, Wayne read comic books voraciously. In the forties, comics were the most popular form of entertainment in the country; between 80 and 100 million people were buying them, making them more widely consumed than the radio or movies. Comic books cost five cents each, compared to a movie's twelve-cent admission price, and Wayne tried to collect them all: "There was early Superman, Captain Marvel, names like the Flame, the Green Arrow and Speedy his sidekick; they always had the sidekicks. The Torch and Toro, the little flame. There was the one who swam under the water, Submariner—he came before Aquaman. Submariner had a lady. There was Bulletman and Bulletgirl, there was Hawkman. There was Airboy; he was a teenager and had an airplane with wings that flapped like a bird. It was a smart plane; he talked to it, and it would go places and do things. Of course, we had Mandrake the Magician, Mandrake and Lothar. The Phantom, the Hangman, you name it, the Blue Beetle, the Green Lantern; of course, I have my life-size replica of the Lantern here today. I'm telling you, we had them all."

Comic books were an exciting parallel universe for many kids. For Wayne, they completely defined his world—he inhabited the stories and their alternate realms, and even viewed real people and actual events as a part of his fantastical one. "I was reading so many comic books that I saw people paralleling the characters in those comics," he said. Wayne saw his classmates as character types and made sharp observations about human nature: "In school the superhero type was perverted into Clean-Shirt Boy. He didn't have the cape and superhero uniform; the clean shirt was his uniform. He was the hero only as a teacher's pet who wanted to monitor the windows with the long pole, 'I'll be the pole monitor!'" School certainly didn't offer any opportunities to display the true valiance and daring Wayne knew from comic books. He wondered if there was a way to show people how to bring that mysterious dimension into the real world.

At age twelve, Wayne read his first full-length book, *The Water Babies,* which was written by Charles Kingsley in 1863. *The Water Babies* is a 383-page moralistic and fantastical Victorian fairy tale with vivid naturalist imagery. In the story, a beleaguered and very grimy chimney-sweep boy named Tom falls into a river, goes into a kind of afterlife, and is reborn as a water baby, a little maritime sprite endowed with gills that allow him to breathe freely underwater. The story's sense of wonderment appealed to Wayne. "*The Water Babies* sparked what was already in me," he said. "This wonder about the netherworld, the places that we can't see but that we can enter anytime. After death, I wondered, is it something like that?" At one point in the book, Kingsley steps out of the narrative to directly address the reader on the subject of imagination: "Some people think that there are no fairies. But it is a wide world, and plenty of room in it for fairies, without people seeing them; unless, of course, they look in the right place. The most wonderful and the strongest things in the world, you know, are just the things which no one can see. There is life in you; and it is the life in you which makes you grow, and move, and think: and yet you can't see it."

Kingsley playfully instructed the reader to forgo any distinction between the real world and the world of make-believe. Yet for all the book's inventive storytelling, it was nevertheless a product of its age, filled with cultural valuations of race. The story equated whiteness with goodness: As the soot from Tom's chimney-sweep toils washed away in the water, he became simultaneously white and self-realized, discovering his true soul. Aside from this loaded symbolism, Kingsley espoused common stereotypes about nationalities and races, especially the Irish and blacks. The timeless "netherworld" of *The Water Babies* appealed to Wayne, but its racist propaganda reflected the world in which he actually lived.

When Wayne first read the book in 1945, the civil rights movement was still years away and racial segregation was standard. Wayne's Alabama-born father, Joseph, was as familiar with the blatant racism of the South as he was with its more subtle expression in the North. "My father had a way of standing up to prejudice, whenever people thought they could put something over on him 'cause he was 'colored,'" Wayne said. One time there was an incident during a family car trip through Virginia. After stopping at a roadside store, Joseph noticed that the clerk had shortchanged him. Joseph started to go back inside and correct the error. "Don't argue with these people, you're down South now," cautioned Louise—in her Philadelphia girlhood she'd been weaned on stories of the Southland as a demilitarized zone of racial combat. "I don't let nobody mess with me," Joseph answered. "Goddamnit, I can count."

Many of the European immigrants in the Ironbound District were financially less fortunate than the Shorter family. Wayne's mother would sometimes point this out to discourage racial scapegoating and encourage self-reliance. "What I got from my mother was to be able to be self-sufficient, a lone wolf," Wayne said. These personality traits influenced Wayne's choice of friends. "My friends were never deadweights or complainers," he said. "They wouldn't say, 'Why are you looking at me—is it 'cause I'm colored?' because they were sure of themselves. I never wanted to be in the company of people who were complainers to the point that they formed a club of complaint, which could even take the form of a gang. I liked the swift people who said, 'Even if we ain't got it, let's make believe we've got it and go!'" Those preferences would later influence his choice of profession, too, though it would be a while before he found any true peers. "Nobody wanted to talk about going to Mars anyway. So that excused them from my club. I didn't even get a chance to know if they'd *be* complainers." If Wayne's faraway expression and eccentric interests dissuaded casual approaches or conversation, these qualities also guarded him against hostile confrontation. "I never had any of that dramatic one-on-one, 'I'm gonna kick your ass 'cause you're black' business," he said. "Never let anybody get that close to me. I had my radar up, and it would say, 'Alien coming!'"

No matter how self-determined and proud Wayne was raised to be and however well his strange demeanor may have armored him, he wasn't impervious to racism's psychological effects. As a child, Wayne was deeply impressed by watching the 1934 movie melodrama *Imitation of Life,* the story of a light-skinned black girl named Peola who renounces her dark-skinned mother and tries to pass as white. During the shameful scene in which Peola says, "That's not my mother," Wayne felt like sinking down in his theater seat. "At the movies, I'd often look around the theater at other people, wondering how exactly a film was affecting them," Wayne said. Together they'd all watched the same confrontations onscreen, and eventually those issues were usually happily resolved, in keeping with the code of Hollywood endings. "When everyone went out of the theater and into the street, nothing outside had actually changed," Wayne said. He'd wonder to himself: "Has anything changed *inside* people? How could it be so easy to see something like that and then turn the other way, and not look at things?"

When Wayne was twelve, his grammar school held an assembly with various student performances and speeches. Wayne was chosen to read an essay about Dr. Ralph Bunche, who was championed as the first American Negro in the State Department and lauded for his accomplishments in the United Nations. The essay upheld Dr. Bunche as the exemplar of the exceptional ethics of the "American Negro." (Bunche went on to win a Nobel Peace Prize in 1950, just weeks after he was turned away from prominent hotels in New Orleans and forced to stay in a run-down "black" hotel.)

In the week before the school assembly, Wayne lay awake at night with an uneasy feeling in the pit of his stomach. His mother reassured him that it was just nervousness, butterflies. But Wayne wasn't anxious about speaking in public. For several days, he couldn't determine the source of his uneasiness. Finally, the day before the assembly, he made a connection as he was rehearsing his speech: He felt that twinge of discomfort whenever he came to the word *Negro* in the text.

At the assembly, his uneasiness grew as he went up to deliver the speech. He stood offstage, waiting his turn while another student, a girl, played a

Chopin étude on the piano. *Say Negro, Say Negro*—the words came back to him again and again, carried on a persistent refrain of shame. The time to speak arrived, and walking onstage, Wayne realized *this* would be his struggle with race. He wasn't terribly burdened by public acts of prejudice— those times when a white guy spat a little too close to him on the sidewalk or when the store owner had shortchanged his father down South. Wayne's challenge would be the one Peola had in *Imitation of Life*: managing the mental strain of prejudice so that he didn't internalize it.

Then a small miracle occurred. Just as Wayne reached the podium, the bell rang. The teacher in charge of the assembly apologized; there wasn't time for Wayne to read his essay. *Saved by the bell!* he thought, and couldn't even bother to feign disappointment. So Wayne was rescued from delivering the speech and confronting his demons, but a larger issue went unresolved: Why didn't the speech stir up any racial pride in him? For one thing, Wayne sensed that someone could glorify Bunche as an exceptional Negro and still "look the other way" when it came to more pervasive injustices. The trumpeting of Bunche as a good race man and ideal American was based on the theory that blacks could best succeed by working industriously and adopting the manners and speech of whites. That view didn't address what it meant to live with a black consciousness, to live with the conflict between how one is perceived by others and how one perceives oneself. Wayne's experience of racism was closer to another view, the existentialist one that Ralph Ellison was beginning to write about in the mid-forties, in the work that would be published as *Invisible Man* in 1952. Ellison's perspective on racism took into account its effect on the mind.

Like existentialists, artists try to define and create the meaning of existence in a seemingly meaningless universe. Wayne wanted to be an artist, which primed him to address the intricacies of racial and other social issues through the subtleties of image and narrative. "I felt like I was going to be an artist," he said. "Being an artist like a painter, you're solo, you're alone, you're on your own, punching your own clock, making a great sacrifice. If the sacrifice is going to be that deep, you've got to be the best artist. It's easy for people to turn the other way when it comes to race and other things. You want to shake people, to try to use your art to force people to not turn the other way."

Louise Shorter's careful nurturing of Wayne's creative abilities was bearing fruit: Wayne had started to demonstrate aptitude for the visual arts. At age twelve, Wayne won a citywide art contest with a watercolor he called *The Football Game*. The New Jersey *Star-Ledger* came by to take his photo and ran a short announcement on his win. *Maybe there's a lucky star following me,* Wayne thought, as he lay awake in bed that night relishing the honor. "But then I quickly tucked the thought away," he said. "I didn't want to spoil it."

The prize came at a crucial time. Wayne's grammar school teachers were concerned about his tendency to stare dreamily out the window in class. This confirmed talent for painting gave his daydreaming a sense of purpose, or at least some artistic potential. After Wayne won the art prize, a grammar school teacher encouraged him to apply to Newark's Arts High School, the first school devoted to the arts in the United States. Arts High was founded in 1931 and was the model for the esteemed New York High School of Music and Art, which opened in 1936. The school's curriculum was basic liberal arts, with each student majoring in visual art, dance, drama, or music. Though students were mostly guided toward the arts-education field, trained to become teachers rather than working artists, there was inestimable value in a rare academic environment where, as the first principal mandated, "Art, music, and drama were to be regarded as major pursuits, comparable in importance to Latin, mathematics, and the sciences."

The school was a godsend for teenagers with artistic leanings, and there was no town with a greater need for it than Newark. In 1967 the infamous riots would make Newark an official symbol of urban decay, crime, and despair, but years before that the city was a tough place to get ahead, Wayne said: "Newark was a hell of a place to learn something about how to survive . . . a lot of things, whether you were well-off or very, very down in the dregs of poordom. Poordom. There is only a few people from

Newark now who are somewhere in the world, imparting their knowledge of survival intelligently, or just daily survival." A large percentage of those Newark "survivors" went to Arts High—among musicians alone, singers Sarah Vaughan, Melba Moore, and Connie Francis, and trumpeter Woody Shaw attended the school. Years later Wayne said he would run into Sarah Vaughan out on tour: "I'd say 'What's happenin'?' and she'd say 'Newark,' and that was enough, 'cause you know what Newark does to people."

Wayne experienced the benefits of the school immediately: He quickly made friends with a few fellow students. Elsewhere, Wayne's odd deportment had alienated people. "Reading comic books and science fiction books, when people approached me through life, they had a general sense that I was an oddity," Wayne said. "They'd say, 'Hey buddy, where you think you're going?' And I'd say, 'You're talking to me . . . mememememe?'" (the echo effect implying that his words had to travel from his permanent residence in another galaxy to reach people). At Arts High, talent, self-determination, and even a touch of weirdness were considered hip. Wayne met some genuine peers there, boys with autonomy and personal style. "At Arts High I met Eddie White, my friend who got all A's and ended up going to Princeton. We'd go out to New York on weekends. He was well versed in math, and was driving a car at a young age, his father was deacon in church—he had a certain amount of independence. Another friend, Albert Defreez, I met him right when I started at Arts High. I saw him sitting on a curb with bloodshot eyes, a good-looking black cat. We ate lunch together in the first week and became friends. I wondered how he got those bloodshot eyes, and then I realized that everyone wanted to challenge him. He was independent that way, too."

Wayne drew incessantly and was serious about becoming a painter or illustrator, but he was an average student in his general course work and earned B's in art classes. School was just a tolerable routine compared to his main fascination: the movies. It was a film, *Rocketship X-M,* starring Lloyd Bridges and Osa Massen, that inspired Wayne's first major art project, a thick fifty-four-page comic book of intricate blue pen drawings entitled *Other Worlds.* Wayne created it over the course of a month, drawing nightly at the kitchen table. *Other Worlds* was the story of a space expedition to the moon, and focused on an interspecies romance between an astronaut hero, Rick, and a lunar native, an Amazon-like leader named Doka.

Though Wayne was a fan of all cinema, he preferred films with magical undertones, especially science fiction and horror movies. One film in particular, the 1948 Powell and Pressburger classic *The Red Shoes,* brought together several of Wayne's fascinations: art, the macabre, and magic. The art film includes a ballet based on Hans Christian Andersen's cautionary fairy tale of the same name, in which a cobbler gives a girl some red shoes that provide her with supernatural dancing powers. Like the girl in Andersen's fairy tale, the film's central character, Vicky, is given red shoes that make her dance beautifully, but when she grows tired, she can't stop dancing and ultimately dies.

Throughout his life, Wayne would go on to see the film *almost ninety times,* an excessive number of viewings by any measure, even for a superb film like *The Red Shoes.* A young child will sometimes ask to hear the same story night after night until he resolves a sensitive developmental issue within the plot. Wayne repeatedly watched *The Red Shoes* in an attempt to reconcile its central conflict: living for oneself versus living for one's art. In one of Wayne's favorite scenes, a leading ballerina, Irina, stops a rehearsal to make an announcement. "I'm getting married!" she gushes. All the dancers in the company rush over to congratulate Irina, everyone except the monomaniacal dance director, Lermontov, who stands glowering at her. When the rehearsal resumes, a dancer turns to Lermontov and remarks, "She's in wonderful form."

Lermontov replies, "I'm not interested in Irina's form anymore, nor of the form of any prima ballerina who is imbecile enough to get married. You cannot have it both ways. The dancer who relies on the doubtful comforts of human love may never be a great dancer. Never."

"That is all very fine," the other man concedes. "But you can't alter human nature."

"No?" Lermontov scoffs. "I think you can do better. You can ignore it."

Lermontov's austere creed mandates that service to one's gift must come before all else. For a teenager with naive notions about art as a vocation, *The Red Shoes* was irresistible in its romantic fatalism. Years before Wayne would have to make such difficult decisions, he watched the film and wondered how much of his own life he would sacrifice for his art.

Generally, in films of the era, action unfolded with slow, excruciating precision until finally all the melodrama the world could stand—and then some—would sweep across a character's face to close the scene. Wayne had a capacious memory, and though he didn't know it at the time, he was storing up a huge inventory of images and scenes. He would use them later, when his pictorial mind would immediately associate a particular feeling or mood with a certain scene that depicted it. In this way film would have a major impact on his artistic innovation. When Wayne was a teenager, however, cinema was simply an absorbing world, and he lost himself in it completely: "I remember how the clicking sound of high-heeled shoes would jerk my consciousness back to the theater, when the army of mothers came to drag kids home from the movie theater at midnight."

2.

Bop Fiend:
"As Weird As Wayne"

ONE MEMORABLE EVENING, Wayne's interest in film and the visual arts was replaced by a deeper calling. He discovered a style of music that captured the velocity and mystery of those "other worlds" through sheer sound. Wayne often listened to his father's favorite radio program, the popular *Make Believe Ballroom* hosted by Martin Block on New York's WNEW. Block played Fletcher Henderson, Noble Sissel, Tommy Dorsey, Bing Crosby, Virginia O'Brien, Doris Day, Billie Holiday, Louis Armstrong, Claude Thornhill, Kate Smith—a miscellany of popular styles, though Block's main aesthetic focus was emblematized in the program's theme song, a swinging big-band number recorded by Glenn Miller in 1940. In the mid-forties, *Make Believe Ballroom* commanded twenty-five percent of the radio audience, and Block could "make" or "break" records based on whether or not he included them in his playlist.

One night Block cautiously—almost apologetically—introduced a distinctively different variety of music: "Ladies and gentlemen," Block said, "we'd like to try something a little different tonight. We're going to play a new kind of music, and you can see how you like it. They call this music . . . bebop." The sound was revelatory for Wayne. "He played Thelonious Monk's 'Off Minor,' then something by Charlie Parker, and then Bud Powell," he said. "My ears perked up when I heard it, and something must have clicked, 'cause I wasn't into music at all. That music seemed to reflect some of what was happening, and also some of what wasn't happening. What some people wished would happen."

As soon as *bebop* became part of Wayne's vocabulary, it seemed like the music was ubiquitous. He couldn't escape it. In 1947 Herman Lubinsky moved his influential jazz label, Savoy Records, to 58 Market Street in downtown Newark. This brought some bop musicians to the neighborhood, and their music was in the air around town. "There were the older guys who hung out outside the school, the ne'er-do-wells," Wayne said. "They were a little older, like nineteen or twenty-one, and they'd be talking hip stuff, standing on the street corners like an information kiosk. You'd be walking by, and they'd throw out, 'Have you heard of Charles *Christopher* Parker?' or 'Have you heard *Dewey* Davis?' Instead of doing the dozens, they'd trade off on music references and see who was finally left with a *duh*. If you were left speechless, they got you." To aid in his conversance, Wayne listened to Symphony Sid Torin on the radio, a DJ who came on the air at midnight, catering to a cult jazz audience. Symphony Sid's stylistic bias was clear in his theme, "Jumpin' with Symphony Sid," a bebop tune composed by Lester Young. "Symphony Sid was unique—with a low voice, and he was always talking hipster slang, making you aware that he was tight with musicians," Wayne said. "One night he came into the studio ripped. He'd been hanging out with Basie at Birdland, and he said, 'I don't even want to be here right now. I was having too much fun with Basie.' Then he'd say, 'Some guys decided to "Take the A Train," and they never got off. Duke Ellington's band stayed on the line, but Prez got off, Bird got off . . .'"

With his newfound interest in jazz, Wayne felt the urge to play some music for himself. "First I got a Tonette, a small plastic instrument with eight holes," he said. "I bought it for a dollar, and it looked like a submarine." The Tonette was introduced in 1938, a sturdy recorder-like instrument with the reedy tone of a flute. By 1941 over half of the grammar schools in the United States had adopted it as standard equipment for pre-band music education; and radio and film musicians used it for special novelty effects. "I figured out how to play it myself," Wayne said. "I'd mash notes, which was when you'd cover half a hole to make it sound like other things, or to play half steps. I'd keep it in my back pocket and pull it out to play when no one was around, but I didn't realize the sound was bouncing off the walls. So my mother could tell where I was, she'd open the window and hear me roaming around outside playing. That's what they should have to protect children. The tagline would be, 'The Tonette, the smart child saver, the molester smasher.' And playing a certain note would render an attacker lifeless. He couldn't even afford the next inhale, 'cause he paid so much on the exhale."

After tooting his way around the Ironbound District for a few months, the juvenile Tonette troubadour was ready to graduate to a legitimate instrument. Wayne had started listening to classical music on the radio, and its dramatic narrative structure and distinct cast of instrumental characters influenced his choice of horn. "I liked the storytelling role of the clarinet that I heard on compositions like *Scheherazade*," Wayne said. "And then I saw one just glowing with possibility there in the shop window, with its shiny silver keys." As he told writer David Breskin, the clarinet's sound inspired filmic imagery for him: "I loved when the orchestra would cut out and you'd hear this lone clarinet, like in Rimsky-Korsakov, sounding like it was going over the sand dunes. I said, 'I want a *horn*!'"

Most gifted jazz musicians show promise at an early age—Miles began playing the trumpet at ten, and Charlie Parker asked for his first saxophone at eleven. At the relatively late age of fifteen, Wayne's ever-doting mother bought him a clarinet and signed him up for lessons with Jack Arnold Press, the conductor of the pit orchestra at the Adams Theater and proprietor of a musical-instrument store next door. ("No wonder he had so many students," Wayne said. "His wife was an actress, a beautiful lady, and walking into a lesson, the whole thing was worth it just to catch a glimpse of her.") With Mr. Press, Wayne covered the essentials of instrumental technique: He mastered fingerings and tonguing, legato and staccato styles; he worked to create the full, round tone that comes from proper embouchure. "Use more diaphragm," Mr. Press would encourage. "You're using muscles you never learned to use before. You're going to get tired in the beginning; keep at it, that will all develop." Wayne also learned to decipher the alien codes of written music, identifying the names of notes on the spaces and lines of the G clef; he looked out for the accidental sharp and flat notes that popped up like space invaders in the clef's cosmos. He played major and minor scales and études; he learned to understand time signatures and the related values of notes and rests. Wayne studied privately with Mr. Press for a year, the only formal instrumental training he ever had.

Wayne's developing interest in music was strongly supported by his parents, who were blissfully unaware that their son secretly indulged the extracurricular interest during school hours. In the forties, the Adams Theater in downtown Newark offered an afternoon double bill of a big band and a movie for fifty cents. The theater was temptingly located near Arts High, and Wayne would cut class to catch the double bill, saving up his lunch money for the admission cost, or joining up with a few other empty-pocketed music lovers to climb the back fire escape and sneak into the theater. While he was supposed to be studying the history of the Civil War or analyzing the literary conflicts of *Moby-Dick,* he was hearing the big bands of Count Basie, Stan Kenton, Woody Herman, Jimmie Lunceford, and Illinois Jacquet, as well as the bebop groups of Dizzy Gillespie, Charlie Parker, and Lester Young.

Wayne's high school transcript bears evidence of thirty absences during his sophomore year—"And those were only the times I got caught,"

Wayne said. He forged parental excuses for all the absences. When the principal learned that Wayne skipped school to see stage shows and also took clarinet lessons, he sensed that the boy might have a musical vocation. He opted for a constructive punishment, enrolling Wayne in a music theory class as a disciplinary action. Along with the advanced visual arts courses required for Wayne's major, the music class made the young truant's course load heavy enough to keep him occupied throughout the school day. The principal had no idea that his "punishment" would help create one of the century's best composers.

Isabella Prepara was the high school's well-proportioned vocal music director and music theory teacher. "She was nice-looking, and all the boys looked at her," Wayne said, a fact that motivated those boys to do their best in her classroom. Wayne started Miss Prepara's music theory course in the middle of his junior year, in the second semester, which brought him into the show more than a few beats behind the other students. "Most music majors had been studying voice or piano since they were six or seven," Wayne said. "They learned to read musical notes when they were first sounding out the syllables of Dick and Jane books." By the end of the semester, Wayne felt like he might be catching up to the other students, but shyness prevented him from speaking up in class unless he was called on directly, so there'd been no concrete assessment of his progress.

For Miss Prepara's final exam, students were tested on ear training and transcription, a series of technical questions, and finally some extensive musical notation. Wayne completed his exam in a matter of minutes and stood up. Miss Prepara had expected the students to work for at least another half hour. "If you get up, you're finished," she warned Wayne. "You can't sit back down and work anymore." Wayne didn't want to appear indecisive in front of his classmates, so he walked over and handed in his test; Miss Prepara told him to wait while she graded it. After what seemed like a lifetime, the teacher looked up. "Class," she announced, "this is an example of a perfect exam." She wrote a score of 100 at the top of Wayne's test and told him to go home. His classmates hurried back to their tests, no doubt with an uneasy combination of envy and admiration. Wayne lingered beside Miss Prepara, basking in the very comfortable combination of her beauty and praise. She congratulated him and once again told him he could leave. So he headed home to show the perfect score to his mother, who was, after all, a more long-standing source of feminine approbation.

"I walked home with a new awareness of music," Wayne said, "with a vague but deeply felt sense that music was the direction I was supposed to go." The lucky star that he'd sensed following him when he won the art contest at twelve now brightly guided him toward music: He was charged with the discovery of his special aptitude. "Not that the world became some kind of set for an MGM musical," Wayne said. "Street sounds didn't fall in rhythm with my step, shop windows didn't sing out." It was more like an innate ability had been unearthed and now animated his thoughts, giving him new purpose. "Throughout dinner that night, a riff of *music, music, music, music* buzzed on in the background of my mind," Wayne said. "At breakfast the next morning, music felt like a new skin that had grown on me overnight."

Wayne asked himself, *If music is coming to me like this, so brazenly, shouldn't I do everything I can to meet it?* His brother, Alan, played the alto saxophone, though he'd switch to trumpet in a year. That summer, Alan and Wayne practiced music nonstop, wasting no time on the rudiments: Childhood friends remember them working through the challenging compositions of Lennie Tristano, who had just released his *Crosscurrents* album in 1949. The following fall, in his senior year at Arts High School, Wayne took a double major in music and art, enrolling in harmony, theory, and orchestration classes, as well as band, in which he played clarinet. The director of instrumental music was Achilles D'Amico, a master of precision and discipline. "He reminded us of Arturo Toscanini," Wayne said. "And I'll never forget this moment. On the first day of class, Mr. D'Amico said: 'I'm going to play three records. These are the three directions music is going to go.' And then he played Stravinsky's *The Rite of Spring*, a Charlie Parker tune next, and finally 'Xtabay' by Yma Sumac."

Wayne knew where *his* sympathies lay. With Charlie Parker and jazz: "Everyone was into dancing and rhythm-and-blues and pop, but I said,

bebop is interesting, it has some of that and some of the stuff from classical music going on in it." Like superheroes in the comics, bebop musicians
seemed to transcend physical and social laws with their music. And instead of punishing wicked evildoers, they destroyed tired or trite aesthetic
sensibilities. With this conviction, Wayne decided to pick up the tenor
saxophone. He soon joined an orchestra led by Jackie Bland, which included his brother, Alan, and, at various times, trombonist Grachan Moncur III and pianist Walter Davis, or "Humphrey"—Wayne would later play
with Walter in a professional setting.

The boys spent Saturdays at the YMCA, working through charts with
a music teacher, Mr. Lamar. "Mr. Lamar got some sheet music for us, and
he said, 'I'm going to teach you guys how to read like a band.' The first
thing that he got for us was a Dizzy tune, 'Things to Come,' a bad tune.
But he'd have us do just the first two measures, really slow, 'cause he
wanted us to appreciate how to read music. Then I'd go home and hear it
in my head fast."

While the Jackie Bland Band only gradually gained a grasp on bebop
music, they wasted no time emulating the flashy style and hipster slang of
the beboppers across the river in New York City, to the amusement and
scorn of their classmates. In the mid-forties, big-band swing music was
still overwhelmingly popular in Newark, and a local dance band, the Nat
Phipps Orchestra, drew in the big crowds. Every night, Wayne and Alan
would practice bebop charts for hours, until they couldn't see straight.
When they finally took a break, they'd indulge in their other favorite pastime: mocking the Nat Phipps Orchestra. After months of rehearsal, the
most disparaging insult they'd produced was "Pretty Boy Band." Nat Phipps
was of West Indian ancestry, an impressive-looking young man, but their
"Pretty Boy" slam was aimed at Phipps's swing music, which sounded ornamental to them, like music gift-wrapped for society, for someone's grand-
parents, or other "comfort-zoners," Wayne said.

The Shorter boys had good reason to be jealous of Nat's group. "Over
in the Terrace Room, when their band played, it'd be packed, with two or
three hundred people," Wayne said. "They'd be playing 'Harlem Noc-

turne,' 'Good Night Irene,' 'The Tennessee Waltz,' or 'An American in Paris.' The Gene Kelly kind of stuff, but they'd play it so that you could dance to it, with some tempo. That's what the girls liked. And they had the girlfriends. The girls would compete to carry their horns. It's always about the girls, I don't care what anyone says."

The Jackie Bland Band was decidedly less popular than the orchestra. It wasn't that Newark's teenagers disliked bebop's rhythms or melodies. Bebop's critical flaw was that it flew in the face of music's social function. "I'd go to a party and put 'Two Bass Hit' on," Wayne said, "and somebody'd come along and you'd hear *shhhhhtt*—the sound of an LP being ripped off a record player. They'd put on Larry Darnell, Ruth Brown, you know, meet-a-girl music, a get-close-and-dance track. And they'd start arguing about it. 'Keep it simple, now. Take that progressive stuff out of here.' And that's when I knew we were going to have a long way to go with this music."

Alan and Wayne were discordant in more than their musical tastes. "The Shorters were always set apart," Nat Phipps said. "Their attire was different. We might be dressed for a party, casual, but they'd come in looking like undertakers, in dark suits with three or four buttons. They'd be there, but not really mix. They'd be pulled off to the side." Alan and Wayne communicated in a bebop-inflected, confidential way that could be as abstract as twin language. "They'd do a lot of sounds and grins, and they'd be pointin' and stuff," said poet Amiri Baraka, who grew up in Newark with Alan and Wayne. "Almost like they didn't want to say too much, didn't want to let too much of themselves out free. They talked, but they weren't like 'savage conversationalists.' It was mostly gestures and signification. And if you were *in,* if you were used to talking with them, they had a certain notoriety." Baraka also said the phrase "As Weird as Wayne" was bandied about to connote something especially "out"; Wayne was so determinedly eccentric that he inspired not a nickname but a *simile* for weirdness.

The Shorters reveled in their social estrangement: Wayne painted "Mr. Weird" on his horn case; Alan put "Doc Strange" on his. They embraced their band's marginal status after hearing bebop demonized by radio DJs, who excluded it from their playlists. They resolved to make the same "chaotic" and "disturbed" music that Dizzy Gillespie, Charlie Parker, and Bud Powell were making across the river. "We'd play at the YMCA, and we'd make like a dollar fifty," Wayne said. "There'd be ten people there. And even *they'd* go home—saying you can't dance to this bebop. We were a poor band, so poor we had the drummer walking across town with the naked drum set. We'd be walking along, somebody's carrying the front of the bass and somebody's got the back." Wayne mocked his youthful idealism: "'But we're dedicated!' we'd say proudly, raising our fists in the air. 'We're dedicated and we're modern. We take chances.'"

Jackie Bland's band went through some growing pains as it learned to balance bebop's style and substance. "Jackie couldn't play one note, but he acted like Dizzy Gillespie," Wayne said. "So we got him to stand up front, wearing a leopard-skin coat and horn-rimmed glasses; he had a goatee and he wore a beret like Dizzy. There were no trumpet players in Newark, or no section anyway. So when the trumpet players were supposed to go *Bam!* on 'Manteca,' Jackie would sing 'wah.' I said, 'Hey man, what's he doin'?' So we took our saxophone mouthpieces off and played those in place of the trumpets."

Mr. Lamar, Wayne's music teacher at the YMCA, noticed the rivalry between the orchestra and the bebop band, and began to stage battles of the bands between the two groups. These battles played out like teen parodies of the culture at large, mirroring the shift from swing to bebop that was happening in jazz. The face-offs unvaryingly resulted in victory for the swing band, but the young bebop group did gain some notice for its obstinate modernism, if not for its music. The battles drew such large crowds that Mr. Lamar decided to stage a more formal contest at the Masonic Temple on Belmont Avenue. Its downtown location attracted a broader audience, including townspeople as well as students.

Both bands rose to the occasion and exploited the new location, staging dramatic spectacles and playing as if their lives depended on it. Up in the balcony, Nat Phipps's guys were models of upright composure. "We had just scored a gig opening for Nat King Cole," Nat said. "So with the help of our parents, we bought uniforms, and we were sharp." In their powder-blue pants and rust-red coats, the orchestra strove for the debonair style of the Cab Calloway or Duke Ellington orchestras, though their synchronized horn sweeps and finger snaps were executed with such military precision that Duke or Cab would have swung the little soldiers offstage in two beats. They attracted a garland of admiring girls with waltzes and upbeat dance tunes like "Little Brown Jug" and Count Basie's "Jumpin' at the Woodside."

Shorter's group arrived carrying their horns in shopping bags, having deliberately left their "bourgeois" horn cases at home. The underdogs set up below the orchestra, down on the floor. Unlike the dance band, the beboppers played by ear. To flaunt that talent, the Shorters unfolded copies of the New York *Daily News* and placed them on their music stands in lieu of sheet music—their sound was so fresh, it was taken from the day's headlines. "Earlier that day we moistened our suits and crumpled them up so they'd be wrinkled, for that devil-may-care effect. We thought bop players had to look that way," Wayne remembered. "We even wore galoshes—and you know it wasn't rainin' outside." Alan enhanced the zany effect of his attire by donning a dandy's white-and-gray kid gloves—he put them on one finger at a time, with exaggerated slowness. Finally, the musicians perched themselves on backward-facing folding chairs and began to play.

However affected the beboppers' outré appearance may have been, their music was genuinely avant-garde compared to the swinging danceability of the big band. And there was no question whose talent commanded the band: Wayne's solos were good, preternaturally so. "That group had more of Wayne's influence than the leader's," Nat said. "Jackie waved the baton, but the little tenor saxophonist in the band was its strength." Wayne was the Sy Oliver to Jackie's Jimmie Lunceford, who was then the epitome of the charming nonmusician big-band leader.

After each group had played once, Mr. Lamar, in the guise of master of ceremonies, took the first vote. He pointed up to the balcony, and the crowd registered some heavy appreciation for Nat Phipps and Co. Mr. Lamar gestured toward the boppers down on the floor, and the applause was not as strong, but still respectable. As the night wore on, the big band's extensively arranged swing music seemed somehow cumbersome compared to the nimble quickness and flash of the Bland Band's bebop. "We were surprising ourselves, and I think other people were surprised that we could play when we looked like we did, like freaks," Wayne said.

By the third vote, the beboppers earned the loudest applause. Mr. Lamar promptly ended the contest and declared Wayne's group the night's winner. This decision was not without controversy. "We'd always won before, and it seemed a little funny to end right at that moment, but I guess it was their turn to win," Nat said. Mr. Lamar's suspiciously abrupt conclusion of the contest was no doubt motivated by sentimental pride—the Shorters were now blazing through Dizzy Gillespie charts he'd heard them struggling with only months before.

Winning the contest gave Wayne a profile on the local scene, and his growing skill on his horn gave him the opportunity to make a little money playing private parties. When Wayne was seventeen, he got a job at a club in Elizabeth, New Jersey, just six miles from Newark. His father drove him to the gig and dropped him off. Wayne went inside, took out his horn, and warmed up, making small talk with the other musicians and checking out the club's clientele, which was largely working-class Polish-American— Wayne recognized some of his father's co-workers in the crowd with their wives or dates.

Wayne felt peculiar about the room, and it was only after the band started to play that he realized why. He was the only black man there, onstage or off. So he wasn't too surprised when a drunken man stumbled over in front of the band and singled him out. "Play that horn!" he said, in a voice that was slurred, but forceful enough to seem menacing. Wayne fixed his gaze down on the floor and played his horn, improvising on the tune as well as he could. Meanwhile, some frenetic ad-lib poetry played on inside his head. *I've had a lucky star over me,* he thought, *but now here's the first confrontation. What the hell is going to come out of his mouth next? Where's that goddamn lucky star now? The sky is cloudy out there! What time is this gig over?* As the set ended, the drunk yelled even louder. "Do you know 'How Deep Is the Ocean?'" he bellowed, and then went back to the bar. Wayne knew about the gangsters who would call out for big hits, greasing their requests with big bills for musicians. But this heckler's sense of entitlement was more intimidating—it was subsidized only by liquid courage. Wayne walked over to the bass player as coolly as he could and said, "If this is going to be one of those things where I'm going to have to fight my way out of here, I don't dig it." Word traveled back to the drunk that the "colored musician" was uncomfortable with "prejudiced talk." The heckler hurried over to reassure Wayne. "You know what," he said. "I don't care if you're fuckin' pin-striped. I just want to hear a little horn. I like the saxophone."

Wayne was relieved. In truth, the drunk may have singled him out because he was the only black man in the club. Still, the man's flattering comment introduced Wayne to the possibility that talent alone might make him conspicuous. "It was like an artificial burden just went away," he said, and then joked: "And that's when I started saying 'pin-striped' instead of 'Negro.'"

Back in Newark, the racial balance was overwhelmingly in Wayne's favor at Lloyd's Manor, a jazz club above a bowling alley where musicians knocked around ideas at weekly cutting contests. In *American Pastoral,* Newark native and writer Philip Roth depicted Lloyd's Manor as a "place where few whites other than a musician's reckless Desdemona would venture," a club where white teenagers' parents claimed they'd be "stabbed to death by a colored guy 'high on reefer,' whatever that meant."

For Wayne, Lloyd's Manor was simply the place to hear Manhattan's best jazz musicians, who made guest appearances there on Monday nights. Just before Wayne graduated from high school, Sonny Stitt had a gig at Lloyd's. In 1951, Stitt was a top bebop alto saxophonist—though he was prickly on the matter of his musical resemblance to Bird, whose pioneering flights cast shadows of insecurity over all saxophonists at the time. Stitt invited Herbie Morgan, a young local saxophonist, to join him for the show. Morgan had developed a reputation as someone to watch, and Stitt meant to salvage the young talent from the wrong side of the river and spirit him over to Manhattan's sanctuary of high bop. To heighten the show's drama, Sonny decided to invite another young tenor saxophonist onstage. Someone recommended Wayne for the gig. Despite his mother's repeated warnings to "stay away from that Lloyd's Manor," and notwithstanding his technical limitations—he could play in only three keys at the time: C, B-flat, and G—Wayne decided it was an opportunity he just couldn't pass up.

Sonny Stitt was already there when Wayne arrived. "You ready, you ready?" Sonny asked. "Sonny always talked fast and said everything twice," Wayne remembered. They went onstage, and Sonny called a tune in the key of E-flat—not one of the keys Wayne had mastered. "He played the blues, all through the keys. I was struggling but I was thinking, *Okay, I'm here, and I've got to play.*"

Nat Phipps was at Lloyd's Manor that night. "Wayne was always a very youthful-looking person, and at that time he looked like he was twelve. He was quiet. Not shy, but retiring. So this unassuming kid came up and started playing, and then fifteen minutes later the house was crazy. The other players wanted to fade away." Amiri Baraka heard Wayne at many cutting contests. "Wayne was precocious," Baraka wrote. "I heard many pretty astounding things he was doing at seventeen and eighteen. Even then, when he couldn't do anything else, he could still make you gasp at sheer technical infallibility."

When they finished playing, Sonny excitedly pulled Wayne aside. "You want to come on the road with me, you want to go on the road?" he asked. Wayne explained that he would soon graduate from high school and wanted to go to college. Sonny replied so quickly that Wayne almost couldn't understand him, "Shit, you got to get your education." Sonny said that only once. Wayne thought to himself, *He's been playing so fast and talking so fast that he don't know which is which. He's playing fast, but it's still Charlie Parker. It's still Bird you hear echoed in every note. Maybe Sonny wants to enhance himself with two younger players.* Working with Stitt would have been the next best thing to playing with Bird—a prestigious offer for an unknown seventeen-year-old from New Jersey. But as much as

Wayne was enthralled by his hero's style, he wanted to go to college and study composition; he wanted to create something original for himself.

In Wayne's junior and senior years at Arts High School, his absences were reduced from the thirty days of his sophomore year to a reasonable total of four days for the final two years. The music classes had succeeded in reforming the young cinephile and stage-show zealot of his truancy. He earned straight A's in harmony, theory, orchestration, and band and was awarded the Sozio Music Award at his high school graduation, in 1951. That year, the Arts High School yearbook featured a "1,001 Arabian Nights" Scheherazade theme. In an extravagantly mythic tone, the yearbook chronicled the "Tale of the Realm Known as the School of the Arts." Though the yearbook's style was naive and overwrought, the caption for Wayne's senior photo hit just the right pitch. It was an uncanny divination:

> In Wayne's future could be seen a tour of the U.S. and Europe, possibly with a band. His esoteric expressions often escaped his listeners, but his musical ability spoke for itself, he also being a "bop fiend."

3.

The Newark Flash

THERE'S A PERSISTENT MYTH that great artists simply emerge as geniuses after they've discovered their creative gifts, kind of like superheroes miraculously empowered by their costumes. And there's a misperception that great artists create with little effort. Much later in his life, Wayne saw some rough drafts of Beethoven's scores. "You know the Fifth Symphony?" Wayne asked. "He made sixteen attempts at that, with crossed out notes and everything. It was *dum, dah,* then *dah, dah dum,* . . . there was a *whole* lot of trial and error before he came up with that rousing *dah-dah-dah dum!*" The score drafts affirmed Wayne's own years of hard work. He spent most of the fifties perfecting his craft as a composer and crafting his cunning as a player—and running around New York City having a great time.

Before Wayne could begin this work, in college, he had to earn some tuition money. In the fall of 1951, he got a job as a stock clerk at the Singer sewing-machine factory in Elizabeth, New Jersey, where his father worked. Wayne spent a year wheeling carts of bobbins from one factory department to the next. By the end of the following summer, Wayne had saved $2,000. College credits were $22 each, so combined with some support from his parents, he had enough money to start school.

Wayne entered New York University in the fall of 1952 as a music education major, and he took all required courses for the major. "I took music history, where we were looking at the twelve tribes of Israel and Saint Francis, all that stuff as it traveled through Europe. There were lots of music history classes throughout college that would climax in your senior year with your music history final exam. Music history was used as a barometer to see where you were as a total person, your overall understanding of culture and music." Wayne also studied piano proficiency, demonstrating his competence on "The Star-Spangled Banner" and the eighteenth-century ditty "Drink to Me Only with Thine Eyes." In his harmony and orchestration classes, he did his homework with an experimental slant. Already schooled in bebop, Wayne had an ear for other sounds. "When I was in music class at NYU, the teachers would give me assignments and say, 'If you want to experiment, do it on your own time and do it outside of class. When you're in class, you have to do it in the way it is supposed to be done.' But a few of us would do an assignment and sneak in what we wanted anyway. And they would say—they didn't exactly know what was wrong because we'd sneak it in so well—'This is incorrect.' Sincerely, they thought it was incorrect. But they didn't know what was going on in my mind . . ."

Except for one teacher. Wayne's modern-harmony professor, Modena Scoville, was a sharp-eared progressive. "She said, 'This may be incorrect, but it's all right. I know you're sneaking around on the subway doing all this stuff.' We used to ride the subway and experiment, 'Hey, why don't we move this C-sharp over here, and let's do some perfect fourths *anyway*,' because they said we couldn't do that. And we'd try to hide 'em. But that one teacher would catch 'em. Every time." Scoville encouraged Wayne to mix styles, but told him he had to *know* those other styles. He got right to work on an opera called *The Singing Lesson*, a story of the Italian gangs he watched near the NYU campus, down in the southern part of Greenwich Village. He stopped working on it in his third year at school: "I heard that Leonard Bernstein was doing something called *West Side Story*, and I thought, *I'll catch up to mine some other time.*" Wayne began to write other compositions and tunes. He didn't give them names right away. Later on he'd call them "Nellie Bly," "Ping Pong," "Hammer Head," and "Sincerely Diana."

Wayne also played in a college concert band, which was no badge of honor for him, he said: "The head of the instrumental department got everybody in this concert band, all the music majors. They knew this band would be the workhorse, bring money in for the school, be the mascot, the rooting thing at football games and parades—sort of a living banner that fostered the school's accomplishments." As a music education major, Wayne had no formal studies on the saxophone in college. That education happened in clubs. The best jazz musicians had instrumental technique that was more than adequate by classical education standards. "Miles Davis told me they asked him to demonstrate triple-tonguing on the trumpet for his Juilliard entrance exam," Wayne said. "As soon as he figured out what they meant, he ran through it like nothing and they passed him." Wayne studied instrumental performance off-hours at Birdland and the Café Bohemia, leading a double life as a student and jazz-club scenester, checking out the acts there. "I took the bus and two other trains to get to NYU," Wayne said. "Then I'd hang till one or two in the morning at clubs in New York and get home close to three. Then I'd be up by seven to go to school. I'd do that every day and night."

In the clubs, Wayne picked up more jazz jargon, and especially admired gems of speech from his idols, Charlie Parker and Lester Young. "You'd always hear Bird talking like a professor, saying 'My inimitable cohort' onstage. And Lester Young, he created a whole new vocabulary." The writer Whitney Balliett collected a sampling: "'Bing and Bob' were the police. A 'hat' was a woman, and a 'homburg' and a 'sombrero' were types of women." Wayne remembered a time when he heard Lester talking to a friend in a club: "Prez said, 'You come in here with a different woman every night. Last night it was a homburg, but tonight it's a sombrero!'" The second date was a little more voluptuous and flashy. Balliett's Lester Young vocabulary included other entries: "An attractive young girl was a 'poundcake.' A 'gray boy' was a white man, and Young himself, who was light-skinned, was an 'oxford gray.' 'I've got bulging eyes' for this or that meant he approved of something. . . . 'Left people' were the fingers of a pianist's left hand. 'I feel a draft' meant he sensed a bigot nearby. People 'whispering on' or 'buzzing on' him were talking behind his back. Getting his 'little claps' meant being applauded. . . . 'To be bruised' was to fail. A 'tribe' was a band, and a 'molly trolley' was a rehearsal. 'Can Madam burn?' meant 'Can your wife cook?' 'These people will be here in December' meant that his second child was due in December. 'Startled doe, two o'clock' meant that a pretty girl was in the right side of the audience." Lester's bon mots weren't just cool and clever plays on words. When Lester mocked color schemes by calling himself an "oxford gray," he anticipated just how blasé some blacks would become to periodic shifts in their designation. Lester certainly would have preferred the absurdist humor of Wayne's "pinstriped" over the later common term "people of color."

On the weekends, Wayne started to make regular money playing music around Newark. A while after his winning performance at the battle of the bands, he got a call from Nat Phipps (the Shorters had just gotten their first telephone). Nat invited Wayne to join his band. "I'd been writing and playing another kind of music for the Jackie Bland Band, but Nat made more money, sometimes fifteen bucks a night," Wayne said. The invitation presented Wayne with his first dilemma between art and commerce, and he talked the matter over with his mother and father. "Think straight, now," Louise said. Wayne took her advice and decided to be pragmatic. "I had to work through college," he said.

After the battles of the bands, Nat's musical interests had begun to evolve away from big-band swing and in the direction of bebop. His band's personnel changed as its members drifted in and out of the service. Wayne was surrounded by talent: There was Nat's brother, Bill Phipps, who went on to play with Dizzy Gillespie; trombonist Grachan Moncur III, who recorded with Tony Williams and Jackie McLean in the early sixties; trombonist Tom McIntosh, who wrote for Dizzy, composing the musicians' favorite "Cup Bearers," and was a longtime associate of James Moody, himself raised in Newark. After he was released from his tour of duty down in Fort Benning, Georgia, drummer Bobby Thomas joined Nat's group, and he later went on to work with the Billy Taylor Trio throughout the sixties and seventies. Even saxophonist Kenneth Gibson, an engineering major who would become mayor of Newark, was an excellent sight reader.

"It was eyelash music," Wayne said, meaning the band's music was light and fluttering, easy enough to read through the delicate curtain of half-closed eyes. "I saw this band was a place to sharpen my musicianship." Wayne's skills were pretty sharp when he started, Nat Phipps said: "His technical facility was always there, from the beginning. So was his ability to hear harmonies in a different way; he had a very phenomenal ear. I'd been playing piano for years, but after just a couple years on the horn, he was coming up with some very interesting harmonic ideas." And in what would become a dominant trend throughout Wayne's career, Nat immediately made room for Wayne's original arrangements. "As a writer, Wayne was quite comfortable with classical compositions," Nat said. "He was beginning to write classically influenced things. And he arranged charts that were cutting-edge, different than what local Newark bands would play." Wayne arranged "Vagabond Shoes," "Love for Sale," "Four Brothers," "Black Coffee," "Peanut Vendor," and "Jet My Love," a tune popularized by Nat King Cole. Besides these twenty-odd arrangements, Wayne wrote an original piece for the band, "No Minors Allowed," named after the prohibitive signs hanging on the doors of some of the clubs that Wayne had wanted to visit as a teenager. "'No Minors Allowed' was the hippest thing you ever heard," Nat said. As Lester Young said, "Seeing is believing, and hearing is a bitch."

Outeroids

While Wayne was happily losing himself in the urban experience of NYU, his brother, Alan, was not faring so well in college. Their mother, Louise, had cultivated both boys to be resolutely creative and imaginative, and they were both extremely suspicious of socialization. But Alan was always "super-questioning," Wayne said. "I think it started to appear when he was noticing boys and girls dating, the reason why people chose things. The girls chose the 'like' kind of person, the masses of males with 'like' attitudes, 'like' this for the 'like' thats. And someone who was different, really different . . . Alan was wondering what made people afraid, afraid to stick out." Alan was accepted to Howard University, the black Harvard—"The Capstone of Negro Education" was its motto. In jazz culture, especially among beboppers, there was an abiding ethos of individuality: "Originality is the thing," Lester said. Black colleges, on the other hand, were generally very conservative at the time, especially Howard, which had one of the largest endowments of any school in the country. "Before you were accepted at Howard, they asked for a picture," Wayne said. "The bourgeois thing was going on. They wanted to see what shade you were, if you were light brown or a deeper shade on the race color wheel. Wanted to make sure you were not too dark. My mom knew that. They would justify it. They had those legal words, they had a right to deny a person's application based on something."

"Based on what?" Alan asked when he read the application, in his "super-questioning" manner.

As a boy from a lower-class family given the opportunity to attend a top college, Alan was expected to prove himself a credit to his race there. But the enforced conformity of Howard's social life was extremely disturbing to him. When Alan came home from school, he reported on the hazing practices of Howard's fraternities in outraged tones, as if they were war crimes. "Alan told me the first thing that happened was that they were asked to obey something," Wayne said. "And then once they were a novice, or initiate, the seniors wrestled them down to the ground and tried to clip an *H* for Howard into their heads." At school, Alan met up with another loner hipster, Pete Lonesome from West Virginia, and together the two boys rebelled against the bourgeois fraternizing. "We ain't goin' for that," they'd say. "That's not what's happenin'. That ain't where it's at. That ain't copacetic." Wayne said that Pete and Alan flaunted their bop style in Howard's conservative climate. "They were talking about Dizzy Gillespie and bebop and Monk, and they had those long coats. They had hats, and they cut the brim way down, which they called the 'stingy brim.' They'd pull their hats down so that half their ears would be covered and you couldn't see their eyebrows, and they'd walk around with really long sleeves almost down to the ground, which was called 'the raggling,' with the real curved shoulder. And they'd crash those parties. Those fraternity parties."

Alan made no effort to cooperate in his studies, either. Professors returned his essays with the usual red corrections in the margins, requests for explication such as, "What do you mean by this?" Alan would return them without revisions, responding in larger, bold print, "What do YOU mean by this?" Alan's Newark friend Amiri Baraka went to Howard with him. "Alan showed up one time for ROTC in shoes with no shoestrings and no pin in his hat," Baraka said. "He looked over at me in line and just grunted. I guess he didn't want to stay in there very much." Alan dropped out of Howard, though he did eventually graduate from NYU years later. But his die was cast at Howard, as Wayne said: "Every time Alan and Pete Lonesome came along at school, everyone said, 'Here they come, the be-boppers, the weirdos.' That stayed with him." Throughout his life, Alan would never relax, always raging against authority and the limits of the status quo, so much that he sometimes seemed paranoid and schizophrenic. Alan's psychological profile was debatable, but his exasperation with all things normative definitely interfered with his full realization as an artist. Bassist Ron Carter's wife, Janet, was a classmate of Alan's at Howard, and through her, Ron later got to know Alan in New York. "I met him at one of those East Side Alphabet City clubs," Ron said. "He was playing trumpet with a Kleenex box for a mute. I said, 'Man this guy is crazy; I'm going to get out of here.'" Ron's response to Alan's free-form improvisation was in part a matter of taste. Ron's reaction did show that it was one thing for Alan to play "Doc Strange" as a teenager and another for him to obstinately continue in that role as an adult. Alan later moved to Europe, where listeners were a little more receptive to both his musical experiments and his anti-conformist speeches.

Wayne wasn't any more normal than Alan. He may have been more musically talented than his brother, and he was definitely less provocative. And unlike Alan's experience at Howard, Wayne was exposed to a forward-thinking, diverse student population at NYU. Just as Arts High had nurtured Wayne's artistic inclinations at a crucial time, NYU's liberal environment fostered his intellectual latitude. Along with his music classes, Wayne took the requisite assortment of liberal arts classes: psychology, sociology, and also ROTC, which they called Geo-Politics. Wayne was especially stimulated by a philosophy course taught by a progressive professor, Dr. Villamaine. "His class had a real mix of people," Wayne said. "There were three guys fresh from Korea on GI Bills, and there were a couple nuns. The first day in class, we were filling out our registration cards. I raised my head up and saw that Dr. Villamaine had written his name and three words on the board: GOD, DEVIL, and FUCK—all in capital letters. He said, 'This is what this course is going to be about.' I was thinking, *The nuns!* I got an A in that course, and Dr. Villamaine asked me if I wanted to major in philosophy. In that class I brought up stuff about Plato and Socrates, about the destiny of a person, a man is what he is, not what he does. There was lots of opportunity for verbalization in that class."

Wayne's NYU course work opened his mind philosophically, and the school's diversity of identity freed him from conventional thinking about social class. In high school, Wayne had bought into Newark's black middle-class value system, and was ashamed of his family's humble home, a second-floor apartment in a building "with a slight lean to it." "Like Alan, I started becoming more cognizant of the class thing when I wanted to have a girl looking at me in high school," Wayne said. "I wanted her to see what was rare and precious in me, but they couldn't see that at all. A lot of the girls, the black girls, were what you call 'high yellow,' they had fine hair—that mix between white and black hair—and were pleasant shades, kind of vanilla or café au lait. They were living around Montclair or South Orange, New Jersey. They were going after the achievers, the ones with white and brown buck shoes and seersucker jackets. In inner-city Newark, there were also nice-looking girls, but they were going after guys who were sons of doctors, lawyers—people who owned homes in Montclair. When I was turned down for a date on the phone, my mother could tell by the conversation that the girl was asking where I lived. My mother said, 'They want to know if you got something.'"

Wayne lost some of his embarrassment and self-consciousness about status in college. "When I went to NYU, I brought my friends home," Wayne said. "They'd drive me home, and I'd take them upstairs. They'd come inside, and it was sparkling—my mom was really good with house-keeping, and always had something good in the kitchen. My friends would say, 'Can we come over? What's your mother got going in the kitchen?'" Louise noted Wayne's growing self-respect. "That's good, Wayne," she'd say. "You're not ashamed to bring people home." Bobby Thomas was one of the friends who visited Wayne and his family at home. "His mother could sure cook some greens," Bobby said. "And his father was always happy to see me; he was very nice. They called me Nobby. They knew Wayne was so talented, but Wayne would talk in a way, about weird movies and in that Lester Young style, that people might misunder-stand him. So his mother would say, 'Wayne, why don't you stop talkin' that way? Talk like how Nobby talks.'" Bobby had to agree with Wayne's mother on that count. "You're not gonna get tight with any girls talking like that," he'd tell Wayne.

Wayne received a scholarship his senior year, but still didn't have quite enough money to finish his studies. After a couple of years working with Nat Phipps's band, it didn't seem to pay so well: With anywhere from nine to thirteen players in the group, each musician could make only fifteen dollars a gig. Wayne wanted to work in a more lucrative small combo, so he formed a group with an Arts High buddy, bassist Eddie White. Eddie was on scholarship to Princeton, one of only two black students at the school. Wayne visited him there, once even spotting professor Albert Einstein walking across the lawn—Eddie's Princeton friends couldn't figure out why Wayne got so excited about it. Eddie and Wayne recruited a pianist for their band named Jacqueline Rollins, "the only one who played like Bud Powell," Wayne said. "She was beautiful, but nobody messed with her—you ain't gonna mess with nobody who can play, and she could *play*." Jacqueline alternated with Nat Phipps in the piano chair of their quartet, and with Nat, Wayne's group won first prize at the Apollo Theater for the Wednesday night new-talent contest with "September in the Rain."

Midget Mambo at the Palladium

While he sharpened his skills as a performer, Wayne began to write original tunes, including mambos, for the smaller group. In the mid-fifties, the mambo held popular sway over all other dance steps. Wayne hadn't been very fond of swinging big-band dance music in high school, but he had to give into the mambo craze. "You couldn't get a date if you couldn't dance the mambo," Wayne said. "You didn't have to be Latino. All the people I knew could dance the hell out of the mambo." Wayne's friends noticed that he danced like he played, with complex flourishes and frenetic outbursts, but altogether slick and controlled. The mambo's musical form had absorbed the serious big-band experiments of Machito and the "Cubop" of Dizzy Gillespie, and Wayne had no trouble composing a few models of the form. "The first mambo I wrote was called 'Mambo X,' then I wrote 'Mambo Moderato,'" Wayne said. "But the one that got it was 'Midget Mambo.' Every time we played it, people got down with it."

Wayne's original mambos made the group a popular band-for-hire at high school proms. With that success, they got a gig as the opening act for the mambo dance king himself, "El Rey del Mambo" Pérez Prado, at the Starlight Roof in the Waldorf-Astoria Hotel. In 1954 Prado had an extended appearance at the Starlight, and his popularity with general audiences reached its height with his 1955 hit "Cherry Pink and Apple Blossom White." This success damaged Prado's standing in New York's Hispanic community, however, where people thought his mambos had lost their edge.

The Palladium club on Fifty-second Street was the multicultural mecca for hard-core mambo aficionados, with the rival groups of Tito Puente and Tito Rodriguez battling there regularly. "After word started getting out about us, we were invited to play at the Palladium," Wayne said. "Tito Puente and Tito Rodriguez were playing there, and Celia Cruz was there in a fishtail dress; she was very young. In our band we had one of the cousins of Nat Phipps, Harold, who played the conga drums. In most of the Latin bands, they had two or three guys drumming, but we just had the one guy, and he played kind of like Chano Pozo or Candido from Cuba. When we played 'Midget Mambo,' I said, 'Uh-oh!' 'cause even Celia Cruz got out there and was dancing! Years later, I was on the bus in Europe, and my band junctured with Tito Puente someplace. Tito came over to me and said, 'Hey man, I remember that time at the Palladium, man. You came over with that band from Newark, man, and you kicked our asses.'"

Jazz Fugue

Wayne graduated from NYU in 1956 with a degree in music education. He was offered a job as the musical director of a school district in Florida, but he barely considered the offer. The job's meager salary wasn't enough to tempt him away from the opportunities in New York. Along with all the live performance prospects around town, Wayne was asked to play at his first professional recording session just after graduation, on June 8, 1956. The session was with pianist and composer Johnny Eaton, a Princeton student whom Wayne met through Eddie White. Wayne joined Johnny to play dances and other social functions around Princeton. "Charlie Parker played bar mitzvahs to get the money, doing bebop versions of 'Hava Nagila,'" Wayne said. "I had to work my way through college, too. With Johnny we played the types of social functions where everyone came out in seersucker suits. Mostly, Johnny was a Dixieland player. Onstage they wore straw hats, vests, with garters on their sleeves. Sometimes Johnny sat on the floor in front of the piano with his back to the keys, raised his hands backwards behind him, and started playing with his thumbs sticking out."

Eaton's skills went well beyond frolicsome ragtime antics. At Princeton, the pianist studied composition with Milton Babbitt, Arthur Mendel, and other proponents of contemporary classical music. Eaton was signed to Columbia Records, and his first recording, *College Jazz,* was issued in the spring of 1956. A *Playboy* magazine review of *College Jazz* noted Eaton's classical influences: "Ringleaders in a cult of progressive jazz on the campus, *Johnny Eaton and His Princetonians* blast off on a winding, flute-filling journey through a milkyway of originals and standards. By admission, pianist Eaton and the rest of his group are students of 'serious' music, and it isn't too difficult to discern the influence of Schoenberg, Milhaud and even Rossini cutting liberally across their polytonal orbit."

At the session with Wayne, Eaton ran through a collection of jazz standards, including "Too Close for Comfort" and "What Is This Thing Called Love?" as well as a couple of classically informed original compositions, "Fugue" and "Hallelujah." The studio had the collegiate atmosphere of relaxed and confident young men at play. At one point, the amateur trumpeter inadvertently made a distracting fluttering noise on his horn that was picked up by a nearby microphone. The producer interrupted the take and joked, "You can't flutter valves like that, because it sounds like somebody running past the picket fence." The producer came off like a good-humored professor indulgently correcting a favored pupil. The musicians all laughed sheepishly, except Wayne.

Fresh out of college himself, Wayne was working through influences as a player. He flexed his bebop chops; on one tune, he briefly quoted from "Hot House," Tadd Dameron's popular bop tune. On the ballads, the lyrical economy of Wayne's melodic lines was more than a little suggestive of Stan Getz, especially the saxophonist's then popular West Coast Sessions for Verve. Wayne's musical inspirations were always manifold, and Getz was as likely an influence as anyone. But Wayne was emphatic about Getz's debt to Prez. "Lester's sound was velvet and whispering, and that sound was so well-known," Wayne said. "When he heard Stan Getz, Miles Davis said, 'That's Prez.' Getz himself would say, 'It's Prez, man.' Lester just wanted the credit for his sound. But here was Lester, still with the Jazz at the Philharmonic. That's why he wouldn't stop drinking in his final days." Wayne's Getz/Young impression was actually very appropriate to the Eaton session, as fitting as his mambos were at the Palladium. Just before the fifth take of "What Is This Thing Called Love?" the producer gave the musicians some positive feedback on their performance. "Cool," Eaton replied, and then riffed, "cool jazz." A cool-jazz style is what the group affected, the loose and easy spirit of Getz's fresh sound. Wayne said he consciously played what the music needed. "I was acting, more than I was influenced by anything," he explained. "The music was such that it was like being at the university, and some propriety was in order. I was not being proper exactly, but I was definitely not playing 'street.' I knew what I was doing."

If Wayne's style was reminiscent of Stan Getz or Lester Young on the ballads, he came into his own on "Fugue," a tune with an introductory counterpoint section. In keeping with the traditional fugue form, the tune began with a single instrument, vibes, and then added successive instruments individually. After the vibes stated the melody, Wayne entered with a countermelody, delivering it with the marvelous facility and tone of classical French saxophonist Marcel Mule. The baroque counterpoint demanded absolute precision, and the slightest deviation from metronomic accuracy would disrupt the tune's delicate solemnity. Wayne's performance was steady and elegant throughout several takes of the tune, thanks to his having run classical scales in workhorse practice sessions.

Those Who Sit and Wait

Wayne's classical music studies had given him the capacity to work with Johnny Eaton and his Princetonians. His basic proficiency gave him the flexibility to play and write mambos. But Wayne's heart lay with the hardcore bop scene in the clubs. In the 1950s, talent still spoke for itself on the jazz scene, and Wayne began to earn a reputation around town as "The Newark Flash." Just as Wayne was getting a name, he was drafted into the army—the service was mandatory for American men in the fifties. A few days before Wayne entered the army, he took part in a memorable jam session at the Café Bohemia. "I was just standing at the bar having a cognac, and had my draft notice in my back pocket," Wayne said. "On that stand was Oscar Pettiford, Art Blakey, they were taking turns, Bill Hardman had come into town, Jackie McLean, Walter Bishop, Jr., Art Taylor, who'd play the drums and alternate with Art Blakey. And Percy Heath came in. Cannonball had just come into town, and had heard that Miles was looking for him. A hearse drove up, and it was Jimmy Smith bringing his organ in there! And I was thinking, *I'm going to miss all this stuff, 'cause I'm going into the army.* So I said 'Shit,' and I got ripped." Drummer Max Roach spotted Wayne over at the bar. "You're the kid from Newark?" he asked Wayne. "You're the Newark Flash? I've been hearing about this Newark Flash, man. You got your horn?" Wayne went out to the car to get his saxophone. When Max called him up to play, Wayne imagined it was his curtain-call performance: *Damn, the place is jumping, but this is it for me,* he thought as he played. "Going into the army meant the River Styx, so I was playing like it was the last time," he said.

Though it was peacetime—the Korean War had ended in 1953—the potent mix of youth, booze, and poetic license caused Wayne to equate army service with death, or at least the demise of his fledgling musical career. The twenty-three-year-old couldn't predict how many exciting, productive years he'd have as a musician. And he certainly didn't anticipate the mundane reality of army routine. Wayne was stationed in Fort Dix, New Jersey, where army life was anything but dangerous. Mostly, there was the tedium of following the same schedule, day in and day out. And as a small, retiring guy whose height maxed out at five-foot-six, Wayne didn't have much brawn to throw around. Fortunately, Wayne discovered he had a talent that spoke for itself in the army: He was a spot-on sharpshooter. "My army days brought out something special in me when I found out I was number one on the rifle range," he said. "Then I didn't have to say nothin'."

Wayne was lucky enough to get a spot in the army band, though that proved to be a mixed blessing. As he told *Jazz UK* in 2003: "When we went to New York City, we had to march down Eighth Avenue. Some of us who played jazz would put our helmets way down 'cause we didn't want anybody to recognize us . . . we didn't want the people on the street goin' 'Look there's Wayne—what's he doin' in there?'" Back in the barracks, Wayne continued to compose during the slow times, and had an ever thickening book of charts. Wayne met pianist Cedar Walton at Fort Dix. "We met in the army in 1956 when he was in the band up there," Cedar said. "I was trying to get into the band. They already had a pianist, so I went to Germany. Wayne and I exchanged musical ideas—he showed me music he wrote, and said he even wrote an opera. I always admired his compositional talents."

Still, army existence was drudgery, and Wayne picked up a classic, timeworn habit to escape its drab monotony. "I really started drinking in the army, on the weekends," he said. "Nobody wanted to be there. Everybody I knew was drinking. Some of these guys would go home on weekends to wives cooking succotash, to forget. But no matter what you did, it'd be back to the barracks after the weekend was over." Naturally Wayne drank a lot in jazz clubs, where drinking was de rigueur. "You'd stand there posed with a cigarette in one hand and a glass in the other, and everybody else was posing, too." Wayne was generally nonconformist but modified his behavior to suit the jazz lifestyle, which condoned drinking as a distraction from the difficulties of making it as a musician. "Also we knew there was the handicap of marketing and commercial stuff. Some of us felt that if you just party and keep a little buzz, it was a filter, and would exorcise thoughts of what you were doing falling on deaf ears—especially the ears that could help carry it somewhere."

While Wayne served his time in the army, his friend Bobby Thomas attended the Juilliard School of Music. Bobby mentioned his friendship with Wayne to his fellow classical music students, who'd heard of "The Newark Flash." Bobby told them that even though Wayne played jazz, he had an ability to sing music and play the piano and "just sorta compose classical music on the spot." Bobby's friends didn't believe him. "They had a whole conception of what a jazz musician is, playing blues licks and everything," Bobby said. "I told them, No, really, he writes organ pieces and operas." Bobby finally convinced Wayne to come over and demonstrate his talents. Wayne was shy, especially with the Juilliard students sitting there so curiously and expectantly. So Bobby loosened him up by talking about their days playing back in Newark, and then dropped Stravinsky's name. Wayne excitedly picked up the thread, talking about Stravinsky's *Firebird,* and then went over to the piano and started singing. "Yeah, how about it?" Wayne said. "What if Stravinsky did a thing like this together with Bird, with Charlie Parker?"

"The way Wayne was singing and playing, you could hear the cymbals, brass, everything," Bobby said. "My friends' eyes were popping out of their heads. The next day in school, all the students were saying, 'It's true about Wayne Shorter!'"

Lester Left Town

Once, on a ten-day furlough, Wayne went on vacation to Toronto. Lester Young was playing there at the Town Tavern, a club that opened in 1949. By 1956, it was the city's premier showcase for international talent. Wayne was familiar with the Town Tavern from having played there with Nat Phipps's band, and he naturally wanted to hear Lester, who was a musician's musician. Prez had been one of Wayne's favorites since he was fifteen and first began checking out musicians at Newark's Adams Theater. Wayne arrived at the Toronto club in flashy New York style, sporting a pin-striped suit and paisley tie. After the first set, Wayne fought his way through the packed club to the bar, where he tried in vain to get a drink.

Asked about his ability to read music, Lester Young once said, "I don't like to read music, just . . . soul." Lester apparently read style as well as soul, because that night he picked the nattily dressed Wayne out of the crowd. "In the middle of the crushing throng, I felt someone tap me on the shoulder," Wayne said. "It was Lester Young. He said, 'You look like you're from New York. You're trying to get a drink, right? Let's go down to the wine cellar and get some real cognac!' He had the run of the place, with all these barrels down there. Lester poured himself a brimming pint glass full of cognac, but he only gave me half a glass. I don't remember what we talked about, 'cause I had a heavy buzz. It was vacation, and everything was happening!" Lester went up to play the second set, and Wayne stood listening, thinking, *I'm on vacation, and here's Lester Young comin' up to me out of nowhere. What does that mean?*

Wayne went back to camp and impressed his army buddies with the story of this happenstance meeting. They were much more impressed a few months later, when with only a few weeks remaining in his tour of duty, Wayne's company commander called and said, "There's a Horace Silver who wants to know if you can get away to play something with him." Wayne had been asked to stay in the army for another year as an instructor on the rifle range, but the lenient commander released Wayne early. Wayne played only three jobs with Horace Silver, which was long enough for the bandleader to note the rapidity with which Wayne was turning out quality compositions. "The first person who hipped me to the procedure of getting your own publishing was Horace Silver," Wayne said. "I put my stuff in Horace's publishing, and Horace has sent it back to me since then; he reassigned about thirteen songs back to me." Publishing was one area where Wayne definitely didn't want to follow in the footsteps of bebop idols like Lester Young, who died almost penniless. Silver was one of the first to take care of the publishing side of business, which made him a baron among musicians. When hip-hop artists started sampling riffs from his Blue Note recordings, Silver claimed that the first royalty statement he received for this usage was more than he made on all his Blue Note records combined.

Everything Was Happening

After his brief stint with Silver in 1957, Wayne started playing jam sessions at Count Basie's, the bandleader's club at Seventh Avenue and 132nd Street in Harlem. At Count Basie's, Wayne met a young trumpeter from Indianapolis named Freddie Hubbard, and the two started practicing together. Freddie lived in Brooklyn, so he had to catch two trains and a bus for the multi-leg trip to Wayne's house in Newark, but he felt like he was compensated for the long commute with the musicianship Wayne inspired in him. "We became very close and worked together a lot because he had a sound that I could blend with without overplaying," Freddie said. "Some guys played too hard, and I always played too hard myself, but Wayne made me play softer." Wayne and Freddie sometimes played in Brooklyn at a place called Turbo Village, or over in Newark at Sugar Hill, where Wayne sat in with Sonny Rollins. Wayne played as much as he could, making up for lost years in the army. He got some especially good training when he got a six-week gig in the house band at Minton's Play-house. As Miles Davis once noted, if you got up on the bandstand at Minton's and couldn't play, you were not only going to be embarrassed by the audience's disdain, you might also "get your ass kicked." By the time Wayne played there in the late fifties, he was less likely to get his ass kicked, though he was scrutinized. "The main guy who was playing there was Willie Bobo," Wayne said. "He was known to be around the bebop guys and Afro-Cuban guys. Dizzy was there, and Monk came in, to see the young blood. I was the youngest one." Wayne had to know a broad jazz repertoire for the sessions at Minton's, where anything from Benny Golson's tunes to the blues might be called for. "You didn't have to totally know the repertoire as much as you had to be able to hear," Wayne said. "They'd say, let's see if this guy can 'see,' which meant 'read music.' You'd hear, 'Jimmy So-and-so can't improvise, but he can sure see.'"

Late one afternoon when Wayne was working a matinee with Horace Silver, a calm, well-mannered lady approached him. "My name is Naima," she said. "My husband wants to meet you. He likes what you're playing." Wayne went into the kitchen to mess around on his horn a little, and Naima came back with her husband, who was John Coltrane. "You're playing that funny stuff, all over the horn, like me," John said. Wayne had seen Coltrane play with Miles Davis in Washington, D.C. "It was nice to meet John because I knew he was the only one that was on to something musically that was moving," Wayne said. Coltrane invited Wayne over to his house at 103rd and Broadway. "I'd go over there, and they would never let me leave!" Wayne said. "They were cooking, and we'd eat and then sit and talk about life." Naima told Wayne he was going to need a very strong wife, a strong life partner for what he intended to do with music. After they ate, Wayne and Coltrane would play the piano, practice scales, and talk shop, comparing their horns—Coltrane told Wayne he should upgrade to an older Otto Link mouthpiece.

Around this time, Freddie Hubbard was in the unique position of jamming with both Coltrane and Sonny Rollins, the two titans of the tenor saxophone. He was a kind of double agent, delivering reports back and forth on the other's progress. Coltrane famously labored over exercises in harp method books until he could lay down arpeggios like a sheet of sound, and Freddie was around sometimes when Wayne practiced with him. "When I'd go over to Coltrane's place, him and Wayne would play out of those string books, for the challenge," Freddie said. "They'd use the method of another instrument to think outside of the lines. Sometimes Wayne could play the stuff that Coltrane couldn't, which is saying something, since Coltrane was supposed to be the technical guy. But then sometimes Wayne would play just like Sonny, and I'd say, 'Hey, wait a minute, you're not supposed to do that.'"

Mostly, Wayne and Coltrane shared a similar mental capacity. They discussed how they wished they could speak "backwards," starting a sentence in the middle and going in both directions at once. They were looking for a freedom in speech that they found in jazz's vocabulary. Coltrane asked Wayne if he'd ever heard about something called *om*. Wayne wasn't into the idea of chanting, but understood the kind of universal sound Coltrane sought in the word. Friends noticed that the two men had the same personality, a kind of investigative thinking, a low-burning fire that could flare up in sound when they took the stage. "Right away with Coltrane, you noticed, *Damn, this guy is not worried about selling any records*," Wayne said. "Trane was always going for the impossible, and to go for the impossible is to sacrifice all the niceties. Trane cared so much about people that he eventually had to destroy things in music, to break down the layers of illusions for people."

One Monday night, Coltrane called Wayne, Freddie, and several others to play a session at Birdland. One of Coltrane's bandmates in Miles's quintet, alto saxophonist Cannonball Adderley, also took advantage of the night off from Miles's group to lead his own band at the club. Cedar Walton, Tommy Flanagan, and George Tucker were also there, along with Elvin Jones, who played drums with Coltrane as he would countless times later. "We were playing all this new stuff," Wayne said. "We were actually playing the music from *Giant Steps*. John had written *Giant Steps* by then. I was like walking through it. And then we did some standards. Cannonball's group would come on with the rhythm-and-blues thing, then we'd come back on with the new thing, looking to the future. People twenty-five years after that said, 'That was a hell of a night!' " Excited about his own rapidly developing music, Coltrane was eager to leave Miles's group in 1959. He tried to hand over his tenor spot to Wayne. "The gig is yours if you want it," Coltrane said. On that recommendation, Wayne called Miles up. "I'll let you know when I need another tenor player," Miles said crossly, not having yet realized that Coltrane, his cherished saxophonist, wanted to quit his group.

Birdland

Another world of opportunity soon opened up for Wayne when he met a young pianist named Josef Zawinul. Joe was sharp and swift, a confident Viennese player and composer who was classically trained as a child in Austria. He was attracted to jazz as a teenager, based on an alliterative association of the word with his own name. Joe made his way to the U.S. from Austria in 1958 on a scholarship from Boston's Berklee College of Music. After only a couple weeks at Berklee, Joe filled in for a pianist one night at George Wein's Storyville club. Jake Hanna, the drummer at the gig that night, recommended Joe to Maynard Ferguson, who tried him out in traditional "sink or swim" fashion, with a gig at the Apollo Theater. Ferguson not only hired Joe but also helped him secure a green card and a cabaret license.

Like Wayne, Joe seemed to arrive on the scene as a fully realized player, though his knowledge of American jazz culture was largely based on repeated viewings of the film *Stormy Weather*. Joe had been in New York only a few months when he met Wayne. "Everybody was already talking about Wayne as the new kid on the block, the young lion," Joe said. "We met at Ham and Eggs, a place on Fifty-second Street just down from Birdland. The place we'd go to a lot was called the Green Lantern. We used to drink there, and *that's* when it started. It'd be me and Wayne and Booker Little. When I first met Wayne, I couldn't speak English that well, but we had such amazing communication."

Joe Zawinul biographer Brian Glasser once asked Wayne how he initially managed to communicate with Joe when the pianist's English was so limited. Wayne gave a vivid account of a jazz scene so thriving that it spoke for itself, where encounters and sightings took the place of conversation. "[Joe and I] met on the corner of Birdland, and we'd go from one place to another—myself, him, and Slide Hampton, and some of the other guys. Freddie Hubbard. We'd just move around, runnin' around, and I didn't realize that what we were doing was in place of talking, the action. There was a lot of action going on. Now that I think back, we were always with people and running into people and things. 'There's Thelonious Monk. There goes Miles. There goes—hey! Sonny Rollins!' And then we'd go in a place to eat and while we were eating, late at night, everyone came in there—Dizzy Gillespie, all of them—and it seemed like . . . They say a picture's worth a thousand words? Well, we viewed. And to me, I thought it was language. . . . Seeing people was more like a conversation than talking with them. We were all in amongst that—Sarah Vaughan, Dinah Washington, and in Birdland. We worked there many nights, and as I'm thinking, Joe and myself, people getting to know us and us getting to know them, that I thought we were talking. But maybe we were not. A lot of shaking of hands and hugging goin' on. A lot of huggin' goin' on."

Joe and Wayne did manage to speak the international language of music. For Joe, their friendship was sealed when he discovered Wayne's comprehensive familiarity with classical music, even the obscure twentieth-century Viennese composer Friedrich Gulda. "Wayne and I talked about Schubert, and he could sing the lines," Joe said. "I was amazed. And then all of a sudden I began to talk about Gulda and Wayne knew about Gulda, and Wayne is younger than me! I thought, *Damn, man, this guy really knows!*

And then he said, 'I wrote an opera when I was nineteen,' and he was singing it. It sounded like Alban Berg, not exactly Berg but in that style. And I told everyone, '*This* is the guy.'" Wayne and Joe naturally shared an appreciation for jazz artists as well. "During this time we were talking about Charlie Parker, about Miles Davis—Wayne was a big Miles fan and knew everything he was doing, everything Blakey was doing. Wayne was, number one, a great student of the game. We'd talk about Ben Webster, Coleman Hawkins, about the different chords Duke Ellington used to orchestrate."

When one of Maynard Ferguson's tenor players had to go into the army, Joe convinced Wayne to audition for the vacant spot in the big band. Joe's roommate, trombonist Slide Hampton, organized the audition, which included saxophonists Eddie Harris, George Coleman, and Wayne. Wayne got the gig. Just after Wayne joined Ferguson, his old high school friend Amiri Baraka went to see him play in the big band at Birdland in June 1959. Baraka wrote about the show in a Wayne Shorter profile for *Jazz Review,* the first published article about him. Baraka's glowing description of Wayne's playing gave some indication of why he might have won the audition: "The playing is characterized by an almost literary (in the best sense of the word) sense of musical relationships. Everything that comes out of the horn seems not 'premeditated' (the fire and surprise of instantaneous extemporization is always present), but definite and assimilated . . . no matter how wild or unlikely it might seem at first. He seems to be willing to try anything. He usually makes it."

That night at Birdland, Wayne "made it" in a solo that Baraka wrote was "taken at a seemingly impossible double-timed tempo" but was "full of fierce and certainly satirical humor." Wayne was more concerned with hearing his original composition, "Nellie Bly," played by the band, and Baraka volunteered to request the tune during the show. The tune was already on Maynard's set list. During its performance, Wayne excitedly blew a "long, long sustained Ammons-like honk throughout an entire passage." Throughout the fifties, Wayne had worked his way through college, where he gained the basic knowledge to become a composer. He survived the army, which motivated him to sharpen his playing and become more determined about the direction of his musical career. Finally, he won a professional gig with an established bandleader. "What it comes to is seriousness!" he told Baraka that night. "Nothing comes to anything unless you're serious about it."

4.

Hard Drinking, Hard Bop
with the Jazz Messengers

A COUPLE OF WEEKS LATER, on July 24, 1959, Wayne played with Maynard Ferguson at the Toronto Jazz Festival. Art Blakey's Jazz Messengers
were there, too, or at least most of them were. Their tenor player, Hank
Mobley, was missing in action: His recurring drug problem made him an
unreliable sideman. When Messengers trumpeter Lee Morgan saw Wayne
up on the bandstand with Maynard, something clicked. Lee remembered
Wayne from the Sugar Hill jam sessions, and Wayne's performance with
Maynard at the festival was consistent with the solid quality of playing
he'd heard from the saxophonist in the past. Lee approached Art about
giving Wayne a shot with the Messengers. Art was always happy to entertain Lee's suggestions—the bandleader adored the bold, brash nineteen-

year-old trumpet prodigy. "Lee is the apple of my eye," he'd say, like a proud grandfather. But Art didn't need much convincing about Wayne's worthiness. He was desperate for a dependable tenor saxophonist.

When Wayne stepped down from the bandstand after Maynard's set, the offer to join Blakey's group came out of nowhere. "Lee Morgan ran across a field," he said. "It was a racetrack; they had the bandstand set up in the center of the racetrack. Night was falling, so Lee could go across without anybody seeing—he was like coming up in the shadows. He popped right up in front of me and said, 'You want to join the Messengers?'" Wayne definitely did want to join one of the most successful bands in jazz. He also didn't want to be disloyal to Maynard, jumping ship after only four weeks in his group. Art intervened, applying his powers of persuasion to the situation. "Come on, you know Wayne's not a big-band player," he told Ferguson, who had to admit that Wayne was in fact just one horn among many in his large ensemble—Wayne's talent did deserve the showcase of a small-group setting. So after a final gig with Maynard at Birdland, Wayne joined up with the Messengers on August 1 in French Lick, Indiana.

The Messengers' sidemen sometimes speculated about how Art had become the group's leader. At one time, Art and pianist Horace Silver had co-led the Messengers, with Horace composing most of the band's charts. *Shouldn't the one who was writing be the one to lead it?* Wayne wondered to himself. Lee, characteristically, was more direct in his inquiries. "You probably gorilla'd it from Horace, didn't you?" he'd ask Art. "You bogarted it, right?" Art Blakey did have a strong-arm, rough-and-ready reputation—he'd worked in the steel mills of his native Pittsburgh—but the truth was that he did originally own the Messengers name. Blakey came of age in big bands in the late thirties and forties, when he also became interested in Africa and converted to Islam, assuming the name Abdullah Ibn Buhaina. In 1947, he formed an orchestra called the Messengers, named for the group's preponderance of Islamic musicians and dynamic sonic delivery. He also recorded an octet under the title for Blue Note in 1947.

The Messengers name then went unused until Blakey teamed up with Silver in 1954. The two musicians made a live recording with trumpeter Clifford Brown, saxophonist Lou Donaldson, and bassist Curly Russell, *A Night at Birdland with the Art Blakey Quintet.* Wayne saw this group at Birdland and the Café Bohemia, toting his books to the gigs after NYU classes. Blakey and Silver released *Horace Silver and the Jazz Messengers* and made a live recording, *At the Café Bohemia, Volumes One and Two,* in November 1955. And that's when the band's ownership came into question. No one knows what happened exactly, and Horace himself denied any power struggle, but Blakey came away as commander of the group. This was not uncommon in jazz: For example, bandleader Marjorie Hyams was displaced by George Shearing, a blind musician from England. "It was Marjorie Hyams's band," Wayne said. "But the William Morris Agency wanted to use the gimmick of the blind man, the gimmick that could sell. And they put the George Shearing name out in front, and Marjorie Hyams played in the background, wearing gowns all the time." Wayne implied that Hyams was marginalized into a more ornamental role in the group when George took the lead.

So, depending on who was telling the story, Horace Silver left the Messengers peaceably or under some duress. His replacements at the piano were Junior Mance, Sam Dockery, and on a couple of recordings, Walter Bishop, Jr., and Thelonious Monk. Saxophonists Jackie McLean and trumpeters Bill Hardman and Donald Byrd were members of the evolving front line. Then in 1958, Art settled in with four Philadelphia musicians who brought the group some down-home soul and sturdy compositions. This Messengers grouping of saxophonist Benny Golson, trumpeter Lee Morgan, pianist Bobby Timmons, and bassist Jymie Merritt recorded *Moanin',* which included some of the group's biggest hits: the title track, "Blues March," and "Along Came Betty." In reaction to the more intellectual cool-jazz phenomenon, this edition of the Messengers embraced the feel of the blues and R&B, and had a fiercely percussive sound with never ending swing.

The Messengers were riding this wave of popularity when Wayne joined them in the summer of 1959. Working with the challenging band-leader was a rite of passage for Wayne, as it was for many musicians throughout the Messengers' thirty-year existence. Art's tough-love leadership style gave each band member the chance to find and prove himself, as Wayne remembered: "Blakey told us that every time we go on the stand, we should remember this one thing: We should always remember that God has given us another chance to come out and clean up the mess we might have made the night before." This sense of responsibility to the music was born of Blakey's deeply held belief in jazz as an American treasure. "Good, bad, or indifferent, it's the *only* culture America has brought forth," he said.

By the time Wayne joined the Messengers, its members were no longer primarily Muslim, but identified instead as aesthetic missionaries, as hard-bop jazz emissaries. They looked the part, sporting matching tailored suits with blazers, their shoes polished until you could see a fuzzy reflection of their horns in them. Certain hidden elements reinforced their solidarity—they wore matching socks and underwear, and their shirt cuffs bore the group's monogram, *JM*. When anyone in the group lifted his arms for a solo, his jacket sleeves fell back to reveal this emblem of team spirit to the audience. And the band did keep its audience in mind. For Blakey, music was entertainment above all: "When people come in to relax and enjoy themselves after a hard day's work, it's my job to make them happy—to wash away the dust of everyday life. That's what jazz music is all about."

Art Blakey's own thunderous percussion style was enormously entertaining. It was controlled, hard and loud, even when he played several rhythms simultaneously, keeping an eye on the time with the ride cymbal while accenting the offbeats with his hi-hat. But audiences were always waiting for the Blakey trademark: a dramatic press roll on the snare that seemed to announce the arrival of Armageddon itself. Propelled by this fusillade of percussion, the well-oiled Jazz Messengers put on a slick show. "The kind of timing I learned with Art was almost always consistent," Wayne said. "Building your expressions into some sort of a climax, ending your solos on something very worthy of sharing with or being remembered by everyone." The Messengers' shows usually climaxed with "A Night in Tunisia." "Art would do the whole thing with drums and all that, and we'd play percussion instruments—usually I clapped away at the clave—and it would be a showstopper," Wayne said. "So we'd do the showstopping stuff, and then you'd get that hell of an applause from everybody. They didn't care what the name or style of the music was if they had a good time that night."

The Messengers' crowd-pleasing formula garnered them steady work, which gave Wayne the financial freedom to move out of his parents' house and into his own apartment. He rented a one-bedroom in a new building at 2185 Fifth Avenue, up in Harlem at the corner of 135th Street. Thirty years before, the area had been a hotbed of the Harlem Renaissance: The street was immortalized in Gershwin's 1922 jazz opera *Blue Monday,* which spawned the jazz standard "135th Street." In the 1920s, Leroy Wilkins ran a popular cabaret club on this corner, a spot frequented by all the "dictys" from the black show world. Willie "The Lion" Smith kept up a rigorous performance schedule at the club, playing seven nights a week from 9:30 p.m. till dawn.

The Harlem Renaissance was long over by the time Wayne moved into the neighborhood in the late fifties. Its black writers such as James Baldwin and Chester Himes had migrated to Paris. Vestiges of Harlem's glory days were mainly found in its residents' sense of style. "When you were buying a new suit, you'd say, 'I'm going down to Bond's to get some new vines,'" Wayne said. "Then you'd come back, and if someone tried to touch it, you'd say, 'Don't put your hands on my vines.' And with your hat, if you didn't want anybody to take your hat off you, you'd say, 'Don't touch my sky!' That might mean your head, too, 'cause touching someone's head is an act of familiarity." Style was more than mere ornamentation; it was an indication of a man's soul. In an *Esquire* article from the period, writer Al Calloway equated style with soul: "It is the self-perception that informs you how and when to groove in your own way while others groove in theirs, and it is the sophistication that knows better than to ask,

'Understand me,' and settles instead for, 'Don't mess with me; I'm in my own thing, baby.'"

No group embodied that attitudinal and performative stance better than jazz musicians. Wayne understood the power of presentation: His own slick style had attracted the attention of Lester Young up in Toronto, and the Messengers certainly had a sartorial sense of purpose. The jazz world was style in action: One night at the Café Bohemia, Wayne and his brother, Alan, walked past Miles Davis. Miles noticed that Alan was wearing the same style of suit and jodhpurs that he was. Miles said, "You're trying to look like me!" Alan retorted, "No, you're trying to look like me!"

Up in Harlem, the burgeoning Black Power movement dominated local discourse. Over on Seventh Avenue and 125th Street, Malcolm X and his Fruit of Islam entourage were building the grassroots power base that would soon drive him to national attention. At "buy black" meetings on street corners, community organizers stood on soapboxes and urged residents to stop trading with the white man and to establish a separate economy. To Wayne, they seemed angry and bitter. The world of jazz already comprised a self-governing nation, and leaders like Art Blakey had a sense of authority and equality enlivened by wit and panache. "We sometimes played Monk's tune 'Evidence,'" Wayne said. "Blakey would announce, 'We'd like to play a tune by the high priest of bop. He calls it 'Evidence,' but we call it 'Justice.'" Thelonious Monk's tune was based on the Tin Pan Alley hit "Just You, Just Me," so Art's clever wordplay referenced that source for the tune, and also critiqued the concept of "evidence" and "justice" in the days of cabaret-card busts and drug-user sweeps by city police.

The jazz world's headquarters, Birdland, was the place to be for musicians. Its Monday-night jam session was frequented by Coltrane, Miles, Mingus, and anyone else who mattered on the scene. Birdland attracted distinguished blacks who were as elegant as they were empowered. Actor Sidney Poitier and prizefighter Sugar Ray Robinson were regulars in the audience. Willie Mays would sometimes come by and have a glass of milk at the bar, sticking strictly to his training diet. On Saturday nights at the club, the Messengers played alongside comedy acts such as Bill Cosby, Lenny Bruce, and Flip Wilson, whose "ugly baby" routine drew big laughs every time. A few more-notorious characters, like mobster Joey Gallo, also haunted the club. "Wayne and Gallo sometimes hung out at the bar—an unlikely pair, for sure—drinking cognac and discussing the philosophy of Camus," Joe Zawinul said. Black or white, Birdland's regulars were the "swift people" Wayne had looked for as a child. Jazz devotees seemed to be fun-loving, poised, and proud, unlike some of those "clubs of complaint" up in Harlem.

These were "hard-drinking hard-bop years," as Wayne called them, when the Messengers worked and played as hard as they could. In many ways, the end of the fifties was an ideal time to be a jazz musician. The Beatles hadn't yet hit the U.S., and jazz was still pop music—heading to a hot spot like Birdland or the Apollo was *the* thing to do after a Broadway show. Birdland even had a "peanut gallery," a small section of about ten discounted seats where teenagers on prom dates sat nursing Cokes all night. And as much as jazz enjoyed popularity during this period, it also experienced major innovation: Miles Davis's *Kind of Blue,* Ornette Coleman's *The Shape of Jazz to Come,* and Coltrane's *Giant Steps* were all recorded in 1959.

With his Messengers gig, Wayne gained new access to this scene and greater visibility among jazz fans, who were quick to hear his resemblance to one innovator in particular. During Wayne's solos, fans urged him on with cries of "Go on and play, young Coltrane!" With his new prominence, Wayne was also subjected to critical scrutiny. Early on in his Messengers stint, one prominent writer, Martin Williams, effectively reduced Wayne to a Coltrane clone, an opinion that colored Wayne's critical reception for years. Wayne had picked up some undeniable influences during those months he practiced with Coltrane. You could hear Coltrane in his keening sound; in his cadenzas, which seemed longer than the songs themselves; and in the sheer profundity of his musical ideas. Even if Wayne hadn't practiced with Coltrane, you would have heard it. By 1959,

Coltrane had become so dominant a figure on the tenor saxophone that he influenced nearly everyone. (Or sent them into exile like Sonny Rollins, who, as the story goes, dealt with Coltrane's genius by banishing himself from performance and claiming the Williamsburg Bridge as an open-air practice room.)

Other musicians heard the difference between the two players, and they were emphatic about the distinctions. "Wayne never struck me as an imitator," Sonny Rollins said. "He liked Trane and maybe me a little, but Wayne was an innovative guy himself, and that would come out in the way he put things together. He was an honest boy and a real player. A real player." All musicians were conscious of their influences then, as pianist McCoy Tyner pointed out: "We all were inspired by somebody, and then we moved on. I think in Wayne's case he was interested in John, but he definitely moved into his own sound and concept. Just like I was interested in Monk, and then I moved on."

Even if Wayne's style and sound were similar to those of Trane or Rollins, his ideas and approach to chord changes were his own. "Wayne had a straight tone, and Trane did, too," Joe Zawinul said. "They didn't have a vibrato like the older guys did, you know, like Coleman Hawkins. Wayne and Trane each came up individually, though. Trane was doing a lot of arpeggiating, running the chords. Wayne had a wonderful way of blowing chords, but he wasn't just arpeggiating. Wayne could already weave melodies as a part of the chords, and we became masters of that as time went on." Coltrane himself perhaps best acknowledged the difference in their approaches. "Yeah, you're scramblin' those eggs," Coltrane once told Wayne. "You're scrambling them differently than me, but you're doing it, too."

Still, Art liked to tease Wayne about the rampant comparisons. "You've gotta get past all those guys, Wayne. Past Coltrane, past Sonny," he'd say, and then cite a mock biblical lineage of saxophonists back to Lester Young. Art used this comedic bit on all his new players, but Wayne knew that the joke conveyed an important message: Get your own style, so that *no one will ever mistake you for someone else.* For that, Wayne would need a few years. It was his nature to paint with his horn rather than preach, as Coltrane did. As Wayne matured, he'd become more comfortable with his own impressionistic leanings and settle in to a more succinct style.

Whatever Wayne's musical resemblance to Coltrane or Rollins, his Messengers appointment gave him the imprimatur of an "important tenor saxophonist on the rise." Onstage, Blakey introduced him as "a new star on the jazz horizon." Blakey's group had produced top saxophonists like Benny Golsen, Hank Mobley, and Johnny Griffin, and that track record was enough to secure Wayne his own recording contract with Vee-Jay Records. In 1959 the Chicago-based label began to add jazz musicians to its roster of R&B and gospel artists. Vee-Jay built its jazz catalog with the young, emerging sidemen of established bandleaders like Miles Davis and Art Blakey. Wayne played as a sideman on Wynton Kelly's *Kelly Great* recording for Vee-Jay just after he joined the Messengers, on August 12 (the record included Wayne's "Mama G," a tune he'd written for Maynard Ferguson). Wayne was signed to Vee-Jay himself a couple months after his Messengers enlistment and recorded his first record for the label on November 9 and 10.

This debut, *Introducing Wayne Shorter,* featured Lee Morgan, pianist Wynton Kelly, bassist Paul Chambers—all Vee-Jay artists—and drummer Jimmy Cobb. In effect, the group was Miles Davis's rhythm section and Art Blakey's horn front line. As a leader, Wayne had a chance to test out that reserve tank of tunes he'd written back in the army barracks. Some of them were a little odd: "Blues A La Carte" had an irregular 21-bar form, with a 13-bar main melody followed by an 8-bar vamp. As a composer, Wayne again revealed a Coltrane influence, but also asserted remarkable originality. Trumpeter Dave Douglas, who later recorded a tribute to Wayne, characterized the difference: "On his Vee-Jay records, Wayne begins with the leap that Coltrane took in 1959 with the composition 'Giant Steps,' and then takes the harmony to the next step. So instead of having the harmony in 'Giant Steps,' where it's always tonic-dominant, tonic-dominant, Wayne was just kind of like, tonic, tonic, but found the voice leading that made it work in a way that no one had before." Most important, Wayne's tunes featured dreamy melodies that stayed in your head—if you mentioned one of his titles, someone would start singing it.

Wayne's unique and plentiful compositions immediately made him indispensable to the Messengers. On November 10, the second day of the *Introducing Wayne Shorter* session, Wayne and Lee had to hurry over to New Jersey for an 8 p.m. session with Blakey. After a couple days in the Vee-Jay studios, Wayne should have been dead tired, but he was actually elated: He'd only been with the Messengers for a few months, and on his very first recording with the band, they were already recording two of his compositions! One tune, "Africaine," became the record's title—Wayne would prove to have a gift for colorful and evocative names.

Wayne's other contribution to *Africaine* was a tune he wrote for Lester Young, who had died earlier that year on March 15. Though "Lester Left Town" was an elegy, there was nothing mournful about it. The tune had a descending melody line that ambled along at a relaxed pace in tribute to Lester's unique gait—the first thing Wayne had noticed about the saxophonist. "The music represented the way Lester walked," Wayne said. "He had a very cool walk, with his feet very close to the ground, and a little bit turned in, like he was on the verge of being pigeon-toed. They'd say, 'Here comes Prez, you can tell by his walk.' There he'd come, with his gig bag, porkpie hat, and long black coat, moving just as slow as he wanted to, you know. He had this look on his face like, 'Hey, isn't this the way it's supposed to be?'" Something about the tune must have appealed to Blakey, who immediately adopted it into the Messengers repertoire.

The second half of 1959 was turning out to be a pivotal period for Wayne: He joined Maynard Ferguson's band, was quickly recruited by the Messengers, signed a recording contract with Vee-Jay, and moved into his own apartment. But the most significant events happened at the very end of the year, when Wayne had some magical encounters with jazz elders that would impact his artistry for years to come.

5.

The Elders

ON NOVEMBER 14, just four days after Wayne's first recording session with the Messengers, the band went to Paris. It was Wayne's first European tour, and his first trip abroad. The Messengers flew over in a Stratocruiser, occupying the plane's cocktail lounge in the bubble space above the main cabin. The ten-hour flight flew by for the band as they drank liberal amounts of cognac and worked out some tunes.

It was a good time to be a Jazz Messenger in Paris. A year before, the group had a triumphal premiere at the Olympia theater. Following gigs at the more intimate Club St. Germain had further popularized the group's soulful brand of hard bop. Though the French maintained a preference for decades-old Lester Young–style balladry—a style near their native chanson—bop had become the default soundtrack for younger Parisians, and a literal one for new-wave film directors. In 1957, Miles Davis composed the soundtrack to Louis Malle's film *Elevator to the Gallows.* In 1959, jazz's frenetic, impressionistic sound would support the street scenes in *Breathless,* the first feature film by Jean-Luc Godard.

That autumn, Godard was shooting in the streets near the Messengers' hotel, the Hotel Cristal in the heart of St.-Germain-des-Prés on Rue St.-Benoit. The Hotel Cristal was chosen primarily for its proximity to the Club St. Germain. "But Art always reminded us—he was always repeating important stuff—that the hotel had a rich history," Wayne said. "It was where the black culturati stayed, like [jazz pianist] Mary Lou Williams and writers like James Baldwin and Chester Himes."

Their tour began in Paris at the Théâtre des Champs-Elysées on November 15, continued on a swing through Europe, and came full circle with a closing gig back at the Champs-Elysées on December 18. For the final performance, promoters planned to feature a number of expatriate musicians in concert with the Messengers, including pianist Bud Powell, who'd set up residence on the Left Bank the previous May.

Bud was doing well in Paris. The French reserved a romantic benevolence for black American artists, and didn't seem to care that performing had become a challenging high-wire act for the pianist. By the end of the fifties, the genius of bepop piano was as legendary for his instability as he was for his music. These days, Bud started sweating before he even sat down at the piano. Once, his piano playing had raised a daringly imagined arch between the opposing poles of Art Tatum and Thelonious Monk. Now he was just walking the line, trying to keep his balance and see his way safely through to the other side, wherever that was, and finish the gig. Still, Bud was working a lot, thanks to his lady companion, Buttercup, and young fan and helpmeet, Francis Paudras. They tag-teamed on the full-time job of steering Bud clear of bars and into clubs for his gigs.

Paudras invited Bud to the Messengers show that night, unaware that his friend was actually already on the bill. In the middle of the show, Walt Davis, Jr., the Messengers' pianist, stepped up to the mike and asked Bud to come onstage. Bud wasn't exactly eager to play. He sank down into his chair and tried in vain to use his trademark beret and overcoat for camouflage, but his fans picked him out right away. Paudras prodded him, the audience clamored, and finally Art enticed him onstage. "All I could think was, we're playing with Bud Powell now, this is Bud Powell onstage," Wayne said. "I was thinking of his music, and what he always played himself, and how to respond to that." The Messengers honored their guest pianist by calling two of his tunes: "Bouncing with Bud" and "Dance of the Infidels."

The Champs-Elysées audience caught Bud on a good night. With concentration, he shunned inspiration and played straight, giving a crowd-pleasing performance—though no matter how Bud played, he was bound to be the night's sentimental favorite. More impressive musicianship actually came from the Messengers' two horn players. Only a few months into Wayne's tenure with the band, he and Lee Morgan had settled in to the front line as comfortably as an old married couple: They formed a striking contrast, a musical yin and yang.

Lee strutted across the stage with a bop walk, his lankiness and high-water pants lending the step a particular insouciance. His trumpet solos were as gutsy as they were virtuosic, with strong flashes of funk and blues. In contrast, Wayne's stage demeanor was absolutely wooden. Messengers fans had begun calling him "The Sphinx"—his displays of emotion were so rare that his slightest smile had the impact of a man coming out of a coma. In his solos, Wayne effected subtle drama, with long, elliptical narratives that he developed with the slowness of a symphonic piece. Wayne's studiousness complemented Lee's expressiveness, establishing a formula that would play out again and again throughout Wayne's career. He'd later be the studious straight man to the heart-melting trumpet of Miles Davis, and then to the provocative keyboards of Joe Zawinul in Weather Report. This equation played out even in more brief partnerships—for instance, when he foiled the expressionistic rock riffs of Carlos Santana.

After the show, the Messengers gathered backstage with Bud and their other guests. Bud's tough-love warden-wife, Buttercup, cornered each of the Messengers and warned them about Bud's tactical disappearing acts. "Whatever you do, don't let Bud out of your sight," she said. "And don't give him any money. He'll use it for wine, or worse." Buttercup was roundly ignored. The Messengers were focused on some friends from the States who had joined them backstage. Prizefighters Rocky Graziano and Sugar Ray Robinson, both Birdland regulars, were in Paris on a showbiz tour. The actress and pianist Hazel Scott was a newly free woman in Paris, having just left her husband, Adam Clayton Powell, the prominent black congressman. According to Francis Paudras's account in his memoirs, Buttercup was so affronted by the Messengers' disregard that she retaliated by calling the police. Paudras claimed that Wayne was among a group of musicians who were taken to the police station, strip-searched, and made to spend the night in jail. Paudras didn't specify the exact nature of the crime that would have justified this quick rallying of the French forces.

In Walked Bud

But Wayne was not among that group. He took a cab back to the Hotel Cristal from the theater. On this night, like the others, there were tempting reasons to stay out—adulating French girls and free-flowing *vin rouge*—but Wayne didn't feel like warming himself at the fire of human companionship. He'd stay in his room, drink a bottle of wine on his own, and work on some tunes. Wayne had been writing for a couple hours when he heard a knock on the door at around 3 a.m. He opened it, expecting to see Lee or Walter, flush with drink. Instead, Bud Powell stood there in his beret and overcoat, sensible enough attire for the damp chill of Paris in December. But Bud wore this uniform year-round, even in the asphalt oven of Harlem in July. Mindful of Buttercup's warnings, Wayne looked anxiously over at his night table, which held a mound of francs. Bud didn't seem to notice the money. He walked into the room, sat in a chair, and looked over at Wayne's horn, which was out of its case on his bed. "Play me something," he said, in his mild child's voice.

Wayne hesitated. He didn't know what to play. When he picked up his horn, he reflexively set in on one of the tunes they'd covered earlier that night, "Dance of the Infidels." After a slow start with some nerve-rattled lines, Wayne relaxed into the tune, staying close to the melody but stretching the rhythm a little according to his own design. After he played, Bud thanked him, stood up, and walked to the door. He turned around and stared. "Are you all right?" Wayne asked. "Uh-huh, it's all right," Bud mumbled in response.

"Bud had that wild look," Wayne remembered, "but it was contained. I knew about Bellevue psychiatric hospital and something-otomy and how they tried to shock him. But when he went down the hotel stairs that night, he walked straight, with his hands in his pockets. He wasn't wobbling, he wasn't ripped or anything." But if Bud wasn't looking for a fix, Wayne didn't know what to make of his late-night visitation. He vacillated between convincing himself it had been an apparition and puzzling over possible motives for the visit. Why him and not Lee? And why had Bud requested the solo concert? Wayne deposited the episode in his memory banks, though with time his interest in understanding its significance only grew.

Wayne related the story to director Bertrand Tavernier years later, in 1985, when he performed and acted in Tavernier's film *Round Midnight*. Dexter Gordon played the film's lead character, an expatriate American jazz musician in Paris who was a fictionalized composite of Bud Powell and Lester Young. The film was based on Francis Paudras's memoir, *Dance of the Infidels*, though Wayne hadn't read the book and was unaware of Paudras's conflicting version of that night's events. Tavernier was altogether unconcerned with veracity and considered putting Wayne's meeting with Bud in the movie. But a scene in which a lucid Bud Powell sought out new music from a younger player was not much in keeping with the film's portrayal of him as a wine-crazed, talent-squandering character. Whether it was a practical or aesthetic choice, Tavernier ultimately decided not to include Wayne's Hotel Cristal episode in the film. Besides Gordon, musical director Herbie Hancock and vibraphonist Bobby Hutcherson are the musicians with the most significant acting roles in *Round Midnight*. Wayne's main appearances are musical—he performs onstage at the Blue Note club and at a recording session. His one extramusical appearance is in an atmospheric scene at the session, where he is briefly shown entertaining some fellow musicians with a story about his favorite movie, *The Red Shoes*.

Bud Powell's daughter Celia was also on the set of *Round Midnight*. She was particularly struck by Wayne's story of her father's appearance in his hotel room. "You all had played together, and Father was a guest with the band that night?" she asked him. "You know, Father didn't go up to see you to get money; he didn't sneak and hide from people to see if he could find someone to help him get drunk. Father followed music, and he went to see you for the reason that he said. To make sure that everything was all right." Wayne couldn't imagine what she meant. "For the future of music," she explained. "He heard something going on with you that night when you were playing."

After talking to Celia, Wayne listened repeatedly to the show's live recording, *Paris Jam Session,* which was originally released on Fontana Records and later reissued on CD by Verve. Such deep investigation of a record was extremely rare for Wayne. It was unnecessary—he'd usually commit music to memory after one or two listens. But this time he set the needle down on the record's edge dozens of times, hoping to solve the puzzle of what Bud might have heard. "That night, Lee played good stuff," Wayne said. "And Barney played very nice, but . . ." Wayne trailed off. "Maybe he must have heard something with me that he felt in his inner being? Like he never detached himself from knowing where he had wanted to go with his music before he fell off."

What might Bud Powell have heard in Wayne that night in 1959? On side two of the record, there's really not much to hear. That side features two tunes that the Messengers played alone, without their guests. On "The Midget" and "A Night in Tunisia," there was more than a little Coltrane in Wayne's sound and style.

The record's side one, on which Bud joined the Messengers for two of his own tunes, was more revealing: Wayne's handling of Bud's compositions got to the heart of the pianist's musicianship. The rather cliché version of Bud's story assumes that his brilliance was forever dimmed by tragic events early in his career, that police beatings and then shock treatments unleashed in him an innate potential for madness. And whatever Bud's genetic predisposition, abuse of such severity could certainly trigger insanity in anyone. But Bud was resilient, and his career wasn't so much a downward spiral as it was a seesaw between brilliance and incoherence. What perpetuated Bud's insanity was his frustration with being unable to realize his potential. Genius doesn't guarantee madness, but the torture of frustrated genius does. That night in Paris, Bud set out boldly on "Dance of the Infidels" with an inventive solo. He walked the tightrope for a few bars then fell back on repetition like a net. When Wayne took the lead solo on "Bouncing with Bud," the next track on the record, Bud must have noticed that Wayne never repeated himself—not a single riff. For Wayne, repetition was stagnation. He simply couldn't traverse old ground. More than that, Wayne's playing reflected Bud's in the way he pushed the tune's melody away from its harmony, in the way he courted dissonance with the master plan of a classical European composer.

Wayne played like the Bud Powell of "The Glass Enclosure," Bud's 1953 masterpiece composition. The tune began as a fragment that producer Alfred Lion heard on a visit to Powell in the apartment where he was kept, and was titled in reference to that prison-like space. "See, Bud's inside the glass enclosure," Wayne said. "He's breaking out with this tune, but in a subtle way. The music is right on the crossroads of classical and jazz. Like, you can hear Shostakovich and Stravinsky doing that stuff, if you had the good fortune to hear either of those composers alone at the piano. You're eavesdropping on their reverie. There you can hear where Bud might have gone." "The Glass Enclosure" certainly points to a talent for composition that was sadly underdeveloped. Like Wayne's compositions, it has the sheer drama of a soundtrack, and unfolds like a narrative. Its chords are so dense that the notes seem to clench one another, but the breadth of their structure allows the sound to bleed away in opposite directions. Alone at the piano, Bud contained the instrumental scope of a symphony and bottled all the sprawling cruelty of *The Rite of Spring*. And though jazz musicians didn't start playing Lydian augmented chords with any frequency until the 1960s, Bud Powell played a few on "The Glass Enclosure" in the early fifties.

In his penetrating analysis of Powell's music, Gary Giddins concludes: "The reason we read more deeply into Powell than into many of his contemporaries may be quite simple: no other pianist, and precious few musicians in any age, speak to us with such electrifying intensity." Wayne sometimes says, "Jazz for me is, 'Do you have the guts to do it?'" There was urgency in Wayne's playing at the Théâtre des Champs-Elysées that night, an inner logic to his solos, but a mercurial aspect as well—Wayne blew back at Blakey's hi-hat jabs like they were in the boxing ring. The seeds of Wayne's style and his initiation as a composer were there. Maybe Bud heard that, Wayne pushing toward the future with music that could only move forward.

Bird

The December 18 show at the Théâtre des Champs-Elysées—and Wayne's dramatic visit from Bud that same night—ended the Messengers' European tour. The band flew back to the States for their next engagement, a weeklong run at Chicago's Regal theater over the winter holidays. Before the Chicago gig, Art invited the band to an early holiday party at his comfortable home in New York on Central Park West. Art lived there with his wife, Diana, and their two children, Sakeena and Gamal.

Sakeena was an unusual two-year-old who had developed the precocious habit of sizing up visitors like a hanging judge the moment they stepped into the Blakey house. "If they were cool, Sakeena was cool," Wayne said. "If they weren't, then she wasn't either. Art said, 'Sakeena's hip to them all,' and let the child have the run of the house." The toddler made an impression on Wayne, enough to inspire a composition with a difficult, penetrating melody line. "Sakeena's Vision" was recorded by the Messengers on *The Big Beat* the following March. In the record's liner notes, Wayne told writer Nat Hentoff that he wanted the composition to be "symbolic of a child's thoughts that adults can't understand. Sort of like out of the mouths of babes come innocence and purity." Blakey immediately adopted most of Wayne's tunes into the Messengers' repertoire, and this one's catchy variation on the old 12-bar structure made it as compelling as any of his compositions. But it was especially hard for Art to resist his daughter's namesake. As Wayne later told *Down Beat* magazine in the seventies, "Art Blakey used all my tunes right from the beginning. I wrote 'Sakeena's Vision' about his daughter, who is now nineteen, and 'Sincerely Diana' was about Art's wife."

Wayne spent most his time at Art's holiday party talking with Sakeena's governess, a pretty Frenchwoman named Joelle. Joelle was the namesake of a composition as well, though for another reason: That day, she passed along Charlie Parker's legacy to Wayne, just as unexpectedly as Bud Powell had walked into his life a few days before. Wayne discreetly guided Joelle away from the others at the party, and they became deeply involved in conversation as they looked out a window on the winter scene in Central Park. He told her about his recent meeting with Bud in Paris.

Joelle's reminiscences turned to a snowy day in 1955 when she was sitting on a bench in the park. She saw a man walking in her direction, coughing violently and sputtering blood on the white ground. Under his arm, he carried a large package. He sat down next to her and stared ahead in silence, until finally Joelle spoke to him. They ended up talking about music for some time, and then he handed her the package. He told her to give it to someone someday, someone whom she thought "deserved it."

She gave the package to Wayne, and told him the man who gave it to her was Charlie Parker. "The package contained," Wayne remembered, "a record by classical alto saxophonist Marcel Mule—a concerto for saxophone—and a violin practice book from Germany, with a fancy design on its cover—ivy, leaves, and a cameo. And music staff paper, with some handwritten music. The handwritten tune was titled 'Sentimental over You.' It had the original ballad's chord progression, but supplemented a new melody. Kind of in the way that Monk might have done it."

For Wayne, the package represented the many ways he felt connected to Bird. The concerto record was indicative of the musicians' shared love of classical music, which is what originally inspired Wayne to play the clarinet. The violin practice book suggested a similarity in their instrumental techniques: Bird used a violin book to practice his alto saxophone, just as Wayne practiced his tenor saxophone with cello parts. When he practiced with Coltrane, they had speculated that Bird worked with classical technique books—now Wayne could be certain. But the key item in the package was the sheet music for "Sentimental over You," which confirmed that Bird composed and recomposed as religiously as Wayne did. "Wayne was the only person . . . who wrote something like the way Bird wrote, the only one," Miles Davis would later note.

These first- and second-hand encounters with Bud and Bird, the bebop elders, made Wayne feel like a chosen one of his generation. They gave him artistic conviction, which he carried quietly within himself: Regardless of the health of his career, he could draw from this reserve of artistic purpose at will. There would be times when he needed it.

6.

Children of the Night

WAYNE'S NASCENT SENSE of personal mission coincided with the Jazz Messengers' growing cultural ambassadorship as globe-trotting musicians. "Art used to say, 'We are world citizens,'" Wayne said. "Even though we had an American passport, our profession superseded our nationality. And I gained a lot of worldly knowledge early on because of all the places we visited." On his first European tour, Wayne experienced the benefits and responsibilities of his Messengers status. One evening after a show in Marseilles, he went for a walk around the city's hilly, cobbled streets, still dressed in his gig suit. Some Russians spotted the young Jazz Messenger and spontaneously invited him to dinner in their restaurant, which they'd already closed for the night. The Russians cooked up a lavish meal for Wayne and talked with him for hours. Any potential Cold War hostility was thawed in their enthusiasm for American jazz music.

Two days later Wayne had a much different experience in Algeria, where the Messengers' politics made them decidedly unwelcome. It wasn't the best time to be in the country. That winter, the fighting between the French Colon and the native Algerian rebels was intensifying. French president Charles de Gaulle had begun to withdraw support for the French colonists in September 1959. Left to their own devices, the colonists stepped up their retaliation against the native rebellion.

When the Messengers arrived at the Algiers airport, Art's valet, Goldie, was whisked off to the police station because of his suspicious bearing—his slightly hooked nose made him look vaguely Algerian. Goldie's detention was disturbing to the Messengers. They adored the valet; in Paris they had just debuted a 12-bar blues tune by Lee Morgan titled "Goldie." The tense atmosphere escalated as the band set up for its show to the sound of cannons and gunfire in the Atlas Mountains outside Algiers.

Conscious of the colonized country's socioeconomics, Art requested that the show's price of admission remain low enough for natives to afford tickets. His request was ignored. At the show, predictably, the Messengers looked out on an audience of white French faces. Art decided to take action. Midway through the concert—just before intermission—he stood up and announced, "Ladies and gentlemen, we're unable to continue the performance due to certain inequities."

"I'm not sure if people knew Art was a practicing Muslim or not," Wayne said. "But when we started leaving the stage, people started throwing things at us. Somebody threw a coin with a hole in the middle and hit Jymie Merritt's bass really hard, cracking the wood. So Art, or I guess I should call him by his Muslim name—Abdullah Ibn Buhaina—pulled out his Koran and said, 'Gentlemen, are you ready to die?' I said yeah, 'cause I was just out of the army. We walked through wall-to-wall people, all hissing at us, with Art carrying the Koran under his arm and wearing one of those hats that was a symbol of Arabic something. We got to the limos and got inside real quick. Someone spit at the car just as Lee Morgan was rolling up the window, so you saw it splattered all over the glass." The Messengers returned to their French-owned hotel, then rebelliously decided to go out for drinks even though the streets were thick with young French soldiers carrying machine guns. "We went to a bar and were clearly making ourselves available to rumble," Wayne said. "But nothing happened. I guess someone knew we were Messengers, so they left us alone."

There were various other skirmishes and confrontations on international tours, some instigated by Art's combative personality and others resulting from the inherent confusion of cross-cultural encounters. Sometimes it was hard to tell the difference. During a Messengers engagement in Helsinki, Finland, Art became embroiled in an argument with Russian border guards at the Finnish–USSR frontier. "I argued with them," Art told *Down Beat* magazine. "These are good men; they just have an idea. The only way we can overcome this is to come up with a better idea."

The Messengers made their most memorable trip abroad when they toured Japan in January 1961, the first modern jazz group invited there by Japanese promoters. Previous jazz tours, such as Norman Granz's Jazz at the Philharmonic production or those organized by the U.S. State Department, had featured primarily big-band musicians and singers. The Messengers were a unified front with the look and sound of a progressive bop band, and the Japanese greeted them like hipster royalty. They were met at the airport by hundreds of screaming Japanese girls in kimonos, as ecstatic as the U.S. fans who would greet the Beatles three years later. "I never saw anything like it," Art said. "When we first went to Japan, they had Lee Morgan shirts, Wayne Shorter overcoats, all that kind of stuff, in the department stores. The same kind of publicity the Beatles got in the U.S., we got in Japan, and plus. I think we're the only American artists that had an audience with the emperor. But this country [the U.S.] never said a word about it, never a word."

On tour, musicians were typically responsible for covering the costs of their own accommodations. "We stayed in some hole-in-the-wall hotels over the years," Wayne said. Japanese promoters provided each Jazz Messenger with a princely hotel room and limo, complete with a deferential driver in white cap and gloves. Gliding down highways to gigs, the musicians saw large roadside advertisements for Messengers shows alongside toothpaste ads. In the United States, the group usually played for club audiences of around a hundred people, who mostly sat in sedate appreciation of the music. In Japan, auditoriums were packed with thousands of dancing fans, heads bobbing in unison, humming along to every note of the band's performance. "The night after our first concert at Sankei Hall, we signed autographs until two in the morning," Wayne said. "But we didn't mind, because we went to carry the message of our jazz, the freedom of jazz. Art said that Japan was our second home." The youthful performances of Wayne and Lee stirred up a special fever of excitement among Japanese girls.

On July 28, 1961, Wayne married Irene Nakagami, a Japanese-American woman born in Chicago. When Irene was six, she and her twin sister were shipped to an internment camp in Delano, California. "She told me that's why Japanese-Americans play lots of games, because they had to pass the time in the camps," Wayne said. "She was pretty. She looked like a Japanese Audrey Hepburn. I never really had a girlfriend. My first date became my first wife. We met, and before I knew it I was married; it was the fast lane." They had a daughter, Miyako, on August 8, 1961. Just after her birth, Wayne wrote a song for her that he'd later call "Infant Eyes." "I saw all infancy in Miyako's eyes, everyone who's ever been an infant," he said. "People reminisce about past stuff and let it take over the present, but with every moment, you're reborn."

After their dynamic Japanese debut, the Messengers returned to more prosaic aspects of jazz life that spring, playing nightclub dates and putting in some long studio hours. They cut *Pisces* and *Roots and Herbs* in February, *The Witch Doctor* in March, and *The Freedom Rider* in May. "Art played the drums on *Freedom Rider* to feel like a ride, with a strong backbeat," Wayne said. "From the middle of my time with Art on to the end, Art had a lot of bills to pay. And Blue Note had made some money on records like Jimmy Smith's *Walk on the Wild Side* and Grant Green's grits-and-gravy stuff, so they were looking for that kind of shuffling sound, which Lee Morgan eventually got to on *Sidewinder*." Wayne remembered an instance when there was an attempted negotiation of art and commerce in the studio. The Messengers had done several takes of a tune, and producer Alfred Lion asked them to play it one more time with a stronger backbeat.

"You're looking for somethin' more down-home?" Lee Morgan asked.

"Yes, could you perhaps give it a little more grease, a little more gravy," Alfred Lion said, in a strange patois of his native European formality and jazz lingo.

"He means more commercial," Alfred's partner, Frank Wolff, translated.

"But now you've spilled the beans!" Alfred reprimanded Frank.

Art spoke up to remind everyone that he was the leader of the session: "This is *our* domain. You're all jivin' back there in the sound booth."

By this time, the Messengers had enough competence and cohesion to take certain liberties in the studio. They clowned around and took on different personae, just for their own entertainment. Wayne's solo on Lee Morgan's "Afrique" at the *Witch Doctor* session was typical of the band's antics. He began with an impersonation of a staggering drunk, blowing low honking sounds that could have drowned a duck. Then his parody of inebriation and ineptitude gave way to a sober and smooth conclusion in his horn's middle register, but his bluesy tone remained in a roadhouse, not too far from the bar. "In those bands, when we would play a certain number in order to imitate someone else, we would do it with fun," Wayne said. "Sometimes, maybe, I would imitate something that Eddie 'Lockjaw' Davis might do. Lee would imitate a lotta people, y'know, like Fats Navarro. For a while, Walter Davis played piano with us, and he would go through all of the piano players of the day. And not only Bud Powell, but every once in a while he'd put an Erroll Garner thing in there."

Like gifted, bored students in need of a challenge, this expert class of Art's finishing school had a little too much time for horseplay and histrionics in the studio. The band's proficiency was certainly remarkable. Unfortunately, it was easy to reduce this spate of recordings to a few more examples of the Messengers' stylized hard-bop formula. It was sometimes hard to tell one record from another. Blue Note couldn't possibly justify glutting the market with so many simultaneous releases. Some recordings were bound to be shelved for a while, and *Roots and Herbs* was one of the unlucky selections. This record, which wasn't released until 1970, might as well have been a Wayne Shorter date—its six tunes were all his. It was a collection of cockeyed, ear-catching charts like "Master Mind," "Ping Pong," and "Look at the Birdie" (Wayne's clever take on the Woody Woodpecker theme). This small treasure foreshadowed the fortune of composition Wayne would create in the mid- and late sixties.

Wayne's growth as a composer accelerated rapidly when the Messengers' personnel changed later in 1961. In June, trombonist Curtis Fuller was brought into the fold, enlarging the group from a quintet to a sextet. In early August, Lee Morgan left the band to form his own group, and Wayne's former bandmate Freddie Hubbard took his place on trumpet. Cedar Walton, Wayne's old army buddy from Fort Dix, came over from Art Farmer's Jazztet to replace Walter Davis at the piano. The group's expert musicianship was evident from the start. "Freddie Hubbard and I joined the Messengers the same day," Cedar said. "On that first day of rehearsal, I brought in 'Mosaic,' a tune I'd been trying to record with Art Farmer. His band had difficulties with it. When I brought it in to the Messengers, Wayne, Curtis, Freddie, and Art ate it up like it was Post Toasties."

The addition of Curtis Fuller's trombone expanded the compositional possibilities for the group, and Wayne exploited the broadened setting. With only two horns, trumpet and saxophone, it had been a challenge to compose harmonies continuously throughout a tune. Wayne could use harmony at the end of musical phrases on the held notes, but was otherwise pretty much confined to writing unison passages. There were exceptions: On tunes like "Those Who Sit and Wait" and "Master Mind,"

Wayne had made a game of patterning harmonization between two horns. But the third horn changed everything.

The first studio album featuring the new grouping, *Mosaic,* was recorded on October 2, 1961, and included Wayne's tune "Children of the Night." Wayne said the title referred to one of horror film's most famous scenes: "I was thinking about when Dracula said, 'They are the children of the night. What beautiful music they make. Come here.' I'd never write no 'Children of the Day,' that's for sure." Wayne seemed to draw on his memory of film scores in the tune's rich chord voicings, which gave the three horns an expansive sonority that sounded like a full orchestra. One source of inspiration for the tune was drummer Philly Joe Jones, who was well-known for his impressions of Bela Lugosi's Dracula. Philly Joe recorded his own "Blues for Dracula" on Riverside in 1958 and included a Lugosi impression as an intro to the tune: "I am the bebop vampire, everybody must drink . . . but Master, Master what are those strange sounds? . . . Ah, the children of the night make such, such beautiful music. Ooooh, ooooooh."

Always a prolific composer, Wayne started to write more than ever. "He would turn out a tune a day!" Curtis said. When Blakey schooled later generations of Messengers, he'd tell them that Wayne had the imagination of a child: probing, playful, and always busy. But the harmonic complexity of Wayne's tunes was advanced and could be hard to master, as his bandmates' long practice sessions attested to. He was promoted to musical director, somewhat controversially, since many of the Messengers were strong composers. "We had a great front line, and it was good to write for that extra trombone," Freddie said. "It opened Wayne up as a composer, too, made him more innovative. I had to practice Wayne's shit all the time! So Wayne was the musical director, but we'd all write things. I said, 'I want to be the leader,' and Art said, 'No, you're not the leader yet.'"

"*Was* I the musical director? I didn't know it at the time," Wayne joked. His responsibilities didn't really change, and whatever direction he provided was very low-key. Sometimes he simply initiated a conversation in the music or stepped up its level of discussion. "We had a very high level of dialogue, on and off the bandstand," Curtis said. "As Wayne was walking up to the front of the stage approaching the microphone, he'd still be talking and joking, and then he'd stop and give you that half smile, with those big eyes. When he started to play his horn, it was just like a coin flipping over—he was still talking, but now it was through his horn. He'd use an excerpt from Frankenstein, maybe this Igor character thing he liked. Then he'd look back and smile. And you got the picture. Everything he did was something like that. We had a talking band. Dave Brubeck's groups did that. And I heard the same thing about Charlie Parker. They'd be playing along, and a girl would walk into the club in a red dress, and they'd play [mimics a suggestive noirish wah-wah trombone sound], something related to a red dress or maybe what was inside the dress. That was going on with the Messengers all the time."

Blakey fostered a strong group identity with band retreats at the country home of his wife, Diana, in Vermont. The house was large and octagonal, with a wraparound porch, situated on 120 acres of land, which Diana's father, John, had bought years before for twenty-eight dollars an acre. For musicians like Wayne who were raised in cramped apartments in cities, the country house and grounds were a "beautiful never-never land," though at times Art had to defend the guys from the natural hazards of the woods. "One time the whole band was out in the woods drinking white lightning, some of that cornfield whiskey," Wayne said. "We were in a swimming hole, it was nice and clean. Then this bear comes out of the woods into a clearing, some yards away, maybe twenty-five or thirty. Art said, 'Gentlemen, don't move! Stay where you are.' Well, everybody got sober! We were decently ripped, but those who could swim, did. Those who didn't think they could swim suddenly learned how to tread water. I was holding on to a rock in the water. We all backed out of the water. The bear was still coming, coming at a leisurely pace, and we backed over to Art's car, one of those Wagoneers that was first on the scene. The tailgate was down, so we got inside, and moving very quietly Art got in front and turned the key. When he started the car, the bear growled and we took off." When Art wasn't protecting the Messengers from bears in the woods, he was busy shielding his wife's three sisters from his sidemen's advances.

These pleasure excursions weren't all slapstick wildlife encounters and lighthearted fun. Art was famous for his fiery temper, which could strike anywhere, anytime, anyone . . . and anything. "They had some horses up in Vermont, and Art would haul off and hit the horses in the head," Freddie claimed. When Art encountered a pugnacious personality like Freddie's, the results could be explosive, especially if Art was a little juiced up. "When Art was drinking, you stayed out of things," Freddie said. "One time Art Blakey beat me up in Boston. Then he got on his knees and begged me to come back to the band." On the bandstand, even less contentious Messengers were subject to verbal thrashings if they gave lukewarm performances. "He'd admonish you if you weren't giving one hundred percent," Curtis said. Wayne said that when someone hit a nerve with Blakey, he'd unleash a sharp street tongue. "When he got mad, Art Blakey used to say, 'You jive so-and-so, I'll chase you back up your mama's womb.'" But Art's admonishments were usually directed toward strangers who feigned familiarity with him, or at outsiders who attacked him for his Muslim beliefs. Mostly, Art was protective of his sidemen, and in essence, he was as smart as he was strong. Art's sidemen respected their bandleader, who embodied a whole new paradigm of savoir faire. "Prior to meeting Art, I thought intelligence was aligned with college education, but he gave intelligence a new meaning," Cedar said, "because we could travel the world and play for and interact with all levels of society."

In March of 1964, Lee Morgan rejoined the Messengers, just in time to record *Indestructible*. It was a vamp-heavy session that featured Wayne's "Mr. Jin," a bombastically imperial "oriental" theme he wrote for Akira Jin, the Japanese promoter who first invited the Messengers to tour the country in 1961. Another Wayne tune, "It's a Long Way Down," wasn't included on the original LP, but did make the CD reissue. These were Wayne's final compositional contributions to the band.

On April 29, Wayne recorded his first Blue Note album, *Night Dreamer*, and this session as a leader revealed a very different side of his personality. Throughout Wayne's five years with Blakey, he composed and played programmatically, with the Messengers' assertive style specifically in mind.

Wayne's musical vision had meanwhile grown to encompass an extensive palette of moods and textures. Wayne's work as a sideman was a mere sketch of the genius that his Blue Note sessions would present as a complete picture. For this first session, Wayne was joined by Elvin Jones on drums, Reggie Workman on bass, McCoy Tyner on piano—Coltrane's rhythm section—as well as Lee Morgan, his collaborator from the Vee-Jay recording sessions. Wayne had just recorded "Mr. Jin" with Blakey; *Night Dreamer*'s "Oriental Folk Song" was a mellower homage to the Orient, with the musicians conjuring the mood of an opium haze. Throughout the record, Wayne's solos were measured, evocative, and quietly emotive. "I'm playing more emotionally than I used to," he told Nat Hentoff, for the record's liner notes. "There are fewer passages of being complicated for the sake of being complicated. And that comes from learning to relate your music to life. When you get down to fundamental emotions and relationships, there's no need to rely excessively on technical devices."

Wayne's affiliation with Blue Note would extend over seven years and eleven albums, a period in which his music would evolve in unexpected ways. Even on this first recording, Wayne demonstrated that his skills surpassed the Messengers' hard-bop style. He left the group in July. "I figured five years, that's enough for a cycle," Wayne said. Wayne told Art he was thinking about forming his own group. He recorded a second Blue Note album, *JuJu*, on August 3, and did want to take some guys on the road to see if he could carry his accomplishments beyond the studio. It would actually be another six years before Wayne led his own band. Another bandleader had invited Wayne to join his quintet, and that prospect had been on Wayne's mind when he gave Art notice.

Back in 1959, Wayne had called Miles Davis to ask for Coltrane's job, on Coltrane's recommendation. "I'll let you know when I need another tenor player," Miles said crossly. Wayne joined the Messengers, and Miles followed his progress with the group. "Miles used to love the Messengers," Curtis Fuller said. "Even when they were saying that *his* group was the group, he cited the Messengers as the one. He hired J.J. [Johnson] and Hank [Mobley] from the Messengers to work with his group. What Miles liked about us is that we sounded like a big band, because of the background roles some of the horn front line would take. Miles thought the Jazztet was stiff, but he loved the Messengers. He'd say, 'How does Art get you guys to write all the best shit for him?'"

By the time Coltrane left Miles for good in 1961, Wayne had developed greater finesse as a player and composer, and Miles both wanted and needed him for his group. "I'd go over to see Miles," Freddie said. "He would have one of Wayne's songs on, and he'd say, 'Freddie, what's *that?*' Wayne had some weird chord changes that he wrote. Miles liked those chords, like he liked Bill Evans's chords. Miles wanted to find the center tone to lead through all those changes."

But Wayne was a Jazz Messenger, and jazz's unwritten code of ethics demanded a certain restraint—Miles couldn't just waltz in and steal an elder's sideman, especially when that elder was Art Blakey. Miles's respect for Art was compromised, however, by an old grievance—in his memoirs, he wrote that Art had informed on him in a 1950 drug arrest in Los Angeles. And for Miles, the musical end always justified the means. He began to actively recruit Wayne, though he was typically unorthodox in those recruitment methods. He first called Wayne at home in New York in 1961. When Wayne picked up the phone, he heard someone strumming a complex progression of chords on a guitar. Wayne was captivated: It sounded like something he might write himself. The playing continued for several minutes. Finally, Miles spoke. "The guitar is a motherfucker, ain't it?" he asked. Wayne agreed. Miles asked, "You happy where you at?" "Nobody likes a Benedict Arnold, Miles," Wayne said.

Miles turned up in the front row at Messengers shows, fixing a voodoo gaze on Wayne as he soloed. "I'm glad Miles wasn't looking at *me* like that, for whatever reason," Freddie said. Miles continued to call Wayne intermittently but discreetly, always at Wayne's apartment in New York. He did lure Wayne into the studio for a one-off date with his sextet and Bob Dorough, released as *Jingle Bell Jazz.* But that was just a couple tunes. Over time, Miles's impatience made him reckless enough to call Wayne on the road in the Messengers' backstage dressing room. Art answered the phone and immediately recognized the voice asking for "Mr. Shorter." "Dewey, is that you?" Blakey asked. Miles couldn't have disguised his trademark rasp if he'd wanted to. But he didn't want to, and spoke with his usual cool impudence.

"Hey Wayne, Miles wants to talk to you," Art said casually, handing Wayne the phone. Then the bandleader paced agitatedly around the room, muttering, "Miles is trying to steal my tenor player," over and over, like a mantra for unhappiness. A distressed Wayne cupped his hand around the receiver to mute his voice. "Are you still happy there?" Miles asked, again. Despite the prestige of Miles's offer, it was sensible for Wayne to remain with Blakey. In the Messengers he was given encouragement to compose, and even more vitally, to hear his compositions tested out on the bandstand night after night; Miles, on the other hand, was still playing the standards he'd popularized in the late fifties.

Miles's courtship of Wayne gained some momentum in 1963, when Miles began assembling his "second classic quintet." He enticed drummer Tony Williams from Jackie McLean's band, and anchored the group with Ron Carter on bass and Herbie Hancock on piano. The saxophone spot proved more difficult to fill. Herbie had moved to New York from Chicago in 1961 to become a permanent member—as permanent as a jazz sideman can be—of Donald Byrd's group. Herbie knew Wayne's playing well: The two had worked together on Byrd's *Free Form* recording.

"A few months after I joined Miles, the idea of Wayne being in Miles's band began to seep through to all of us," Herbie said. "George Coleman was playing tenor saxophone with the band at the time, but there was something about Wayne's playing and the kinds of compositions he wrote that felt like he was the piece we really needed." George's style frustrated the free-leaning Tony, who found his approach too conventional and "inside." Conversely, George resented what he considered the band's willful experimentation, though he did play "out" one night, to the surprise of the other players. (Musicians tell a story about how years later there was still bad blood between George and the others. At an anniversary party for the Village Vanguard, Herbie, Ron, and Tony reunited for a trio set.

George Coleman came backstage with his horn, hoping to sit in and relive old times. "Don't even think about it," Herbie cautioned George, with uncharacteristic venom.)

Miles let George go, in part to appease his prodigious young drummer, and replaced him with the avant-gardist Sam Rivers for a tour of Japan. "Sam joined us on very short notice on that tour to Japan," said Herbie. "Tony wanted Sam in the group, 'cause Sam had been like a father figure to him, from when he'd been a kid in Boston. Sam had groomed Tony." Tony lobbied to bring his mentor into the group, hoping Sam's liberated musical presence would energize the quintet. But the rhythm section had discovered a unique chemistry, and Sam's irregular phrasing reacted badly to that mix. Miles felt like he had to rein in Sam's freewheeling style, which was more in keeping with the experimentation of Ornette Coleman and Coltrane. "It didn't really work out that well with Sam; it didn't quite mesh," Herbie said. "Sam's a great player, of course. He just wasn't quite what we were looking for. We all became more certain that what we were really looking for was what Wayne had."

When Miles heard that Wayne had left Blakey and was finally free, he commissioned his agent and "wheeler-dealer" Jack Whittemore to call Wayne. Tony and Herbie also worked to convince the elusive saxophonist to join them. This peer pressure finally succeeded. "So Wayne was getting all these calls begging him to join the band," Miles wrote in his memoirs. "When he finally called me, I told him to come on out. To make sure he did, I sent that motherfucker a first-class ticket so he could come out in style. That's how bad I wanted him. And when he got there the music just started happening. Our first gig together was to be at the Hollywood Bowl. Getting Wayne made me feel real good because with him I just knew some great music was going to happen. And it did, it happened real soon."

Miles Smiles

WAYNE STOPPED BY to see Miles's tailor, who fitted him for a tuxedo. He used Miles's first-class "incentive" ticket to fly out to L.A., heading directly to the Hollywood Bowl for his premiere performance with the bandleader. The band was already waiting backstage. "You know my music?" Miles asked Wayne. "Yeah, I know it," Wayne quickly replied, with a little too much assurance. "Uhh-ohhhhh," Miles said. "I guess you're bad then, aren't you?"

There was no luxury of a rehearsal to test out Wayne's avowed readiness. It was showtime, and Miles preferred a "trial by fire" method of sideman initiation anyway. But when Miles called the first tune, his initiation was "show no mercy, take no prisoners, and give no quarter": Miles started with "Joshua," a slippery Victor Feldman tune with sly meter changes. "The parts that the saxophone had, they ran all snaky and flowing," Wayne said. "But I had been listening to the records and playing along at home." The band played a few other tunes, then yielded the stage to the Duke Ellington Orchestra. Nobody commented on Wayne's performance after the show. Back in his hotel room, Wayne wondered how he'd done. Finally, the phone rang. "We're ready to record tomorrow," Miles said, getting right to the point. It was the highest praise possible.

The group actually didn't record for a while, but that same week, the Miles Davis Quintet did tape an appearance on *The Steve Allen Show*. Allen was a jazz composer himself—his tune "Gravy Waltz" won a Grammy for Best Original Jazz Composition in 1963—and he was always happy to host Miles on his show. For an outfit that would become the most celebrated small group in jazz history, this early TV performance was pretty uneventful. Miles's sidemen were as sharply dressed as their leader, but as smooth as they looked, they sounded a little stiff on their three tunes, "No Blues," "All Blues," and "So What." The latter two tunes were first recorded on Miles's 1959 masterpiece, *Kind of Blue,* with his "first great quintet," which included Coltrane. They were the most recognized tunes in his repertoire, smart choices for a TV audience. Though he would have preferred to start out with some fresher material, with placid determination Wayne tailored the secondhand tunes to his own style.

Miles must have heard something he liked. After he finished his first solo, he walked away from the stage, listening to Wayne play. When Miles mistakenly thought he was off camera, he shook his shoulders in an irrepressibly giddy dance move. It was a rarely seen burst of emotion from the stoic trumpeter, whose self-expression onstage was typically funneled through his horn. It did look like some great music was going to happen.

Wayne had played with Herbie on Donald Byrd's *Free Form* recording, and had been on the bandstand with Tony, too. "Tony played with the Messengers, at the Storyville in Boston when he was thirteen years old," Wayne said. "Art asked him to come up and play. For a few minutes, he would play exactly like Art Blakey, kidding around, and then he'd mix in a little Max Roach thing. Mixing it all with some of his own beginnings."

If Wayne knew the other players as peers, he had admired Miles from a distance. As a college student, Wayne had felt the crowd's frisson when Miles made an entrance at the Café Bohemia with French actress Juliette Gréco and Columbia Records producer George Avakian, just after Miles had signed to the label. When Miles played the trumpet, he had an aura. With his regal bearing, he cultivated that aura into a mystique. Miles reminded Wayne of actor Ronald Colman, who was born to middle-class British parents but strove to maintain the standards of a "high-born" Englishman on and off the screen. "Miles wore that country gentleman stuff, all that was missing was the stables and horses," Wayne said. "Some guys would hide behind their instrument and not think that looking good had anything to do with it. Miles projected a certain class thing with clothes."

Backstage with Miles, Wayne witnessed him assembling that genteel character firsthand. "If he had two ties in his room," Wayne remembered, "He'd say, 'Which should I wear, this one or that one?'" Miles fussed over his sidemen's appearance, too, and tested their fashion sense. "Put your handkerchief over here," he'd say, or "Let me fix that shirt. Don't you know Versace?" And Wayne quickly saw that behind the Prince of Darkness mystique, Miles was actually a warmhearted man. Like Art Blakey, Miles had a reputation for scathing commentary. "People assumed that his nasty tongue created a hardship for his cohorts," Wayne said. "But he directed that at outsiders. Miles was fun, and just wanted to be entertained himself. More than anything, Miles became like a big brother to me."

As a bandleader, Miles did exact high standards without giving much instruction, which could be disturbing if not shocking for new guys in his band. Wayne wasn't too bothered by it. He'd never trafficked much in systematic music-making anyway, instead relying on his sixth sense to sound things out. Besides, it was all part of the tradition: Miles had learned his "sink or swim" style of bandleading from his own mentors. Miles told Wayne about when he moved to New York from St. Louis and played a gig with tenor saxophonist Coleman Hawkins. After Miles's first night on-stage with the group, Coleman said, "Dewey, what you played tonight, that ain't it." So Miles worked on "it." In the middle of the week, Coleman told Miles, "You're getting closer, but that still ain't it." Miles worked with Coleman for two weeks, and at the end of the gig, Coleman finally told him, "That's it."

"Sometimes you have to play for a long time to be able to play like yourself," Miles once said. After five years with the Messengers, Wayne was ready to come into his own, and Miles occasioned this metamorphosis. "It wasn't the bish-bash, sock'em dead routine we had with Blakey, with every solo a climax," Wayne said. "With Miles, I felt like a cello, I felt the viola, I felt liquid, dot-dash and colors started really coming."

The rhythm section of Ron, Herbie, and Tony had already been with Miles for a year, during which time they learned to trust their instincts. Herbie said: "The group's defining quality was trust, and acceptance. Whatever happened musically was supposed to happen, and you were supposed to make it work." Wayne was well suited to this sensibility. "Wayne seemed to have a sense of our curiosity as to what it would take to make the music feel different," Ron said. "Wayne left the counter space that would allow us to help him help us. Sometimes the music worked out great, sometimes less than great, but it didn't matter, 'cause we were in this laboratory, trying to find the thing that was going to work tomorrow night."

The next week, the quintet went on a European tour. Their first date was at the Berliner Philharmonie, a West German temple for orchestral music and rarefied jazz acts. A recording of that show, *Miles in Berlin,* revealed how quickly the group gained momentum, with Wayne bringing a new depth of interplay to the rhythm section. Wayne's puckish style—his "now you see it, now you don't" approach to improvisation—gave the rhythm section room for a broader balance of tones and timbres, and on tunes like "Autumn Leaves," the group's communication became almost telepathic.

But it was as Miles's resident composer that Wayne made himself indispensable. "Wayne would just write something and give it to me and walk off," Miles wrote. "He wouldn't say shit. He'd just say, 'Here, Mr. Davis. I wrote some new songs.' Mr. Davis! Then I'd look at the shit and it would be a motherfucker." Miles noted that Wayne wrote like Charlie Parker. "It was the way he notated on the beat. Lucky Thompson used to hear us and say, 'Goddamn, that boy can write music!' When he came into the band it started to grow a lot more and a whole lot faster, because Wayne is a real composer." With Miles, Wayne's trusty book of compositions thickened by the day. When the quintet hit the studio for the first time on January 20, 1965, Miles simply told him to "bring the book."

Wayne contributed two tunes to *E.S.P.*—the title track and "Iris." A tuneful melody built on intervals of descending fourths, "E.S.P." originally credited both Miles and Wayne as composers and was issued through Miles's publishing company. In trumpeter Kenny Durham's *Down Beat* review of the record, he hinted that Miles's faltering delivery of the melody suggested that Wayne might be the sole author of the title track. After a few years, Wayne got a call from a publishing administrator. "Guess what?" he said. "Miles returned your song. He returned the rights back to you."

"You never heard of Miles doing that," Wayne said. "I said, 'Miles, you gettin' religion?'" Miles's reversion of the tune's ownership was kind, but was probably not spiritually motivated; Miles simply had to acknowledge that the piece bore Wayne's unmistakable stylistic imprint. Miles typically performed surgical reconstruction on his sidemen's compositions, but he made only minor cosmetic changes to Wayne's tunes. Wayne knew that Miles granted him rare autonomy: "When I wrote stuff, Miles would say, 'There's no need to change any of Wayne's music. It's all there.'" Miles didn't need to abstract the essence of Wayne's music—Wayne wrote with the fine points in mind. (Though when the stakes were higher, Miles wouldn't always be so considerate about recognizing Wayne's exclusive ownership of his work.)

As Wayne's playing style evolved and his compositions grew more vital to his bandmates, the man behind the music remained an enigma to them. While the other musicians socialized after gigs, Wayne usually retreated to his hotel room. "Tony and I would hang together a lot," Herbie said. "We'd be out in the world seeing what kind of trouble we could stir up, but Wayne had a tendency to be a loner."

"I was a lone wolf," Wayne said. "I'd be in my hotel room with room service, fantasizing about books I was going to read, or actually reading them. Then I'd put the book down, and a musical drama would come on-screen in my mind. The music would become a story, with the notes taking on dimensions, sounds took the form of a background setting, and then it'd be like, 'Hey! What's that over there?'—the rhythm would enter the picture as another character. And then I'd have to stop myself."

Miles was intrigued by Wayne's hermit-like habits. "What does that motherfucker *do* in his room all day?" he'd ask Tony or Ron. "Does he write music all day?" In those first few months, the band's social dynamics didn't involve much face time between Miles and Wayne. "Miles and I were together sometimes, talking about politics, and art and sports," Ron said. "And Tony lived in Miles's building, and Herbie would be there lots of times, so he knew what those guys did during the daytime hours. Not really knowing Wayne off the bandstand, Miles was curious about what Wayne was doing when he wasn't playing."

On tour one time, Miles sent Ron up to Wayne's hotel room to investigate. "Go see what he's doing, man," Miles said, casting Ron in an undesirable role of secret agent/butler. "I'll look, but I'm not going to tell you what he's doing," Ron told Miles. "You've got to walk up your own steps." Ron didn't remember exactly what Wayne was doing when he dropped by. "Wayne was probably reading a book by a Stephen Hawking type or watching an old sepia-colored movie," he said. And ultimately, the secretive routine behind Wayne's strangely appealing compositions didn't matter much to Miles, who was a sorcerer of sounds himself. "Miles didn't really care where Wayne got his 'thing' from," Ron said. "He just wanted to know what Wayne was doing during the daytime. He was just being nosy."

"I didn't know that Miles was so interested in what I was doing, but I knew that he was always watching soap operas during the day," Wayne said. Onstage, Miles revealed that soft, romantic side of his personality when he played, just as he also expressed his more aggressive instincts. And he created musical scenarios that encouraged the others to sound out their own quirks. The sensitive musical interplay of Miles's quintet demanded such individuality and subjectivity from players that it brought out certain character traits lurking below the surface. In Wayne's case, his inner "Mr. Weird" made a big comeback. Shortly after Brazilian drummer Airto Moreira moved to New York, he met Wayne and Alan Shorter together at Wayne's apartment in Harlem. "Alan and Wayne walked out of the building, and I saw them briefly," Airto said. "I didn't understand a word of what they said. It was like they were from a different world. But I thought it was me because I didn't speak English well. But then later on I talked to them individually, and I found out that I felt the same way about them even when I could speak English."

When Wayne did emerge from his room and get out among the band, his character could be bizarre, and his language tended toward the far side of oblique and the denser part of opaque. Wayne's random sighting of a stranger in red shoes at the airport might set him off on a long monologue on the merits of his favorite movie, *The Red Shoes*. Backstage between sets, one of the guys would comment on the measurements of a striking woman in the audience, and Wayne would respond with a mathematical principle of astrophysics. In many ways, Wayne's manner of speaking was like his style of playing. His conversational non sequiturs usually involved mind-twisting metaphorical leaps. Half the time, no one was sure *what* Wayne was trying to say, but it seemed like it *might* be profound.

"I didn't know whether Wayne was crazy or a genius," Herbie said. "I knew something was there, but I couldn't get a handle on it." Herbie decided he had to find out. "We were playing some club outside of Boston," he said. "After the gig, I got a bottle of cognac and went back to his hotel room and we drank. And we talked for hours. And I began to see that there were word games that Wayne would play. His whole approach was much more like poetry, if anything, than how we normally perceive standard conversation. His way of speaking was on a much higher plane. I did come to the conclusion that he was a genius, not crazy. He really blew my mind." It was fortunate that Herbie managed to crack the idiosyncratic code of Wayne's personality. This was the beginning of the deepest friendship and most long-running musical association of Wayne's life.

Just as Wayne began to ease into a friendly rapport with the others, Miles developed some health problems that took him out of commission. He had hip surgery in April 1965, then broke his hip in August, so he was forced to cancel dates from April through October. His sidemen fended for themselves admirably during those seven months, putting their energy into lots of studio work, mostly for Blue Note Records.

"Blue Note was like going to the bank for us," Wayne said. Musicians were paid $500 for a recording and additionally for each day of rehearsal. The label typically allowed one week per record date: three or four days of rehearsal, and a final day for the actual recording. It was just enough time for extremely skilled musicians, who usually came from various ensembles, to refine and tighten their music into the illusory sound of a working band. "These were one-shot things," Wayne said. "There was nothing developmental as a band. A recording was just one movie, and then the next was another movie, in a kind of dream away from Miles. The thing was that you didn't want to get ridiculous." For Wayne, the studio simply never measured up to the stage. He preferred the spontaneity of live music. "You know, all these other things come into place sometimes when you get into the studio," Wayne said. "The studio becomes like a citadel. 'We got to stay here a whole week until we get it, or no one goes home!' That kind of thing. 'I want to see some dedication here.' That kind of stuff. To me that's surface stuff."

Recording engineer Rudy Van Gelder was technically responsible for the coherent sound of the Blue Note sessions. His studio, built in 1959, was in Englewood Cliffs, New Jersey, just a twenty-minute drive from downtown Manhattan. Van Gelder engineered all of the label's recordings there, manning the console with such remote and precise professionalism that he came off as a little robotic to the musicians. Wearing white gloves, he would greet musicians with a warning to keep their hands off everything. The engineer's personality was better expressed through his magnanimous studio space. With its atrium-like shape and huge wooden arches that intersected on its ceiling far overhead, Van Gelder's studio had the exalted air and awesome reverberation of a cathedral sanctuary but the homey feel of a cabin or chapel in the woods. "My goal in building the studio was to create an environment in which musicians felt comfortable, so they could concentrate on their performance," Van Gelder said. "In short, a nice place to play. I believe Wayne appreciated it."

Wayne enjoyed the studio, but he and his peers didn't realize the rareness of their opportunity to record there so frequently. When everyone was so prolific, it was easy to take it for granted. "We didn't think about it much," Wayne said. "A fish is too busy swimming to notice that it's in the water." Blue Note producer Alfred Lion did recognize that the musicians were at a creative peak. "If [Alfred] liked an artist, he would record them frequently, rather than just do one session," Van Gelder said. "This resulted in the musicians becoming comfortable in the studio environment, and placed the music as the fundamental focus, rather than all the technical things that go on. This allowed Wayne's music to develop."

During their break from Miles's quintet, his sidemen recorded some of their finest work for Blue Note: There was Herbie's *Maiden Voyage* and Tony's *Spring,* on which Wayne served as a sideman. Wayne also played on his former Messengers' bandmate Lee Morgan's *Gigolo.* And between March and October 1965, Wayne made three records of his own as a leader, *The Soothsayer, Etcetera,* and *The All Seeing Eye,* which brought his total Blue Note output to six records in eighteen months.

Alan Shorter played flugelhorn on *The All Seeing Eye.* Wayne hadn't seen much of his brother since he'd moved to Europe. Alan lived in Paris and Geneva, where he played solo avant-garde shows in clubs. "He would play and some people would be booing and some people would be yeahing," Wayne said. "He'd stop playing and curse the audience and say, 'You're not ready for me yet. Nobody's ready for me yet!' And then walk offstage." Alan was also working on his magnum opus, a colorful book on philosophy and culture. "Alan wrote a great big book on his thoughts about life, about seven hundred pages," Wayne said. "He had one chapter dedicated to his time in France. He wrote, 'France: A Dedication. When I was leaving France, a customs agent asked me a question. He asked, "Do you ever intend to return to France?" I answered "Pourquoi?"' That was Alan's whole chapter on France! My mother had two copies of the book. She later went to publishers, did some footwork. They all basically said the same thing: 'This is way ahead of its time, too advanced.'"

Wayne's music was too advanced for Alan to master without a fair amount of practice, as it was for most musicians who worked on Wayne's Blue Note sessions. "A lot of people don't know that Wayne's one of the best writers that we got on the jazz scene," Freddie Hubbard said. "I did some of his best records, *Speak No Evil* and *The All Seeing Eye,* but I had to take that music home and practice it. I played with all these guys, with Sonny and Trane, the heavy guys, but Wayne wrote the strangest songs, the ones that got you." With the broad harmonics and expanded instrumentation of *The All Seeing Eye,* navigating Wayne's chord changes was a challenge for the best readers and improvisers.

Joe Chambers was a kind of house drummer for Blue Note at this time, playing on Wayne's dates and those of Bobby Hutcherson, Andrew Hill, and Freddie Hubbard. Like most musicians who often recorded for Blue Note, he didn't remember much about any specific date, but did recall how Blue Note's key personnel handled the artful dance of the recording process. "Alfred was around all the time, but Duke Pearson was the A&R man," Joe said. "Duke was a musician himself, so he acted like a buffer between the musicians and Frank and Alfred." Wayne said the producers mostly left him to his own devices, but were clearly looking for the kind of soulful vamps that made Lee Morgan's *The Sidewinder* a success: "They never tried to get me to go commercial. They'd pull the drummer aside and ask him to put a little more groove in something. *Adam's Apple* responded to those suggestions most." That record's title track was as close as Wayne ever got to the soul-jazz formula.

These recordings charted Wayne's growth as a cosmic philosopher as much as a musical thinker. For the liner notes to *The All Seeing Eye,* Wayne told Nat Hentoff he was working toward "a wider range of colors and textures" while also continuing his search for added dimensions in his ideas "about life and the universe and God." Wayne said the inconsistent meter of "Genesis" represented the "immensity of the act of creation," and its overall feeling of open-endedness pointed to the fact that "once begun, the creative process keeps going." The chance to make an extramusical statement as a leader was as important to Wayne as the music itself. "Once you begin thinking about the nature of the universe and the nature of man, there's no way of stopping," he told Hentoff. "It's all so open, without finite limits. The universe keeps changing, man keeps changing, and I keep changing."

In addition to their recording projects, the musicians used their break from the Miles Quintet to gig around New York. In June and July, Wayne played six weeks with drummer Roy Haynes at Slugs, a jazz club on East Third Street between Avenues C and D. This was a rough and isolated neighborhood. No subway lines serviced the area, and cabs rarely ventured there. If you didn't own a car, the club was accessed only by a walk east from the Bowery through housing projects and "teenage gangbangers" territory. Slugs's remote location discouraged tourist traffic and invited fringe characters like drug dealers and their clients, who included more than a few musicians. The musicians gradually took over the place, and by the summer of 1965 practitioners of the "new black music" such as Sun Ra and Albert Ayler were regulars. It was the kind of scene where artists did live action painting to the music, and a couple of painter Robert Thompson's spur-of-the-moment pictures were hung on the wall before they dried. Slugs remained an unofficial after-hours musicians' hang until Lee Morgan was shot to death onstage by his mistress there in 1972.

That summer, a gang from Brooklyn was prowling the neighborhood around Slugs, and Philadelphia saxophonist C Sharp was mugged heading home from the club. It was no secret to anyone on the scene that Friday was pay night for the club's musicians. Wayne bought a hammer and packed it inside his horn case for protection. One rainy Friday night, he left Slugs with a modest bit of cash and walked west to get a taxi. When Wayne heard two sets of footsteps quickening behind him, he unzipped his case and grabbed the hammer. Its new silver head reflected the street-lights as Wayne lifted it up above his head. With a cinematic sense of lunacy, Wayne affected a strange nasal tone and growled out, "I'm gonna get somebody tonight!" The footsteps behind him halted, and his own nervous stride resounded alone through the deserted neighborhood until he finally reached a cab-friendly street.

"I kind of knew what I was doing 'cause I had been in the army," Wayne explained. "If you act crazy, just for one minute, it makes you unpredictable." Wayne had used that tactic long before, to discourage confrontations as a teenager in Newark. He still had his radar up, and it still signaled "Alien coming!"

Live at the Plugged Nickel

By November 1965, Miles was well enough to play again. The quintet played a mid-November gig at Philadelphia's Showboat Lounge, a week at Detroit's Grand Bar, a Thanksgiving-week run at the Vanguard in New York, and a stint at Bohemian Caverns in Washington, D.C. Reggie Workman and Gary Peacock each subbed for Ron on a couple dates, but the main group played together enough to settle back into a groove.

That comfort was a problem. After only a few gigs, Miles's sidemen began to feel restless. Though the band was thrilled to be on the road with Miles again, they'd become almost too accomplished at playing Miles's classic repertoire—still the same old "Round Midnight," "Funny Valentine," and "So What." "The band was never conventional, so I can't confine it to being that," Herbie said. "But even within our very creative and loose approach to the music, everybody did things according to certain kinds of expectations. I knew if I did this, Ron would do that, or Tony knew that if he did this, I would do that. It became so easy to do that it was almost boring." Especially after they had tried out some fresh ideas during those productive months away from Miles, his music felt predictable and complacent.

Just before their final gig of the year, in Chicago, Tony came up with a solution. "Hey, what if we made *anti-music*?" he asked. "Like, whatever someone expects you to play, that's the *last* thing you play?" The rest of the rhythm section wasn't sure. This onstage parlor game would feel awkward and could sound disastrous. But in the end, they all agreed to sacrifice the gig for the "betterment of the band." They didn't have a choice. It was time to grow, or die.

The Plugged Nickel club in Chicago's bohemian Old Town seemed like a good place to test their experiment. The Plugged Nickel's audience would be expecting to hear the smooth band they knew from Miles's records, but hopefully they'd be more forgiving than New York's scrutinizing jazz cognoscenti. And the adventurous "Great Black Music" of Chicago's AACM (Association for the Advancement of Creative Musicians) proved that experimentation wasn't necessarily antithetical to tradition in the city. Still, expectations for this show were especially high, since Miles had cancelled dates at the club in July, August, and October.

When the musicians walked into the Plugged Nickel, they were surprised to see Columbia Records producer Teo Macero stringing wires across the stage. What was *he* doing there? Miles was waiting backstage, where he confirmed that Columbia wanted to record the gig. Tony glared at the other guys in a silent warning: Nobody was turning back from their sabotage mission. So what if there'd be recorded evidence of the "anti-music" gig for everyone to hear?

Then, for some unknown reason, Miles refused to be recorded on the first night of the gig. On the second night, threatened with a suspension of his contract, he acquiesced. That night and the next, Macero recorded a total of seven sets, capturing the band's dynamic creative process on an album that was later released as *Live at the Plugged Nickel*.

From the intro to the first tune, "If I Were a Bell," it was clear that Miles's sidemen were up to something new. Usually there was a clear statement of the melody at the start of a tune—something you could whistle—but this intro was as abstract and erratic as the wind. A few bars in, Ron uprooted the chord's foundation on his bass; on piano, Herbie pulled away from the tune's tonal center. Miles quickly reacted, testing out some off-kilter phrases of his own, but his final musical phrase had the querulous upward curve of a question mark: *What the fuck is going on here?* It was clear that improvised solos were going to be *collectively* forged by the band. Anything a soloist said would have to be vetted by the rhythm section.

By the start of the second set, Miles was enjoying the band's game. The trumpeter always ran his bands on musical meritocracy—the best ideas ruled, and even the leader had to be hip and selfless enough to follow them. But Miles's chops were still weak from his extended time off. So he challenged the others by simply leaving them extra space. Lots of space . . . while the audience waited for his next phrase, seasons changed, people fell in and out of love . . . and the band faltered. It took the band members almost seven minutes to coax the anti-music from Miles's deep silence. But when they did, they quickly climaxed, and nobody was faking it.

If Miles liked the rhythm section's anti-music game, Wayne was thrilled by it. "When I heard those guys dropping the bottom out from under me, I knew it was 'Go for it' time!" he said. "I'd been in the band for a little over a year, and the next thing I knew we were way out there. It was like . . . this is what freedom means. The awareness was that the great responsibility that came with the territory was to push the envelope. You heard responsibility converted into expression that sounded like a great adventure." The adventurous rhythm section pushed Wayne into some of the most brilliant playing of his career. On tunes like "Green Dolphin Street," Wayne expanded the harmony until he seemed lost. Then he resolved everything with such natural logic that he seemed to be mocking, "Oh ye of little faith."

During the second set, the band relaxed into a more traditional, melodic take on "When I Fall in Love." In his solo, Wayne confidently ref-

erenced jazz elders such as Lester Young, Sonny Rollins, and Stan Getz—
he wanted to fit a little of everything in. After Wayne finished his solo, he
joined Miles offstage. Miles turned to Wayne and asked, "You ever feel
like you could play *anything* you want?"

"Yeah, I—" Wayne began.

"I know just what you mean," Miles interrupted. "But can you also *not*
play everything?"

"Oh, that's a lot harder," he answered.

"When Miles talked, sometimes it was a good kind of convolution,"
Wayne said. While they talked, Ron Carter took a solo. A fan began to
taunt him with shout-outs to esteemed bassists such as Ray Brown, Oscar
Pettiford, and Paul Chambers. Miles hurried out and played the head to
cut Ron's solo short—a gallant rescue by the leader.

It was no wonder the crowd was rowdy. Fans had expected to hear polished pearls, the bop tunes they knew from Miles's recordings. What they
heard instead were rough cuts from a band that was using music like a
philosopher's stone. This band was proof of the reprimand Miles had delivered to saxophonist George Coleman just a year earlier: "I pay you to
practice *on* the stand!" Of course, there was a lot of experimental music
around; artists like Ornette Coleman, John Coltrane, and Eric Dolphy
were reshaping jazz into entirely new forms. But Miles was a direct link to
the bebop era—he'd actually played with Charlie Parker—so if he was
moving his music out of the past, that said something.

Miles wasn't as hostile toward the avant-garde as some believed him to
be. More than once he came backstage after a set and bragged, "I was
really getting into some Don Cherry shit there, wasn't I?"—proud to have
copped some riffs from the daring trumpeter. The difference in Miles's
band was that his musicians always played with controlled freedom, keeping an eye on a tune's chord changes or melody, while some avant-garde
musicians used freedom to disguise a lack of knowledge or talent. "Almost
all the avant-garde people were doing a language they didn't know," Wayne
said. "Many of them would learn just enough of the language to convince

people that they were avant-garde. And just enough is a lot to a person who doesn't know the difference."

In some ways, the quintet's music felt freer than free jazz, more avant-garde than the avant-garde. "Tony could sound like Max Roach or Art Blakey or Philly Joe Jones, in any given second," Ron said. "Freedom was when any one of these five people in the group could immediately identify that and jump to that page in their book. That's freedom for me, to have that kind of musical awareness, where the ego is not part of the music." In an interview with filmmaker Ken Burns, *Plugged Nickel* reissue producer Michael Cuscuna described the quintet's freedom in similar terms: "They were never inhibited by structure, they were never inhibited by pre-dictability, they were never inhibited by musical signposts. They were free to go anywhere they wanted to, and they knew everyone else would follow. That's a luxury that few of us ever experience, in marriage or in music or in, in any kind of art form or any kind of teamwork. It was, it was astonishing."

Chicago pianist Jodie Christian was in the crowd at the Plugged Nickel that night. "Technically, they listened to one another and played together unlike any other band I'd ever heard," he said. "Everybody heard each other and was able to respond to the same thing. At intermission everybody in the audience would talk excitedly about what we were hearing, because they were playing both free-form and conventional. I don't think I ever heard anything like that again."

The guys in the band knew they were onto something special. As Wayne told writer John Szwed, their sense of musical mission lent them the dignified air of a chivalric order: "At the Plugged Nickel we were raising so much hell musically that when we came off we couldn't say nothing to each other. We were lethargic in a princely way. We weren't trying to put on airs . . . it was like 'Let's not touch this.' You were in the royalty of the moment, and such royalty need never be tampered with." When Wayne looked at Tony, Ron, and Herbie, he flashed to movie scenes of crusaders reclaiming the throne for King Richard. He felt something like transference in levels of his being, as if the musical experience were promoting him from an earl to a duke.

Reality did intervene. Most nights, the Duke of Bass flew back to New York to see his newborn son, who was born on December 18. "I would finish the gig at two in the morning, and take a three-o'clock plane from Chicago to La Guardia," Ron said. "I'd spend a day in New York with my new son and my oldest son, who was seven years old then, and then I'd take a seven o'clock plane back to the gig." And the rhythm section did have *some* technical discussions about the music. There were questions along the lines of "How does that work? Just show me on paper how you play five against four and maintain the bar lines." Or Ron would say, "Herbie, on an F major chord, if I play beyond the bottom, it gives you these kinds of choices. Then you have to guess what my next note is, so you can build your chord based on following this trend in the voicing." But this talk would come well after a show, maybe at dinner before the next night's performance. The musicians acted on "common knowledge" intuitively, in real time, before it was articulated in later discussions.

On the third night at the Plugged Nickel, which was also recorded, the quintet played some of the same tunes again, but even a Miles classic like "So What" sounded reborn. Usually it was Tony who kicked things into high gear, juggling polyrhythms you just couldn't quantify punctuated by good-natured rimshot tantrums. Ron leapt over bar lines in a single bound. For his part, Herbie would key in on the melody, then change his mind and follow Wayne's smeared path of saxophone into a chromatic never-never land. "In music, if you're going up a ski slope, you usually slide down on the other side," Herbie said. But here, resolution wasn't just delayed, it was sometimes abandoned altogether, he said: "You'd go up the ski slope and all of a sudden there'd be nothing there. Tony would make a crash and it would just be with the cymbal, without the bass drum as usual. Or I would build up to a big chord and Ron would do nothing. Everything we did was the opposite of what everyone expected us to do."

There were times that the band didn't quite make it through a song. "If we were going to get lost, we were going to get lost together," Herbie said. But even with the gig's hits and misses, the group found its "anti-music." When each musician attempted to fake the others out with his own erratic stream-of-consciousness, the group was pushed to a deeper level of musical consensus. They'd found a way to make those old songs new again.

Still, they assumed that the recording must be a disaster, and were relieved that Columbia decided not to release it. When a *Live at the Plugged Nickel* recording was finally issued in Japan nine years later, the guys were astonished to hear that the music actually made sense—their experiment had become a common vocabulary for small-group jazz. *Live at the Plugged Nickel* defined truth in jazz for the next generation of musicians. Later, in 1982, when the record came out in the U.S., a twenty-year-old trumpeter named Wynton Marsalis showed up at Wayne's house with the record in hand. Wynton asked if he could just sit silently and watch Wayne's expression while they listened to the music together.

Limbo

During Wayne's early years with Miles, he had conviction in the value and purpose of art. There was a solid basis for aesthetic faith and good incentive to live for music. In those divine days, the guys in the band possessed equal talent, work was steady, and inspiration seemed limitless. Summarizing Wayne's role in the group, Miles called him "the intellectual musical catalyst." Miles referred to the fact that Wayne's compositions spurred the group on to innovation. But this choice of words also revealed something more about his view of Wayne: A *catalyst* is an agent that stimulates a reaction or change while remaining unaffected by the change itself. In his music and in his life, Wayne seemed to exist in a world apart, uninfluenced by changes in mood or fortune.

But Wayne's personal life was not so carefree. Even at the height of the quintet's success, there were signs that music would take Wayne only so far. In 1966, Wayne and his wife, Irene (who'd assumed the traditional

Japanese name Teruko), separated after marital problems—"She was 'finding herself,'" Wayne said—though they peaceably enough arranged for Wayne to see his daughter Miyako on weekends. (In 1973, Teruko married actor Billy Dee Williams. Williams lived across the street from Wayne and Teruko in Harlem before he moved out to L.A. and became a *Star Wars* celebrity and purveyor of smoothness in Colt 45 commercials.)

Around the same time, Wayne experienced a more abrupt loss. In April 1966, Joseph and Louise Shorter drove over to see the band in Philadelphia on its final night of a gig there. The Shorters had been nearby in southern New Jersey shopping for a retirement home—ideally, a property with a nice, big house, a sizable yard, and maybe an orchard, their own Elysian fields on earth after years of Ironbound life in Newark. After the gig, Wayne and his parents went to eat at a restaurant over on Lombard Street. He meant to catch a ride back to New York with them, but the band was still waiting for payment from the club. So Wayne went back to the band's hotel, and Joseph and Louise drove on without him.

Later that night, Herbie went to his hotel room, where he got a call from Teruko. Her voice was shaking as she told Herbie that there had been an accident. On the way home to Newark, the Shorters' car went off the road and hit a tree. Wayne's father was killed instantly. Teruko thought this bad news should come from Herbie since she and Wayne were estranged. Wayne seemed somehow expectant when Herbie walked into his hotel room to deliver the news. He was lying on his bed awake, still wearing his suit from the gig.

Miles had also lost his parents—his stepfather in 1963, and his mother, whom he adored, in 1964. And Miles was going through a divorce as well. After a tempestuous marriage, his wife, Frances, had finally left him; newspaper reports of her affair with Marlon Brando regularly reminded him of the fact. Over those troubled months, Wayne and Miles made a habit of drowning their sorrows together after gigs. "You want to go home to an empty apartment?" Miles would ask, rhetorically. "I don't either, let's stay out." Miles commiserated with Wayne's Job-like spate of hardships. "When it rains it pours," he'd say, and order another "light" champagne and cognac cocktail—a mix chosen not for its bubbly extravagance but in deference to the liver infection that had laid him up from January to March. Wayne usually drank double cognacs, and in keeping with their code of cool restraint, he didn't become dramatically drunk. There was no dancing on tables or shooting out lights. Wayne would grow silent and his eyes would gradually lose focus. When his eyes began to cross, someone would gently send him up to his hotel room to sleep.

But Wayne's steely constitution sometimes gave out. One night, the quintet played at Lennie's On the Turnpike, a club on Route 1 just north of Boston in Peabody, Massachusetts. Tony's father drove out from his home in Boston for the gig, and he and Tony tap-danced together onstage. With the loss of his own father weighing on him, Wayne gave Tony's father a saxophone as a gift. "All the emotional stuff was building up that night, you know," Wayne said.

Herbie's fiancée, Gigi, was traveling with the band. "Wayne was drinking a lot, as usual," she remembered. "We were leaving the club, and Wayne was standing up, and then he fell over flat on his face. That was the first time I was devastated by the injury a person can do to himself. I realized how much I'd come to love him when I saw that his face was so horribly hurt. It was awful."

"When I fell, I had a sandwich in one hand and a horn in the other," Wayne said. "Nothing happened to the sandwich or the horn. But it wasn't a whole lot of scotch I'd had." It was apparently enough. Luckily for Wayne, Miles was joined on tour by a friend, a pretty lady doctor from NYU Hospital who'd operated on his hip. As she applied pHisoHex to Wayne's smashed lip and tried to clean him up, Miles explained, "He's been going through a lot of shit." *That's why Miles has this doctor girlfriend with him,* Wayne thought, jealously. *He's going through a lot of shit, too.* The soothing doctor told Wayne he'd had a release of anxiety. Slackened by the scotch, his body went where his mind had refused to go, and he literally crashed.

Wayne said that for years the illusion of invincibility protected his mu-

Wayne's mother,
Louise Page Shorter.
Courtesy Wayne Shorter

At age five (right) with his brother, Alan,
around the time they were "making the whole
world" out of clay. *Courtesy Wayne Shorter*

No. 1 in Art Show

From a newspaper item on Wayne's
first-place finish in a citywide art
contest. *Courtesy Wayne Shorter*

A page from Wayne's thick book of blue pen drawings that he created in 1946 at age fifteen. Entitled "Other Worlds," it depicts an interspecies romance between an astronaut earthling, Rick, and the leader of the moon people, Doka.
Courtesy Wayne Shorter

Another page from "Other Worlds": at this point in the story, the astronaut party has returned to the earth.
Courtesy Wayne Shorter

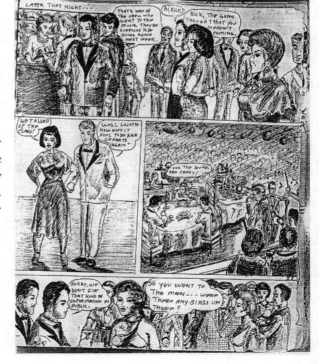

Wayne's first professional gig. He is on clarinet, standing in back, to the right of the bassist. *Courtesy Wayne Shorter*

With the Maynard Ferguson Big Band, Birdland, July 1959. Wayne is seated in the front row, to the right of Maynard, standing, on trumpet. Joe Zawinul is on piano. *Courtesy Joe Zawinul*

Lee Morgan, Wayne, and Art Blakey (partially obscured) onstage. *Courtesy Wayne Shorter*

The cover image for *Introducing Wayne Shorter* (Vee-Jay Records). *Institute of Jazz Studies, Rutgers University*

At the Messengers'
1960 *Big Beat* session.
Francis Wolff
© *Mosaic Images*

The resident composer
makes some musical edits
in the studio, with Art
Blakey and bassist Jymie
Merritt looking on.
Francis Wolff © *Mosaic Images*

At home, absorbed in a long composition at the piano, with his daughter Miyako, who is wondering if her father will ever be finished with his music.
Courtesy Wayne Shorter

Encouraging Miyako to look at the photographer, who is Miles Davis. They are in Miles's home, and Miles's dog, Milo, is on Wayne's lap. Wayne said the dog "died of loneliness" soon after.
Courtesy Wayne Shorter

At an August 1964 *JuJu* session.
Francis Wolff
© *Mosaic Images*

Herbie Hancock ruminates on the complexities of Wayne's music or just grabs a quick nap at the December 1964 *Speak No Evil* session. *Francis Wolff © Mosaic Images*

Miles and Wayne, laughing onstage. *Courtesy Jan Persson*

The Miles Davis Quartet onstage in Berlin, 1964. *Courtesy Jan Persson*

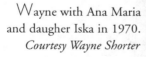Wayne with Ana Maria
and daugher Iska in 1970.
Courtesy Wayne Shorter

Josef Zawinui

Miraslav Vitouf

Dom Um Romao

Eric Gravatt

Wayne Shorter

A publicity shot for an early and short-lived incarnation of Weather Report. *Institute of Jazz Studies, Rutgers University*

Press and Public Information / 54 W. 52nd Street, New York, New York 10019 / Telephone (212) 765-4324

European Joe, African American Wayne, and part-Mongolian Jaco get back to their ethnic roots on tour, 1978. *Courtesy Peter Erskine*

Wayne playing the lyricon, his "instrument of meditation," flanked by his other two horns, soprano and tenor saxophones.
Courtesy Wayne Shorter

Chanting on a Japanese bullet train, during an extracurricular visit to the Yamaha factory in Hamamatsu, June 1978. *S. Uchiyama/Whisper not*

Weather Report in its most popular grouping, with Peter Erskine and Jaco Pastorius. *Institute of Jazz Studies, Rutgers University*

The core members of Weather Report, Wayne and Joe Zawinul, in their traditional duet number onstage. *www.markbrady.com*

At critic Conrad Silvert's farewell fiesta concert in 1982, recorded as *Jazz at the Opera House*. Pictured (left to right) are Lew Tabackin, Charlie Haden, Jaco Pastorius, Tony Williams, Wynton Marsalis, Conrad Silvert, Danny Zeitlin, Toshiko Akiyoshi, Pat Metheny, Carlos Santana, Bobby Hutcherson, Wayne, and Herbie Hancock. The painting behind the group was collectively created by the musicians after the show. *Courtesy Wayne Shorter*

An on-screen appearance in the film *Round Midnight*, 1985.
Courtesy Wayne Shorter

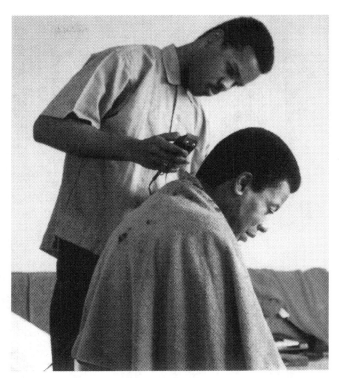

Getting some emergency grooming from saxophonist Greg Osby backstage. *Courtesy Wayne Shorter*

Performing with Brazilian pop star Milton Nascimento in one of their many appearances together in the 1980s. *Institute of Jazz Studies, Rutgers University*

Inspiring some young Japanese Soka Gakkai International members. *Courtesy Wayne Shorter*

With Carlos Santana at the
start of the Santana–Shorter
tour in 1988.
www.markbrady.com

Wayne and Ana Maria on safari in Thailand during a Monk Institute tour in 1996, just months before the crash of TWA Flight 800. *Courtesy Wayne Shorter*

With Carolina, whom he married in 1999. *Courtesy Wayne Shorter*

With the younger players of his current quartet, pianist Danilo Perez, bassist John Patitucci, and drummer Brian Blade, at Columbia University, August 2001. *Tom Terrell*

Speaking in broad terms, as usual, in 2003.
Courtesy Wayne Shorter

sicianship during drinking binges: "When you think you got it made—
king of the road and all that stuff—you don't sway or swagger when you're
playing on the bandstand, no matter how much you drink. Miles called
me 'Iron Man.' They said Lester Young was like that, always cool on the
bandstand no matter what. But Lester was actually discouraged about
people stealing his sound, making money off of it."

Wayne's sadness about his father's death and discouragement over his
divorce weakened his will and made his performances vulnerable to intox-
ication. In the months after his father died, when Wayne had a little too
much to drink, his bandmates began to hear it on the horn. Miles later
commented on Tony's disgust for Wayne's sloshed technique at shows:
"Tony used to get upset with Wayne because Wayne would be drunk
sometimes up on the bandstand and missing shit, and Tony would just
stop playing."

One night in 1966, Wayne showed up at a gig to find tenor saxophonist Joe Henderson backstage. Miles said he'd invited the rival player to test
out the sound of another horn in the band, but he seemed to be relaying
another message, as Curtis Fuller remembered. "To break Wayne, Miles
hired Joe Henderson," Curtis said. "Just to make Wayne take note. He
came to work one day and Joe was there. Of course Miles also wanted the
two tenors to see what would happen musically." Miles's implication was
clear: No motherfucker was irreplaceable, not even a genius composer.
The warning was a sobering one, and Wayne tempered his cognac habit
for a while.

"Mostly when you listen to Wayne or any of the great musicians, you
hear an ability to transcend sadness and malaise and put that directly into
music," trumpeter Dave Douglas said. Only the most astute ears might
have picked up any suspicious slurring in his performances—just as few
modern listeners know that the "Quodlibet" of Bach's *Goldberg Variations*
was based on a German beer-hall song. Wayne's playing on Miles's recordings was as expert as it was soulful. In fact, by the time the band hit the
studio again, the group was so tight that it got all the tunes right on the

first take. On this recording, *Miles Smiles,* the group had only a brief re-hearsal of each tune, just enough to nail down the melody and settle in to a tempo before heading off into orbit with it, with the very first pass around the globe committed to record.

Miles Smiles included Wayne's "Orbits" and "Footprints," the tune that earned him a legacy as a composer. "Footprints" originated with a practi-cal need: "I wrote 'Footprints' when Miles asked me for something to play at gigs," Wayne said. It was a 12-bar minor blues in 6/4 time, played over a repeating five-note bass figure. The tune sounded like Miles, with a re-strained range of melody, soothing as a gentle wave in its gradual ascent and relaxed descent. "Footprints" had the even temper and calm pace of the music on Miles's popular *Kind of Blue.* Wayne had recorded the tune eight months before on his own *Adam's Apple,* but this version with Miles was more memorable. As soon as the horns made a sustained impression of the melody, Tony's drumming washed it away, creating a comfortably melancholic mood that had to be felt before it could be understood. Miles added the tune to the band's live repertoire, and it became a classic, in-cluded in the jazz canon studied by young musicians in theory classes. This was and still is the Wayne Shorter tune most often called at jazz clubs.

Artists can't always count on history to recognize their greatest work, especially when they're competent and generous enough to provide the art necessary to a time and place. The irony was that for all of the haunting beauty of "Footprints," the song offered only a trace of Wayne's talent as a composer. Wayne could easily jot down several such melodies on a cock-tail napkin between sets.

On *Miles Smiles* it was actually another tune, "Dolores," named for Wayne's cousin, which was a step in a new direction. "You can hear the roots of Miles's stuff to come on 'Dolores,'" Wayne said. It was a depar-ture from the old head arrangement concept, not just the same old tidy theme, solos, and restatement of the theme. "Dolores" was a looser sketch for improvisation, a 38-bar piece in five sections of assorted lengths. The first, third, and fifth sections had melodic lines for the horns; the second and fourth sections were open expanses for drums and bass only. "We were actually tampering with something called DNA in music in a song," Wayne said. "Each song has its DNA. So you just do the DNA and not the whole song. You do the characteristics. You say, 'Okay, I will do the ear of the face, I will do the left side of the face. You do the right side of the face.' Everyone took a certain characteristic of the song and . . . you can do eight measures of it, and then you can make your own harmonic road or avenue within a certain eight measures."

After playing mostly 8-bar phrases throughout the tune, Wayne and Miles tumbled their way out of it at the end, repeating the melody line as if they were in search of its source. Tony inherited the ending, and went out with a big roll. Form had usually dictated the course of their improvisation, but by the end of this tune they were improvising the form itself. These formal experiments on "Dolores" planted the seed for Miles's open-ended excursions into electric jazz. "Wayne has always been someone who experimented *with* form instead of someone who did it without form," Miles later wrote. "That's why I thought he was perfect for where I wanted to see the music I played go."

8.

Sanctuary

"WHAT DO YOU DO with your hands when you ain't doing nothin'?" Miles once asked Wayne.

"A lot of people do this," Wayne said, motioning with a palms-up shrug.

Miles said, "That's right, but what do you do with *yours*?"

A jazz musician invests so much in improvisation that his creative mindset can carry over to the most ordinary moments. As Miles's question showed, improvisation touched the heart of everything, even the act of creating being from nothingness and the art of extracting coolness from boredom. In Toni Morrison's *Jazz,* a novel structured like a jazz composition, the narrator concludes the book by inviting the reader to retell its story, just as a tune calls out for a musician to remake it through improvisation. Morrison's narrator points to the same creative source that Miles had wondered about: "If I were able I'd say it. Say make me, remake me. You are free to do it and I am free to let you because look, look. Look where your hands are. Now."

When Wayne examined his hands—and by extension the essence of his creativity—he began to draw inspiration from earlier periods of his life, especially the time when he'd painted and sculpted as a child. "A lot of the songs I wrote in the early sixties had a lot of the New York nightclub feel to them," Wayne said. "As I matured I think my songs began to look back farther, to things in my childhood."

One night in 1967, Wayne came home to his apartment in Harlem, lit a candle, and sat down at the piano. When he put his hands on the keys, a tune he'd call "Nefertiti" emerged as a complete melody. Around the same time, another composition, "Fall," also came to Wayne in a moment of grace. "'Nefertiti' was my most sprung-from-me-all-in-one-piece experience of music writing," Wayne said.

In 1967, a bust of the Egyptian Queen Nefertiti that Wayne had sculpted as a student was still proudly displayed in the lobby of Newark Arts High School. Wayne's image of Nefertiti bore close resemblance to the ancient painted limestone bust in the Berlin Egyptian Museum. Wayne's bust had almond-shaped eyes, a regal nose, strong lips, and high cheekbones, though he endowed his sculpture with cornrowed hair rather than a tall blue crown. The bust was a statement of Africanist advocacy. Wayne said he created it "so people could see another kind of face instead of the faces they saw in the newspaper."

"Nefertiti" was a fitting title for the tune. Much as Wayne had conjured the bust's form from nothing twenty years before, Wayne sculpted the melody of "Nefertiti" out of the darkness of the room. But "Nefertiti" wasn't actually finished until it was submitted to Miles's shrewd editing in the studio. When Wayne took the tune to the next recording session, on

June 7, 1967, the band started out by rehearsing the melody. The tune was a basic 16-bar form built on intervals of fourths and fifths, but its descending melody line was tricky, swinging out from various syncopated starting points.

They practiced the melody again and again. With the horns in repetition mode, a foundation was laid upon which the rhythm section could improvise. Tony's playing grew more dynamic and insistent with each repetition of the melody. In lieu of traditional horn solos, the delayed resolution built tension, and the rhythm section's embellishments created a sense of development.

When they finished the first run-through, it was time to improvise on the theme. But Miles asked, "Hey man, what if we made the tune by just playin' the melody?" It was so obvious and yet so radical an idea that the band could only laugh in response. No one was doing *that* in jazz. "That's it, right?" Miles said. Miles may have intuited the tune's mood of creation, and wanted to preserve the beauty of the fully formed phrase. Or maybe he was just ready to try something new.

After a couple more takes, Miles wanted producer Teo Macero to play back the original take, which he felt had captured the band's epiphany, its spirit of discovery. Unfortunately, Teo had started rolling tape halfway through the first take. Eventually, the fourth take was used on the album. Whatever was lost in previous takes, the horns' unison and ostinato rendering of the melody retained a floating sensation, and gave the music a sense of yearning and mystery.

The critic Martin Williams was in the studio for the recording of "Nefertiti," reporting for *Stereo Review.* Williams wrote that during playbacks, Wayne heard something he didn't like in his solo, and ducked his head and pulled up his coat collar in embarrassment. As usual, Miles told Teo that Wayne's playing was fine. What's more, the stylish economy of the tune and its mythic evocation of the regal Egyptian queen appealed to Miles's sensibilities, and he used *Nefertiti* as the record's title.

A young folksinger named Joni Mitchell heard the record, and had a particularly astute take on it. "It's a very unusual piece of music, in that it's like a silk screen," Joni said. "They start off in unison, and then they get more and more individuated, like a silk screen slightly offset. Through it all, Tony is just boiling, he's the soloist. It's a very simple form, almost like a folk song. Verse, verse, verse, not even a chorus or a bridge. Like repetitive modules. The form is unusual to jazzers—I remember someone saying, 'Listen to the form of this, it's so unusual.' And I thought, it's just a simple folk form, but look at what's happening. You're not waiting for the guys to take their solos, the melody suffices, and meanwhile the drummer's just going crazy. It evokes this image of a late night in New York City; some guy is coming up from Chinatown and he's drunk and he's kicking over garbage cans and yelling all the way uptown. There's escalating anger in the drums, and that makes it a beautiful piece of music."

Nefertiti was the harbinger of a new period for Miles, one in which improvised solos became secondary to mood and fragmented riffs. But beyond musicology, Miles was moving in a whole new direction culturally, one in keeping with the times. In the session data for another of Wayne's tunes on *Nefertiti,* "Pinocchio," producer Howard G. Robiss noted that they wanted "some psychedelic speech on this—maybe tape of Timothy Leary."

When the Beatles hit America in 1964, pop music began to eclipse jazz's audience, and by 1967 jazz was in a state of crisis. As Miles began a venture into popular culture and electric music, he was perceived as a sellout. There was a famous story of his revelation when he heard the funk group Sly and the Family Stone at the Newport Jazz Festival. But jazz wasn't exactly struck by lightning. Miles's interest in pop music had a deeper source, as Wayne observed: "When Miles started getting into the pop stuff, it was about getting back to something he'd absorbed from rhythm-and-blues. Where Miles grew up in St. Louis, if you had an element of that R-and-B thing, you caught people, back in those groovy times in the forties and fifties. He wanted to put what was missing back in jazz and get people to buy some records with the combination of both things in it."

Much was made of Miles's fascination with Jimi Hendrix in the late sixties, but Wayne emphasized another influence: "We went with Miles to see James Brown at the Apollo Theater when he was doing his "Night Train" groove. Not the song itself necessarily, but that feeling. That's when Miles was already saying that jazz didn't have a strong or driving enough motor that got into people's bones. You know, he heard the same old *ding-ding-da-ding-ding-da-ding,* and he was saying it was kind of boring and all used up."

In March and April 1968, the group spent several weeks in the countercultural ground zero of Berkeley, California, where they performed with Gil Evans and his Orchestra and vibed on the spirit of the place. "We stayed in a hotel with the kitchen and everything in San Francisco, 'cause we were living there for quite a while," Wayne said. "And we'd go into Miles's room, and we saw his head beginning to make the pop machinations that led to *Bitches Brew.* Before Miles married Betty, his head was already there." That spring, Miles began dating Betty Mabry, a well-connected and creative woman whose youthful influence on Miles's style and music gave her a rep as the femme fatale of jazz fusion. Betty seemed to embody the funky chic that made younger black performers so popular at the time. "Betty was nice," Wayne said. "Miles would call us into the room when she was dancing, saying, 'Check Betty out, dig her!' And the way she danced was what he wanted in the music."

In 1967, Wayne met his own muse, a beautiful, wild, and fiercely smart Portuguese girl named Ana Maria Patricio. Ana Maria had moved to the U.S. with her family when she was twelve. She spent her early childhood in the Portuguese colony of Angola, where her father was a deep-sea diver and bridge builder. This cultural dislocation cultivated a very self-contained little girl. "Once, on a nine-day trip from Lisbon to Angola, Ana went missing on the ship, and was finally found sitting all sanguine in the boiler room watching film reels," Wayne said. Ana's dynamic personality and beauty made her seem more mature than her years, and attracted plenty of attention: "When she was only ten, a bullfighter showed up at their family home to ask for her hand. Her mother sent him out of the house with a broom!"

Ana Maria's parents were jazz fans with a record collection that included Wayne's Blue Note albums. "Ana's mother told me that when she was twelve, Ana saw my photo on an album and said, 'That's the man I'm going to marry.'"

Ana did feel the pull of Wayne's matchless music. "When I first met Wayne, he was real weird," she said. "I met him through his music, it was love at first listen. That told me a lot about the man, his music. Then I met him in person, at the Bohemian Caverns in Washington; he was playing with Miles. I was after him, and when a woman is after a man, it's only a matter of time until she gets what she desires. I'm from Lisbon, Portugal, and I came from way far away to this country to meet Wayne Shorter, what else? Destiny." At that first "meeting," Ana noticed Wayne, but he didn't see her, because he was "too busy trying to be cool, flying by on the way to the bar, getting another cognac," she later told him. Miles did notice Ana, and stopped by her table to play with the charms on her bracelet.

Wayne was acquainted with Ana through her sister, Maria, who was married to Walter Booker, the bassist for Cannonball Adderley. "My brother told me about Walter Booker," Wayne said. "He said, 'You've got to meet Walter and Maria.' I went over there and Maria was playing Lili Boulanger's music, Nadia's sister, so I knew Maria was hip. Maria always wore silver dresses, and my brother called her 'The Silver Lady.' Later that week we were playing at the Village Gate. I saw Maria and her daughter from a previous marriage, Clothilde, in the crowd. After we finished playing, I was packing up my horn, then turned around and Clothilde was sitting behind me. Someone else was sitting back there, and she said, 'This is my aunt, Ana Maria,' and we shook hands. She was wearing one of those soft doe-leather jackets with patches of many colors with a corduroy skirt and the grandma shoes that were popular then. I went to get another drink, 'cause it was three-for-one just before the bar closed. Then as I was walking out to get a taxi, I saw her standing in the doorway. I looked, stopped, and this sobering thing came over me. I said, 'You want to talk?' We took a cab to her sister's house and hung out there."

"She was not a product of that narrow American high school cliquish thinking," he went on. "Ana had an IQ of over one-sixty and a photographic memory, and you saw it right away—everything that came out of her mouth was different or surprising, and she did math in her head real quick. Ana Maria had it all." Wayne and Ana quickly became inseparable. Teruko and Wayne had shot from flirtation to marriage without much courtship. "Ana Maria was my first real experience of having a girlfriend," Wayne said. They went to the movies to see *2001: A Space Odyssey* on one of their first dates.

As Wayne's relationship with Ana was beginning, Miles's second classic quintet was disbanding. With the exception of a few of Wayne's tunes, the quintet mostly performed Miles's older repertoire to the bitter end. "I would have loved for us to have another year playing the new library before Miles went on to do whatever he did," Ron said. "There's a lot of music we didn't quite get a chance to fool around with. I wonder what kind of dash and daring we could have found if we'd played 'Nefertiti' for three more weeks, but we never got a chance to do that." They were denied that opportunity largely because of Miles's shift into electric music. When Ron left the band in 1968, Dave Holland, who was adept on the electric bass, moved from London to take his place that August. Herbie left in September, and Chick Corea came in on electric piano. Jack DeJohnette replaced Tony in March 1969. Tony left when he heard that Miles might experiment with using an extra percussionist in the band.

Wayne's concern with tone color and texture and with the essence of matter itself made his transition to electronic music smoother. Wayne had a theory: "There's electricity in water, which is organic. And acoustic music has something organic about it, right?" This mind-bending premise supported a basic point: For Wayne, music was music. So he stayed on with Miles and weathered the electric climate with a gear change. "When electronics came along, the tenor saxophone would get buried in the overtones of all the electricity," Wayne said. "In most rock bands, the tenor acts as a backup. They join up with the synthesizers, and just provide accents." Wayne began playing the soprano saxophone to be heard as a solo voice above electronics. Wayne's experience with the clarinet eased his adjustment to the new horn. "I started on the clarinet, and holding the clarinet involves similar positioning as holding the soprano," Wayne said. At fifteen, Wayne had been drawn to the clarinet's soaring sound; for him, its fleetness evoked something flying over sand dunes. He was similarly attracted to the swiftness of the soprano saxophone, though his metaphorical description of this instrument was updated for the Age of Aquarius. "To me, the soprano saxophone is like the dolphin coming from the bowels of the ocean, overcoming and shooting higher than the waves," he said. John Coltrane had died in 1967, leaving a void as the foremost modern player of the soprano saxophone.

The straight and slender soprano was the diva of horns. Its testy temperament posed certain technical challenges, but its distinctive form was capable of superlative beauty. Like the tenor saxophone, it had a conical body, but was very narrow, requiring a huge volume of air to be pushed through a small space. And with its more sensitive mouthpiece, proper pitch was maintained only with a very steady and focused airstream. When played as well as Wayne played it, the soprano's clarion call could cut through the densest thicket of electronic instruments. But Wayne's collaborators said that regardless of his instrument, there was something about the sheer *life* of his sound that projected through any kind of commotion. "On the soprano sax or the tenor, Wayne can always be heard," said Airto Moreira, a percussionist who played with Wayne in Miles's electric groups. "He could go to a war and play the saxophone, and everybody would hear it. He wouldn't have to play much, just a couple notes, and everybody would drop their arms and go, 'What is that?'"

The first release featuring the new horn was *In a Silent Way*, recorded in February 1969. Joe Zawinul's title track would have been a beautiful showcase for any instrument, but it provided an especially exquisite introduction for Wayne's soprano. In the studio, the band first rehearsed the tune as Joe had written it, with percussion, full chord and bass line changes, and with both Miles and Wayne introducing the melody. In

Miles's rearrangement, the tune was reduced to John McLaughlin's pedal-point guitar and a shimmer of keyboards, with Wayne entering alone on the melody. In effect, Miles's edit created a grove within the forest of Joe's tune. A grove is naturally silent, well-shaded so that few plants grow, offering no food or shelter for the animals that make noise elsewhere in the forest. On "In a Silent Way," Miles cleared out the undergrowth of the tune and got the noisemakers out of the way, so that Wayne's entrance was as quietly dramatic as a deer coming out into the open.

This idyllic quietude in the studio was the Pax Romana compared to the riot of the invading barbarians that Miles took out on the road that spring. His electric band with Wayne, Chick Corea, Dave Holland, and Jack DeJohnette toured together for a year and a half but was never officially recorded, which later gave it cult status. The electric band's free-for-all jazz fusion was an attempt by Miles to reach wider audiences: Columbia's archives contain a thick stack of memos by executives trying to figure out how to market Miles to the elusive "underground" element, the hippie generation. Miles's respect for Jack's drumming was deepened by the fact that Jack had previously been with the Charles Lloyd Quartet, a group that gained crossover success in pairings with rock acts at the Fillmore West in San Francisco. Producer Bill Graham masterminded these pairings, which reflected his eclectic vision of presenting quality music of all genres on one bill—rock, blues, jazz, Indian music, *whatever.* In the late sixties, FM was a new frontier of experimental music, and stations such as New York's WVDW played a stylistic mix. You might hear Hendrix, Laura Nyro, and Miles in a single half hour of radio programming. Musicians themselves had little concern for labels, anyway. When Gil Evans contacted Columbia in May 1969 to request a copy of Miles's *Filles de Kilimanjaro,* he also asked for some rock music (Blood, Sweat, and Tears) and something from the contemporary classical genre (Terry Riley's *In C*).

Courting the "underground" crowd, Miles produced concerts at the bohemian Village Gate club. The electric band played there opposite the long-running musical *Jacques Brel Is Alive and Well and Living in Paris* and comedian Richard Pryor. For these shows, the electric band left behind Miles's classic tailored look and took a trip down fashion's modern cat-walk. Miles would turn up in a suede jumpsuit and space-age goggle sun-glasses, with Chick in a glittering purple headband, and Dave accessorized by his own long hair. Wayne also sported some groovy finery. "One time we were on the bandstand at the Village Gate, and I was almost as thin as Miles then," Wayne said. "I was wearing a Spanish leather vest, and chop-per boots with a heel, in two different colors, brown and black, Spanish conquistador riding-the-horse boots. People in the audience were looking up there at me and Miles, and after the set they were asking, 'Which one is Miles?'"

However much the band's appearance flaunted the countercultural team spirit, few casual jazz fans had a taste for the group's bracing mix of free jazz and jazz-rock. "With that band we were playing our butts off, everybody was raising hell," Wayne said. The band escalated into hitherto unknown levels of abstraction. "Each soloist brought out a different aspect of the rhythm section," Jack said. "When Miles played, there was more of a beat to grab hold to, and then when Wayne would play, it would get more abstract, and then when Chick and Dave would play, it would get even more abstract."

Chick Corea, or "Chickie," as Miles called him, was a fan of contem-porary classical composers such as Béla Bartók and Karlheinz Stock-hausen, and used his Fender Rhodes piano to otherworldly effect, with its ring modulator permeating the music with dissonance. The music got so "out," however, that Chick would bring an extra drum kit onstage and play it instead of his keyboards. "Sometimes Wayne would be taking his solo and Jack and Dave's playing would become so vigorous that playing the piano wouldn't make much sense to me," Chick said. "So I'd jump on the drums, and Jack and I would both go at it, making all kinds of wild rhythms, creating even more energy. Jack and I had some fun with that for a few gigs, and Miles seemed to let it go for a while—he was willing to let anything go for a while—then he said, 'That's enough.'"

"Miles liked things to be kept fairly clear behind him," Dave said. "He liked the groove to be kept consistently, not messing with the groove or making it too elastic. And also, he adhered to the form of songs. Obviously there's a lot of freedom in his playing, but Wayne by contrast was just ready for anything to happen. We sensed that, and it gave us a sense of a little more freedom with Wayne in the music." After Wayne soloed, he would move offstage with Miles, who was a bemused witness to his rhythm section's recklessness. "What the fuck is going on out there?" he'd ask Wayne. Miles's sidemen had pushed him to great freedom before—the anti-music experiments of the Plugged Nickel were a good example. But this was a whole other degree of freedom. Chick said that when Miles left the stage, the musicians found themselves "out in the ozone, but happily so"; Dave talked about the rhythm section conducting "outer-space research on the music." Miles tolerated the experimentation as long as he was offstage. When he went back onstage, he would restore order, sometimes with a single note of calm. "Nothing ever flinched Miles—no matter how wild we got, he'd come back in and find something that would anchor all the motion that was going on around him," Jack said.

For Chick, Dave, Wayne, and Jack, it was wonderful to be paid to perform in this creative, changeable environment, groping around for ideas that worked, discarding the ones that didn't. They would have done the same thing for free, and they did, in late-night jam sessions back at home in New York.

After finalizing his divorce with Teruko, Wayne married Ana Maria. They moved to the Upper West Side of Manhattan on Seventy-sixth Street for a couple months and then more permanently to West Ninety-second Street, just off Broadway. When Wayne lived up in Harlem, first alone and then with Teruko, he hadn't had many visitors, just McCoy Tyner one time, and sometimes Bobby Thomas and his wife, Nicole. These monastic tendencies had contributed to his reputation as an exotic "lone wolf." But under the influence of Ana the socialite, Wayne began to entertain people in his home. This hanging-out time familiarized Wayne's bandmates with more ordinary aspects of his personality such as his tastes in food. "I used to go up to Wayne's house," Jack said. "He loved having people around, he and Ana. He'd have dishes that he'd make—fried chicken and greens, mashed potatoes, and stuff like that. But the chicken was the thing for him."

Like Charlie "Bird" Parker, Wayne had a thing for chicken, and he waxed messianic about its supernatural powers. "Wayne told me chicken was good for your imagination," Dave said. But Wayne was no generic chicken booster. "It was fried chicken, or well-broiled chicken, but not chicken made just one way or just any way," Wayne said. The band teased him about his fowl muse, as Jack remembered: "Whenever Wayne was playing really great, we'd say, 'You had some chicken tonight, didn't you?'" Years later, Wayne's passion for the poultry was unabated. At seventy, he would still wrap up a caterer's pan of roasted chicken in the backstage greenroom and carry it back to his hotel.

Wayne and Ana spent a lot of time with Herbie and his wife, Gigi, who lived within walking distance of them, just a couple blocks over on Riverside and Ninety-second. They were also friendly with the musical couple Airto Moreira and Flora Purim, who lived on Seventy-second just up the street from Miles. The Shorters naturally saw a fair amount of Ana Maria's sister Maria Booker, but then so did everyone else on the scene. The Bookers' apartment was the gathering place for a loose conglomeration of Miles's current and former sidemen. All-night jam sessions at Walter and Maria's place were fueled by plenty of music, home-cooked food, wine, and cocaine. "Those were the days of wine and roses, and of lines and noses," Maria said.

In late August 1969, Wayne took this homespun spirit into the studio for his next Blue Note recording, *Super Nova*. The record played out like a late-night jam session, with atmospheric, improvised musical sketches. The personnel included Walter Booker and John McLaughlin on classical guitars, Sonny Sharrock on electric guitar, Miroslav Vitous on bass, Jack DeJohnette on drums, Chick Corea on drums and vibes, and Airto Moreira on percussion. Miles hadn't been too fond of Chick and Jack's double dose of drums on tour, but Wayne did appreciate this embarrassment of riches, and with the addition of Airto's percussion, the session had a ferocious polyrhythmic feel.

In the late-night jams at Walter Booker's place, Flora Purim sometimes sang "Dindi," a classic Brazilian tune by Tom Jobim that was familiar to Americans from Frank Sinatra's 1967 recording with the composer. Wayne loved the song and wanted to record it. Blue Note producer Duke Pearson was friendly with Maria Booker, and knew she sang a very heartfelt version of "Dindi" herself. Duke and Wayne agreed that Maria should be the one to sing it, even though she was an amateur. At the session, Maria recorded the song to the lone accompaniment of her husband's guitar. It turned out that she and Walter were actually splitting up, so this tender and intimate duet setting was very emotional for Maria. At the end of her performance, she broke down into sobs. Wayne preserved Maria's weeping on the record, which was the swan song to her marriage with Walter. "She was going through a crisis, a domestic marital thing," Wayne said. "That's why she cried at the end of it. I said we've got to get this life on the record, get all the life in there. And it was therapeutic for her, too. When she finished the record, she got a divorce." If "Dindi" helped Maria split with one husband, it connected her to the next: She soon married singer Jon Lucien, who popularized the song in the seventies.

As a leader, Wayne rewarded instinct over execution and favored process over product. For Wayne, Maria's candid emotion was far more compelling than the purity of her musicianship, just as maintaining an open mood of experimentation in the studio was more important than any musical goal. On the record, Maria's singing comprised only the middle section of "Dindi." The tune was introduced with a cacophonous jungle of percussion, with Wayne's monotone horn lines punctuating and spooking the proceedings. Emerging from this instrumental tangle was the delicate section with Maria's voice and Walter's guitar. When Maria finished singing, or came undone, the tangle of percussion closed in again, building into frenzied Brazilian *batucada* and samba rhythms.

Airto initiated this final ritualistic rise of percussion on "Dindi." He said the track's loose and spontaneous development was characteristic of the session. "They asked me to set up my drum set," Airto said. "I thought, wow, Jack DeJohnette is going to play, what am I going to do? I play the drums but I don't play like Jack. I set it up anyway, and we were jamming, we had percussion all over the place, and almost everybody was playing percussion from time to time. They'd play something on their horn, then go over to the percussion and shake something. At one point on "Dindi" there was a strong rhythm, something fast, and Jack was looking at me, trying to play this Brazilian rhythm, and he said, 'Come here, come here,' and I sat down at my set and started to play this street samba rhythm. It generated all this energy, and everybody was playing crazily on top of that. That album, seventy or eighty percent of that album, happened naturally like that." Wayne was having some other thoughts while he was making the record. "*Super Nova* gave me a lot of information," Wayne said. "As I was playing it, I was thinking, *What's going on here? I hope these guys can keep going and follow me . . . Well . . . I'm going to remember this, continue this when the audience is ready.*"

Offhand as the *Super Nova* session was, Wayne was in fact its leader, a gentle master of the studio domain. He consciously chose to work with those nebulous rhythms and harmonies that Miles's electric band had been testing out on tour. When Miles went into the studio in late August to record *Bitches Brew,* he did not continue in the same direction. "I think that probably after months and months of experimenting in that direction, Miles was looking more for grooves and vamps and certain things that allowed him to float on the top," Chick said. Miles famously created that vamp-heavy sound on the bestselling *Bitches Brew,* which included two of Wayne's tunes, "Feio" and "Sanctuary."

Named after a novella by Edith Wharton, "Sanctuary" was originally recorded in February 1968, which was when trouble over its ownership began. "During the session Miles asked about his sharing part of 'Sanctuary,' Wayne said. "Miles wanted to get in on it. He said, 'You know how it is, Charlie Parker did that, too.' I said no. And that was before knowing it was going to be a big bestseller. When we left the studio, Miles said, 'Just send me something in the mail.' He said it to Herbie, too. And then he walked out the door with his coat on crooked."

The history of Miles's co-shares in his sidemen's tunes was as complex as Ellington's collaborative relationship with composer Billy Strayhorn. Miles certainly did some radical rearrangement of his collaborators' tunes in the studio. There was a fine line between editing and re-creating a composition. Conflicts arose over whether or not his changes were fundamental enough to merit a co-writing credit. Pianist Bill Evans's compositional voice suffused *Kind of Blue,* which led to speculation about his being the Camille Claudel to Miles's Rodin. Miles had a formal dispute with Joe Zawinul over the rights to "In a Silent Way," a matter that was resolved only with the help of lawyers.

But Wayne and Miles's contention over the ownership of "Sanctuary" was more easily and affably resolved. Columbia's records contain a 1968 memo from Elizabeth Martone of the label's copyright department: Martone noted that Wayne was receiving a 2-cent licensing fee for "Sanctuary," but requested 3½ cents a side, a payment commensurate with full ownership. A few months later Wayne sent Ms. Martone a handwritten letter addressing the matter. In a twelve-year-old's good penmanship that aspired toward businesslike formality, Wayne implied that Miles had granted him full possession of the tune.

This is to inform you that the enclosed license bearing my name as 50% writer of the composition entitled Sanctuary has been rightfully adjusted. Henceforth, my future releases of compositions owned by Miyako Music, have been created from my mind (Wayne Shorter).

I am certain you are very familiar with this kind of "misunderstanding" in the business, therefore, I shall not attempt any further explanation for the readjustment.

Cordially yours,
Wayne Shorter
MIYAKO MUSIC
I know you understand.

"Sanctuary" became a regular tune on the electric band's set list and was performed in the style of "Nefertiti"—Wayne and Miles played the melody unison, or nearly so, while the rhythm section stormed underneath them. On *Bitches Brew,* he recorded "Sanctuary" as a through-composed tune with the expansive crests and falls of an opera. Wayne couldn't help noticing how another *Bitches Brew* tune, "Miles Runs the Voodoo Down," bore suspiciously close resemblance to a song recorded by Betty Mabry on a demo that summer. "That was his wife Betty's tune, called 'Down Home Girl,'" Wayne said. "Miles took it and broke it down with no beat, like he was hearing it through water." Betty's demo, which perhaps coincidentally went unreleased, was produced by Miles and featured John McLaughlin, Hendrix's drummer Mitch Mitchell, Harvey Brooks, and Larry Young. She and Miles split up shortly after the recording.

While Miles continued on his controversial path into electric music, Wayne was finding bliss at home. On September 29, 1969, Wayne and Ana Maria had a daughter, and named her Iska. Wayne had liked Cyprian Ekwensi's 1966 novel *Iska,* and especially admired its girl protagonist, who was a symbol of the winds of change blowing through postcolonial Africa. In Nigeria, *iska* is the Hausa word for wind, but it's also a poetic expression for transition, or for liminal things like ghosts.

A few weeks after Iska's birth, Wayne went out with Miles's electric band on a European tour through mid-November. Sadly, this meant that he missed one of the few healthy months of Iska's life. Just after the turn of the new year, Wayne and Ana Maria took Iska to the doctor for her routine three-month vaccination, the tetanus shot. A few hours later Ana laid Iska down for a nap. When Ana went to check on the infant, she found her awake, her lips blue, and her head, arms, and legs jerking in a seizure. Herbie and Gigi Hancock's daughter Jessica had been taken to the same doctor for her vaccinations. Gigi remembered the day with grim vividness: "Ana Maria called me and was crying and said, 'Iska, she's, she had this terrible thing . . . she was turning blue, and I rushed her to the hospital and she was under the hospital tent.' I think that Iska was brain damaged right then because she was without oxygen for so long."

For years, Wayne and Ana Maria didn't connect Iska's symptoms to the vaccination. A vaccination is supposed to protect a child from sickness, not cause it. And Iska's diagnosis was vague, so they remained in denial about her brain damage. They dressed their daughter like a little princess and looked for signs of normal development, though she continued to have seizures that sent them on frequent runs to the emergency room. Iska's critical medical condition was devastatingly painful for Wayne. The tragedy caused him to question the meaning of everything: music, family, and life itself.

Iska's condition precipitated one career change for Wayne immediately. On March 7, Columbia recorded Miles live at the Fillmore East in a mega-concert staged by Bill Graham. Miles was billed as an "extra added attraction" to Neil Young and the Steve Miller Blues Band. As *Rolling Stone* magazine noted, the Fillmore had programmed lots of rock with jazz pretensions, but Miles was the real thing. Though the audience wondered when exactly they were supposed to clap, the first show was successful enough that on the second night, Miles was moved from the opening act to the more prominent second slot. After the show, Laura Nyro, a passionate Miles fan, gave the trumpeter a dozen red roses, which warmed him up to the idea of opening for her June 19 show at the venue.

He would do that concert without Wayne. Wayne gave his notice to Miles, who had been encouraging him to get his own band anyway. Miles didn't know just how much he'd miss the sideman he called his "intellectual musical catalyst." After Wayne left Miles, the bandleader went through more than five saxophonists in as many years. Wayne had been a vital composer and player on fourteen recordings and countless live dates, and he'd also been dependable. "I never missed a concert, never missed a job," Wayne said. "Only one time with Miles, the plane I was on couldn't take off from Norway. So I got to Newport late for the next gig. I was in my tuxedo walking up the stairs to the stage as they were finishing. Miles was walking down the stairs, and he didn't say anything, just shook my hand and gave me money. Like he knew I never missed a job, and so there had to be a good reason for the one that I missed."

Like Coltrane before him, Wayne had stuck with Miles for five years. "Coltrane told me he learned the most stuff playing with Miles," Wayne said. "Notice how he said 'with' and not 'for.' Everyone who played with Miles came away with the same essential thing, that *you should never stray too far from the fine point.*"

9.

Music for Films That Would Never Be Made

AFTER LEAVING MILES in 1970, Wayne took his first break from steady work in eleven years. He spent a while relaxing in the Caribbean islands. As he stretched out and looked across the water, he also looked back on his years with the Messengers and Miles. The Messengers had given Wayne a career, and Miles had given him much more, a way to approach the barely comprehensible chaos of the world—they *played* the barely comprehensible chaos of the world. What was supposed to come after that? Whatever Wayne did next, he didn't want to do it the same way. Anything besides the same old club routine. And for a while, he didn't even have any interest in the saxophone. "I didn't want to play," he said. "I just looked at the horn every once in a while. Then I started playing a lot of other things, not jazz, but stuff from Yma Sumac, music from Peru, a lot of Latin stuff."

Those "other things" came through when Wayne recorded his next Blue Note album in late August 1970. *Odyssey of Iska* included "De Pois do Amor, o Vazio" (After Love, Emptiness), a bossa nova tune by his old friend Bobby Thomas. Its other tunes were world-beat free-jazz tone poems to the planet with titles like "Wind," "Calm," and "Joy." Wayne wrote the record's liner notes in prose that verged on poetry. He began and ended the notes with a refrain: "Iska is the wind that passes, leaving no trace." The repetition had the feeling of a Negro spiritual, with Wayne wistfully looking beyond his daughter's physical problems to find inspiration in the more ephemeral aspects of her spirit. "Iska knows there is no possessing joy," he wrote, and said the recording represented "the transition of each man's soul as it passes through life: a pictorial-musical journey symbolizing the lifetime and whatever happens after."

His saxophone solos reflected this elusive quest. Rather than strong melodic statements, they focused on the subtleties of tone color and musical texture. *Down Beat* reviewer Larry Kart longed for Wayne's more self-assertive style of previous years, criticizing his "seeming desire to renounce the notion of the improvising musician as the purveyor of a competitive, flamboyant ego. . . . What I hear on this album is a musician trying to disappear. I wish he wouldn't."

Jazz has a long tradition of the soloist as a questing hero. In Coltrane's quartet, for example, no one ever doubted that he was the group's central character. Wayne rejected this role. He didn't flex his chops; he didn't make unifying "Hear me talkin' to ya" preacherly solo statements. But a selfless ego was not to blame for Wayne's style. If anything, his love of film was the culprit. When Wayne soloed, his cinematic imagination took over. He played selected components of a composition as if he were reproducing elements of a movie. Wayne didn't just play the hero. He played the bit actors, too. Then he'd shift to scenery if the mood struck him, or even become the camera zooming in on the action.

With this approach, Wayne improvised aspects of music that were usually written in the composition itself. As he said, "Composition is just improvisation slowed down, and improvisation is just composition sped up." He played what he heard to be right for the music, not for him as the soloist. Wayne was certainly capable of blowing a solo as clear and rousing as a call to arms. Some critics and fans didn't understand why he refused to do that, especially at a time when jazz's declining popularity made heroes valuable to the music. Joni Mitchell had an insightful response to this "disappointment with Wayne" faction: "I've seen reviews of Wayne's work where they say they want more from him, but it's clear they'd be satisfied with a lot less of a player."

Wayne entertained ideas about leading a band and consulted with Miles's manager, Jack Whittemore. Wayne's interest coincided with a period when rock had pushed jazz to the sidelines of marketability. Jack called club owners to test out booking possibilities for a Wayne Shorter Quartet. "They wouldn't say yes and they wouldn't say no," Wayne said. "They said, 'Yes, we would like Wayne Shorter to come to the jazz workshop,' but if an agent calls and says, 'Dizzy Gillespie's free that week,' they're gonna get the well-known established musicians, to build that club up." In the newly precarious environment for jazz, people didn't want to take a chance on a new group.

Weather Report

So instead, Wayne formed a partnership in which he'd generate the most marketable and commercially successful music of his career. When Wayne and pianist Joe Zawinul worked together on Miles's *In a Silent Way*, they made offhand comments about playing together, an idea they'd first tossed around in Maynard Ferguson's band back in 1959. By 1970, Joe was ready to leave Cannonball Adderley's group. Bassist Miroslav Vitous worked with Wayne on *Super Nova* and with Joe on his 1970 recording, *Zawinul.* Miroslav described himself as the "trigger man, like the trigger on a gun" in bringing Wayne and Joe together. "In fact I wanted Wayne to be on my *Infinite Search* album, so I called him first, and he said he only recorded with Miles and his own albums," Miroslav said. "So after he left Miles, I called Wayne and I asked him if he'd be interested in putting a group together." Wayne thought it was a good idea, but needed to talk it over with Ana Maria and Joe. "Joe and I were talking about going out on our own," Wayne said. "Then we hit on an idea to get together with Miroslav and have a band, 'cause it might be stronger to do it like that. And better than starting out separately where you've got to build up sidemen and all. We'd be sidemen as a corporate body."

The music itself would be the leader of their band. After they agreed to form this cooperative group, they had to name it. The Wayne Shorter–Joe Zawinul–Miroslav Vitous Group was far too unwieldy a title. Wayne, Joe, and Miroslav spent an entire evening at Joe's apartment brainstorming group names. Joe threw out "Triumvirate," but it had a political connotation that might be a "drag" for the audience. What they really wanted was a name so simple and elemental that it would carry a subliminal seduction. "The Audience" seemed like a good prospect until they realized its potential for confusion at performances. Finally, Wayne said, "Let's have something that people are confronted with every day, like 'The Six O'Clock News.' Something they naturally tune in to, like the 'Weather Report.'" Everyone simultaneously said, "YEAH!"

Joe was enthusiastic about his musical association with Wayne. For Joe, they'd had a unity of perspective all along. "Our main connection was that independently, not knowing the other was doing it, we both started changing the form of music around, away from the song form," Joe said. "His music and mine. His songs weren't in any standard form. We were very much alike and simply opened up a melody and let it expand where it went. Independently before we worked together, we were both thinking, *Why does a tune have to go as long as eight bars? Why not more or less?*

Wayne acknowledged their musical compatibility, but was more excited about Weather Report's potential to break out of the jazz-club ghetto. "With Joe's Cannonball years and my Blakey and Miles Davis years, we'd accumulated musical information to use in the band," Wayne said. "We were talking about doing music that had mountains and streams and valleys and going over hill and dale. We were trying to do music with another grammar, where you don't resolve something, like writing a letter where you don't use capitals. We wanted to have a fanfare and a chase and an announcement. It was close to film music. Music for films that would never be made. But we were thinking about doing something to not just change the course of music, but also to get out of the nightclubs. We didn't want to work five nights a week in a nightclub until four in the morning. Sometimes five sets on the weekend with a matinee on Saturday. And of course, you fill in the blanks and the spaces of set breaks with drinking. That breaks down your body physically if you spend a lifetime working that way. And also we felt that the music needed to be appreciated on a larger scale, by a larger audience." Rock musicians like Janis Joplin and Hendrix were evidence that you could in fact burn out even when playing large venues. Still, Weather Report's desire to reach a more diverse audience was smart in the new rock ascendancy.

Weather Report hired a manager, Sid Bernstein, who knew something about appealing to a broad audience. Bernstein had famously brought the Beatles to Shea Stadium in 1965. "Sid was cool, he was a big guy who had ten children, and he said, 'I know what you're talking about,'" Wayne said. In December 1970, Weather Report signed to Columbia Records, Miles's label. Joe went to Europe with his family. When he returned, they searched for a drummer, settled on Alphonse Mouzon, and then rehearsed throughout February. Columbia released their first record, *Weather Report*, in May 1971. The label did such a good job on publicity that most listeners were as intrigued by the band's mystique as they were by its music. Joe suggestively called *Weather Report* "a soundtrack for the imagination." Reviewers hailed Weather Report's futuristic vision and used terms like "miracle" and "magic" to describe its music. Its sound seemed to channel mysterious sources. "Milky Way," the opening track, had an intriguing resonance that might have been tolling bells on Mars, but was actually created with only acoustic piano and soprano saxophone.

Overall, the record was polyrhythmic, with the world-beat tone poem concept that had been nascent on Wayne's *Super Nova* and *Odyssey of Iska* recordings. There was a layer of richness added by Airto Moreira, whose percussion was overdubbed onto the initial recording. Joe asked Airto to forgo his spot in Miles's band and join Weather Report, but Airto became nervous. "I was a little bit insecure about Joe 'cause he always talked real big. He was coming on real heavy. I was scared that I'd get into an argument with Joe on the road, and that would be it." Airto told Joe that he had to stick with Miles. Joe was not happy about Airto's decision and demanded that he find a replacement percussionist. Cornered, Airto said, "I know a guy who's better than I am."

He recommended Dom Um Romão, a Brazilian working in Miami with pianist Marcel Prieto. Romão was actually a drummer, not a percussionist, but Airto gambled on the belief that all Brazilian musicians instinctively knew what to do when they got their hands on a *shekere* or some *agogo* bells. Romão drove up to New York with his drum set for his Weather Report audition, borrowed some small instruments from Airto, and did a winning job in his "percussionist" ruse. When Romão joined the band on its first European tour, everyone who'd heard the record naturally asked about Airto. Joe would say, "Oh, we got his master. This is the guy who taught Airto." (Airto later toured Europe with Cannonball Adderley and had to field questions from the press about his "master." "But I never studied with anyone," Airto would say.) Airto's drama of fleeting membership in the band was the first of many personnel problems to come.

It was telling that Airto's brief and troubled tenure with the band played out vis-à-vis Joe rather than Wayne. Where was Wayne? "Wayne was a thinker, always thinking, thinking, thinking," Miroslav said. "He didn't want to influence the other musicians, wanted to wait to see what happens. Because a lot of Wayne Shorter is about waiting. I have never seen a musician who could wait more than Wayne Shorter."

Everyone plays a role in a band. While Wayne thought and waited, Joe acted. Hal Miller, a writer and friend of the band, sometimes joined the musicians on tour. "It was perfect because Joe was domineering and liked to take control anyhow," Hal said. "So he'd be fussing with the road crew and Wayne would be standing by with a beatific, benign smile. I remember once I asked Wayne for the time. He started talking to me about the cosmos and how time is relative. Joe came over and said, 'You don't ask Wayne shit like that. It's 7:06 p.m.'"

Joe once told Wayne that he came to the U.S. looking for a woman like Lena Horne. "Joe wanted a little color in his life," Wayne said. Wayne provided Joe and the band with color, character, and charisma. Joe offered guidance and day-to-day management. He argued with promoters and hired and fired band members—tasks that came easily to someone who had coped with Nazi SS officers as a twelve-year-old in his native Austria. Cannonball Adderley had also taught Joe how to take care of business. Between themselves, Wayne and Joe had an implicit understanding of how the band should work. "I was the bad guy, and Wayne was the good guy," Joe said.

Wayne knew that speaking up came in handy in the music business, but since his days in grammar school, he'd never been one to speak his mind. And he didn't usually need to. His talent spoke for itself. "I think my tendency to not speak up didn't knock me too far out of an advantageous place in music," Wayne said. "There were not many lost opportunities, 'cause I was always being discovered. Maynard Ferguson wanted me for his group, and Art Blakey, too. Then people told me, 'Hey, Miles is watching you,' and Miles called me. I was sought after."

Now his leadership role in Weather Report demanded that he direct others. But when someone asks Wayne how to write or play music, he usually responds indirectly, sometimes with a parable about artistic self-direction, like this one:

Mozart told a story about this young composer who asked him, "How do you do what you do? How do you get creativity going?" Mozart said, "Well, first you start writing songs." Then the guy said, "But you were already writing songs when you were very young, like six years old." Mozart answered, "Yes, but I never stopped to ask anyone, "How do you do great things?"

Wayne's instructive story of Mozart's self-reliance implies a confidence that everyone has the same talent for music. "There's a responsibility that lies within but also an arrogance when you say, 'I'm not going to ask anyone,'" Wayne said. "I thought I could hear anything and everything in music. I never did ask anybody, 'How do you do this, or that?' Whenever I had a question, I thought, *Let me see if I can hear it myself. Like, Stravinsky sure got it together . . . how did he get that beauty and that boom, boom, in* Rite of Spring?"

Wayne trusted Joe's leadership, even when it came to the hallowed ground of his own music. "Too many pieces of music finish too long after the end," Stravinsky once said. Joe made sure that Wayne's music never finished too long after the end—or began too soon before the beginning. In Weather Report's first few years, Wayne began to write longer compositions, sometimes of twenty or thirty pages. "All of it was good, fabulous stuff," Joe said. "I'd play it on the piano, like classical music. It was very intricate, beautiful, and well thought out. Wayne could sit with chords for a long time, but when he was done, it was masterful. I played all of his music for hours, and he'd say cut where it needed to be cut, when it was too long. I never changed a note, a chord, or anything. But he trusted me to edit it down, because the only thing I did was cut it down so we could put it on the record. I said, 'Wayne, you've got to write stuff for chamber ensembles, for orchestras.'" Joe had an opposite compositional style. He improvised, recorded what he improvised, and later wrote it all down without any changes.

Following Weather Report's 1971 European tour, Eric Gravatt replaced Alphonse Mouzon. (Conveniently, if ironically, Alphonse took Eric's place in McCoy Tyner's group when Eric joined Weather Report.) Eric was an imaginative drummer whose questing intellect suited Wayne's own. "The Weather Report drummer who was the all-around hippest one was Eric

Gravatt," Wayne said. "He did trigonometry on the train, or wrote plays. Eric had a way of playing that was open and free, with the cymbals set high, like he was reaching up to the sky to play sometimes. He had some stuff going." Eric played with Weather Report on its next record, *I Sing the Body Electric*, which was actually two records in one: side one was a studio album recorded in December 1971, and side two was a show recorded live in Tokyo in January 1972. With *I Sing the Body Electric*, Weather Report lost some of its self-consciousness, moving beyond what Wayne called the group's early "'Weather Report Presents' kind of sound."

Most significant for the band, the record was well received in the rock press. Bob Palmer gave the record this glowing review in *Rolling Stone*: "*I Sing the Body Electric* is a beautiful, near-perfect LP, especially welcome after Weather Report's noodling, at least half-dismal debut album. . . . Weather Report may be playing for each other, as some detractors have suggested, but they seem to have become their own most demanding audience. Now that they've got their shit together, they're one of the most exciting groups in contemporary music."

10.

We Were Always Here

BY THE END OF 1972, Iska's seizures were becoming more frequent and severe. Doctors suggested that a milder climate might help relieve her condition. Wayne had been thinking about moving from New York. His years in the city had served him well, giving him access to the heart of the jazz scene. But Wayne's days of jamming down at Birdland were long past. As he began to feel like he'd exhausted New York's cultural benefits, the hassles of city living became glaringly apparent. Its scenery was concrete and bricks. He'd stand in the cold rain trying to hail a taxi home to the Upper West Side, passed up by all the cabs on duty—drivers assumed a black man wanted a ride to Harlem, a forbidding, crime-ridden neighborhood with dim prospects for return fares. The Shorters considered buying a car, but then they'd have to pay extravagant parking costs and contend with poorly maintained, pothole-ridden streets. The previous year, Herbie and Gigi Hancock had moved to Los Angeles. They raved on to Wayne and Ana Maria about the gorgeous green wonders of the West Coast. "In New York, no matter how much money you have, you're just surviving," Herbie told Wayne. "Come out to California and start living." So in the final month of 1972, Wayne and Ana Maria left behind the hostile winter chill of New York and moved to Los Angeles. "That's where the new life started," Wayne said.

The couple stayed in Herbie and Gigi's guesthouse until they found a house to rent across the street. Over the next few months, they settled into a new way of life. Many new parents find themselves reevaluating their beliefs in order to pass on a meaningful sense of the world to their children. Iska's brain damage presented special concerns and complications for Wayne and Ana Maria, as they didn't know what was actually going on in her head. Iska would listen to Wayne playing the piano, and seemed to move along with the music's rhythm, but her movements were slight and imprecise. Wayne and Ana weren't sure how she made sense of the world.

They did learn from Iska's example. "People would come for a party, and they'd be talking about Vietnam and politics," Wayne said. "And you know what Iska would say to all this stuff? She'd just crawl around kind of singsong-saying 'doo-doo-doo-doo-doo.' I saw no evil in that child. Iska could only respond to you with kindness. Everything was ice cream for her." Iska's goodness seemed to reform anyone who met her. "It's like, you know, Miles used to cuss all the time," Wayne said. "But in Japan, where people didn't speak English very well, he said it bothered him, 'cause he couldn't even cuss there." Miles's attitude was that if those motherfuckers over in Japan didn't understand the hip transgression of blasphemy, he had to admit that there wasn't much point in it. In the same way, if negative emotions didn't have any impact on Iska, why would anyone bother projecting them in her presence?

In the early seventies, the culture-at-large was becoming more sensitive to "vibe" and spiritual issues anyway. "After the assassinations of Martin Luther King and the Kennedys, everyone started asking, 'Where is the world going?'" Wayne said. "And with the civil rights movement, once you get something enacted, the difficulty is to continue something that's hard-fought. When you win, that's a relief, but then how do you maintain that 'All's right with the world' feeling on the inside of yourself?"

The social movements of the sixties got personal in the seventies, with revolutionaries reoriented toward identity politics and spiritual quests. "There was a period of openness to religious influences," Wayne said. "People were investigating Sufism, stuff from India, the sitar, Beatles lyrics. Whoever thought they were more internationally minded wore a continental suit with the vent in the sides. People were searching for a label— shopping around for a banner to be under, a kind of nationalism, or spirituality."

Improvising musicians are often misperceived as creatures of pure instinct, so they can be eager to appear cosmopolitan and philosophical. "People who played progressive music were usually thinkers," Wayne said. "Charlie Parker could sit and carry on a conversation about anything. He had a photographic memory. But most people didn't know that about him. To dispel the general notion that musicians were like 'Duh,' some of them wanted to seem more facile with encounters about life. Instead of feeling embarrassed or half empty, they wanted to say something." In an era when rock musicians rolled out the notion of Jesus Christ as a superstar, John McLaughlin and Carlos Santana took up with Indian guru Sri Chinmoy, and McLaughlin's Mahavishnu Orchestra played at lots of colleges, delivering and soliciting new sounds and ideas along the way. After Weather Report concerts, college students would ask Wayne questions about John Lennon, or if Weather Report's music represented the band "going head on with the old guard."

Blacks who had allied themselves with the civil rights movement in the sixties began celebrating their African heritage. Wayne's perspective on identity was never so black and white. Again, he told a story about Miles to illustrate his point of view:

Someone asked Miles how he would like to be remembered after he passed away. Miles said, "I don't want people to say six hundred years from now that I was Norwegian. Or a Zulu." One time when we were with Miles, a white guy with a camera came into the dressing room at the Village Gate. Miles said, "What the fuck you think you're doin'?" Miles hit the camera and knocked it on the ground, and said, "You think you can take any kind of pictures 'cause you're white?" Another time a black guy with a camera came back there to take pictures. Miles said, "What the fuck you think you're doin'? You think you can do that 'cause you're black?"

Many younger jazz musicians did flaunt their African pedigree, though the display was often part of a search for something deeper. Herbie took the Swahili name "Mwandishi" for himself and for his electrified sextet, which combined jazz, rock, African and Indian musical influences. "We were always searching for ways to make the music all that it could be with an amount of freedom," Herbie said. "And we were searching for a religion that would help solidify our spiritual foundation." Herbie discovered that religion one night through Mwandishi bassist Buster "Mchezaji" Williams. This religion would structure and support the rest of his life, and Wayne's, too.

In the spring of 1972, Mwandishi played a week at a club in Seattle. The gig started on Tuesday, and each night after the show, the group went to the most "happening" parties, drunken affairs that lasted until dawn and beyond. So the band played its Wednesday- and Thursday-night shows hungover, with only a couple hours of sleep. Sometimes hangovers gave the guys a musical edge, but by Friday they were nearing nervous exhaustion. Unfortunately, Friday was a big night at the club with a packed house. When Mwandishi walked onstage, the crowd's happy expectancy hit them like a challenge, a confrontation. Herbie usually kicked off a set with "You'll Know When You Get There," or another tune that featured his keyboards. But this time Herbie was too tired to jump-start the show.

"I took the coward's way out," he said. "I called 'Toys,' a tune that began with a solo by another musician, bassist Buster Williams."

In that solo, Herbie heard a Buster Williams he'd never heard before. "This expressive music was coming out of him from somewhere else," Herbie said. "His feats went beyond technique—at one point he worked the four-string instrument in three different directions at once, simultaneously trilling, and going up and down on the strings. The audience freaked out over his solo, so by the time the band came in, we were wide awake and inspired. The set played out like magic." After the set, Herbie grabbed Buster backstage. "I heard you were into some new philosophy or something," Herbie said. "If it can make you play bass like that, I want to know what it is." Buster smiled magnanimously and said, "I've been chanting for a way to tell you about this." Instead, Herbie had asked *him*. "The message reached me the only way it could have, through music," Herbie said.

The "message" was the Buddhism of Nichiren Daishonin, a thirteenth-century Japanese monk whose philosophy centered around the final teaching of the Buddha (Siddhartha Gautama). This teaching, the Lotus Sutra, affirmed that all living beings have the potential for enlightenment or Buddhahood. Nichiren's Buddhism emphasizes the interconnectedness of all things—cause and effect—as well as personal responsibility for one's own life condition. These teachings were common to most Buddhist practice. The difference was, Nichiren taught that all the Lotus Sutra's beneficial wisdom could be realized by chanting its title, [Nam] Myoho Renge Kyo. Nichiren claimed that "Nam-myoho-renge-kyo" was the ultimate law permeating all phenomena in the universe. Nichiren Buddhists chant this phrase—referred to as *daimoku*—along with excerpts from the Lotus Sutra, they study Nichiren's writings; and, controversially, they propagate his teachings.

This focus on propagation has sometimes earned the followers of Nichiren a cultlike reputation. Members have an imperative of *shakubuku,* to introduce others to Nichiren's practice. Less than noble motives have corrupted all religions at one time or another, and the simplicity of this chanting practice has made it particularly easy to twist or taint. In the 1970s, before the practice had matured in the United States, new practitioners were often encouraged to chant for material gains—a Mercedes or even cold, hard cash—without any explanation of the deeper Buddhist principles involved. All Nichiren Buddhists *are* initially encouraged to chant for whatever they want, but this is directly connected to the belief that "earthly desires equal enlightenment," which is a rare concept in Buddhism and one that can be easily misunderstood. Ideally, someone chants for an object or goal, and whether or not he acquires or achieves it, he has a realization about why it doesn't actually bring happiness. Overcoming inner hurdles and developing inner wisdom are the more satisfying spiritual benefits of this practice.

Most members take *shakubuku* to this more profound level, first suggesting that aspiring Buddhists chant for a personal goal, and then familiarizing them with more deeply transformative aspects of the practice. With Buster's encouragement, Herbie originally chanted to find the best approach to his musical career, but quickly realized the larger effect Buddhism had on his entire life. With these benefits, Herbie was eager to share the practice with friends, and he fulfilled his duty by introducing Ana Maria to the practice. Herbie thought it would help her deal with the strain and burden of caring for Iska. Ana responded to Nichiren Buddhism immediately, attracted to the prospect of chanting for Iska's improvement. Wayne didn't take to the practice at first, Herbie said: "Wayne didn't feel it was necessary to have a ritual in order to have that kind of growth and clarity we were seeking. There was a hint of arrogance in his attitude—more than a hint—and Wayne was usually too careful to telegraph stuff like that. Usually he was too smart to lay that on somebody."

Over the next few months, Ana Maria's chanting became a regular background sound in their home, like the washing machine, television, or the stop-and-go music of Wayne composing at the piano. When she chanted, each syllable was given even weight, "Nam myo-ho ren-ge kyo, Nam myo-ho ren-ge kyo, Nam myo-ho ren-ge kyo." The chant's foreign sound cast a shadow over its words, but there was also something familiar about it to Wayne. It was like an aural equivalent of Proust's madeleine, carrying him back to one of his earliest thoughts as a child: *We were always here.* After she chanted, Wayne noticed that the atmosphere in the house felt cleaner, like when Miles played a long tone and changed the temperature and color of the surrounding air, the cool blue note settling down into green.

One morning, Wayne listened more closely to the sounds of Ana Maria's chanting. Beyond the pulsing, monotone notes, there was music in the pronunciation of the words. He stood at the French doors to the room where she chanted. Ana sat cross-legged on the floor, facing a shrine with a strange scroll, some green plants, a bowl of fruit, and two large white candles in hurricane glasses. Wayne interrupted Ana and asked her to show him what she was doing. Ana told him that she was performing morning *gongyo,* which meant "making the highest cause for the highest effect to attain an enlightened life." She showed him the small prayer book, which included a section of the Lotus Sutra's second chapter and its entire sixteenth chapter. And Ana pointed out the focus of her chanting up on the shrine: the Gohonzon, a scroll with Chinese characters that depicted the ten realms, or states of life: hell, hunger, animality, belligerence, humanity, heaven, learning, realization, bodhisattva, and Buddhahood.

Wayne started chanting with her on occasion, but was still hesitant to embrace the practice. Initially, he just went through the motions of reciting the words. "I was trying to recite the *gongyo,* the Lotus Sutra, from time to time," Wayne said. "But I'd be messing it up, just making believe I was doing it, like when babies pretend like they can speak English." Down deep he still viewed the ritual as a sign of weakness and wondered if it was just a crutch.

It would require a full cultural immersion for Wayne to make a firm commitment. That opportunity came in the summer of 1973, when Weather Report opened for Santana on a tour of Japan, where millions of Nichiren Buddhists—members of the lay organization Soka Gakkai International, or "Value-Creating Organization"—were based. After a show in Tokyo, Wayne was visited backstage by a small man named Nobu

Urushiyama, a Japanese drummer who practiced Buddhism with his family. Herbie had given Nobu's phone number to Ana Maria. "While Weather Report was in Tokyo, I got a call from Ana Maria," Nobu said. "She said, 'Please take Wayne to a temple and encourage him to become Buddhist,' because at that time their suffering was at a pinnacle with Iska." Wayne was planning to go on to Hawaii the next day with the band, but Nobu convinced him to spend a few days at his family's home in Fujisawa City, a town about an hour west of Tokyo.

The family treated Wayne like a rock star on a hermitage, laying out a cornucopia of fruits and vegetables to accommodate his vegetarian diet, a lifestyle change he made in California. Nobu's family also gave him several English-language books about Nichiren Buddhism. Wayne needed a rest from the rigors of Weather Report's life on the road and used his stay at Nobu's home as a spiritual retreat. "For three days, Wayne just slept, ate, and read the books," Nobu said. "We didn't discuss the Buddhist teachings at all, and we barely talked. He stayed in my room and had complete privacy." Back home in California, Wayne had tried chanting, but hadn't seen how simply reciting Nam-myoho-renge-kyo would lead to enlightenment. When he had time to read about the philosophy behind the practice, it registered with him. "I saw that all the doors were open with Buddhism," Wayne said. Nichiren's philosophy seemed like everything he already believed in anyway, or had once instinctively known as a child but had forgotten somewhere along the way. Back in 1965, for example, Wayne had demonstrated a fascination with the concept of "cause and effect" when describing the title track on *Speak No Evil*: "This piece is about caution, be careful about what you say: What comes out of your mouth can cause some horrendous effects or beautiful ones."

After three days, Nobu asked him, "Are you ready?" Wayne said, "I guess I'm ready." Ready or not, early on the morning of August 7, Wayne recited *gongyo* with Nobu's family and then went to a small temple in the Tokyo suburbs. A priest lightly tapped a rolled scroll inscribed with the Lotus Sutra on Wayne's head and then chanted Nam-myoho-renge-kyo, committing Wayne to the practice. "There was also a small baby there, small enough to be held by his mother," Wayne said. "He was also having his ceremony. It seemed like a good omen."

They hurried to the new Shohondo temple (*shohondo* means "high sanctuary") for an afternoon dedication ceremony with Daisaku Ikeda, president and spiritual leader of the Soka Gakkai Buddhist organization. The event's jazz-loving organizers recognized Wayne standing at the back of the crowded temple and whisked him up to the front row of the 6,000-seat sanctuary just in time for the ceremony's start. During the ceremony, President Ikeda spotted Wayne and smiled broadly at him. When they left, Nobu asked Wayne, "What kind of feeling did you get from that encounter?" Wayne said, "I got this, Nobu. Daisaku Ikeda was saying, *I know what I'm going to do. I know what you're going to do. So let's do it together.*" Wayne felt that President Ikeda's expression meant that they always had been and always would be Buddhas, as if they were both remembering the practice from long before. Nobu said he was impressed: "You listen to Wayne play, and just one note says thousands of things. In the same way, that one smile spoke volumes to him."

Having witnessed this friendly conspiracy between Wayne and President Ikeda, Nobu drove Wayne back to his hometown in a celebratory mood. "We went to a menswear store where my family had an account," Nobu said. "I asked Wayne if he wanted a little something from the store, a small gift, and he picked out four very expensive white dress shirts! The next day he took off to Hawaii." Wayne left Nobu with a memento of his commitment ceremony, a poster with this zealous message inscribed on it:

To Nobu: Rock on—and on—and on! Domo arigato. Arigato goza-imasu. August 7, 1973, a day when the gods roared!

The year 2000 is waiting for birth. Let's give it healthy mothers and fathers: members of Nichiren Daishonin's future truth because of NOW Truth!

Wayne Shorter

True personal change is usually a gradual process, an evolution rather than a revolution. Though Wayne's enthusiasm for Buddhism was genuine, his path to enlightenment has not been a straight and narrow one. In Hawaii, he veered in a 180-degree turn away from the spiritual retreat in Tokyo. In reaction to his new spiritual dedication, Wayne indulged in a three-day marathon of high living. "I like to use the analogy about the water hose in the garden," Wayne said. "You turn the water on and your essence, your intention to be clean, pushes out the rusty stuff that clutters you. The first thing that came out for me, what I did was I disappeared in Hawaii. I was in a hotel off the main tourist circuit, and no one in the band knew where I was. I bought lots of sharp clothes and wined and dined by myself having long so-called philosophical conversations, and eating stuff so that I felt good, you know, and drinking another champagne and another scotch. The whole entirety of my nightlife and entertainment history was encapsulated in a three-day party."

Soka Gakkai Buddhists believe that their dedication to the practice instigates a process called "human revolution," a philosophy originated by President Ikeda in a book of that title. Through this step-by-step process, Buddhists learn to conquer the negative aspects of their character and develop wisdom, compassion, and joy. They also believe that with this commitment, greater negativity arises to stop their spiritual revolution. These obstacles tend to show up in a person's unique area of weakness. Drinking was Wayne's Achilles' heel. "When I started practicing Buddhism, the drinking came to a head," Wayne said. "You can see yourself when you start practicing. So that party in Hawaii told me, in my head, 'Oh, this means that's the fulcrum here.' The bells were ringing."

Wayne may have rebelled against his own commitment to the practice with the bender in Hawaii, but when he returned to California a few days later, Herbie said that Wayne had clearly undergone a profound conversion. "We didn't know when he left for Japan that he was going to receive his Gohonzon. We thought we'd have to continue the conversation to convince him to practice. Wayne not only started practicing but joined in

Japan. He came back immersed in it. Totally into it, not just understanding it from a distance, but in a very internal way."

When Wayne started practicing Buddhism, he began to see himself more clearly, and he didn't entirely like what he saw. So at forty, an age when most men have long settled into an adult identity, Wayne decided he wanted to recover the purity of intent he'd had as a teenager. "I wanted to get back to the fifteen-year-old kid in me who drew the science-fiction comic book," Wayne said. "That would be the jumping-off point. And then I could continue from there. Certain other things were aborted. You know, to thine own self be true."

Mysterious Traveller

The fifteen-year-old budding artist who'd created the comic book was not a jazz musician of international renown with the responsibility of co-leading a band. When Wayne set out on what Buddhists call "human revolution," he began a long-term growth process that wasn't always compatible with his short-term career goals as a musician.

As Wayne began to change his fundamental approach to life, there were greater cultural forces that were also acting to distance him from music. "When I was first getting into bebop in the forties, jazz was the music of social revolution," Wayne said. Musicians such as Charlie Parker, Thelonious Monk, and Bud Powell defined hipness with their auras of serious, engaged artists. Throughout the fifties and most of the sixties, jazz was a respected cultural expression, especially when played by someone like Miles: "With Miles, we were spelling out the details of how the world was changing around us," Wayne said. They were part of something larger than themselves. By the seventies, Tom Wolfe's "Me Decade," music no longer served the same social function. Distinguishing himself in this environment was less appealing to Wayne. "Being original and noteworthy as a musician was not such a concern for me," he said. "I stopped worrying about whether or not originality would be subsumed within the crushing wheels of the music business. Music took second place for me." Both the inner transformation that Buddhism inspired and jazz's loss of meaning in culture caused Wayne to focus on aspects of life other than music.

Wayne's continuing disillusionment with music was inevitable throughout the seventies, as Weather Report moved in an increasingly commercial direction. By 1973, Weather Report was an artistic success, but only to a certain degree. "We always solo and never solo," Joe said, describing Weather Report's collective improvisation ethos. This made for some thrilling musical interplay at times, but it also made the music dependent on magic— everything worked only when the demigods of inspiration were kind to everyone in the band.

So concerts were hit or miss. From one night to the next, fans and critics might see Jesus in the music, or they might just see a band stuck in Dante's seventh level. One *Down Beat* writer caught the band on a transcendent night: "Now I'm going to say it. Weather Report, a five-piece band with roots in jazz but ideas in the universe, gave one of the greatest concerts I've ever heard." During the same period, another *Down Beat* writer heard them on a night when the magic eluded them: "With a group like Weather Report, if the rabbit doesn't appear, all you have left is an interesting-sounding hat. But those who have heard their second album or who were fortunate enough to have attended opening night (when the music was evoking stand-up screams) know that the magic can be pretty heady stuff. When it's lacking, though, said Vitous, the band lets it be, remains calm (their definition) and waits for it to come around again. Then they caress it, beat and kick it, wanting it to stay, knowing it won't."

And even when these moments of glory did come, they weren't enough for the rock audience. Audiences at the Plugged Nickel would sit in expectation while Miles's rhythm section spent seven minutes searching for the best way to fill Miles's silence. The rock audience didn't have the patience for delayed gratification. If Weather Report wanted wider success, its only solution was to find a reliable sound, something as dependable as a net, a musical tool that would carry the band along, no matter what. "I wanted to get into a groove," Joe said. "Weather Report had been dependent on just feeling, and I didn't want it to be about mood. I wanted to have a little more organization, so that sometimes when it's not magical, you could still go on and have a little more punch."

So on the band's next album, *Sweetnighter*, recorded in February 1973, Joe guided the band away from collective improvisation—magic or mundane—and toward compositions emphasizing funk and groove. As usual, Wayne came up with the record's title—"Sweetnighter" was the name of a children's medicine—and he also contributed a couple of tunes. But Joe provided the lion's share of the music, and the dominant compositions on the record were unquestionably his. "I started writing longer, intricate pieces, but also more groove-oriented, like '125th Street Congress,'" Joe said. "This is the tune with the Zawa beat, the first hip-hop beat. I have sixty recordings of rap groups who sampled that recording for their stuff."

Wayne's compositions were less essential, however beautiful. "Manolete" would have fit in nicely on previous Weather Report albums, as would "Non-Stop Home." Wayne talked about the tune's origin: "I wrote that for my grandmother. She used to belong to the Baptist Church, the Black Baptist Church, and that was like her church's song. If you take the rhythm off and let the melody play, that's her song, man." The tune sounded like a church caught up in a twister. Its melody didn't emerge until nearly two minutes into the tune, and was quickly taken up in the swirl of Joe's synthesizer, which he debuted with eruptive force on this record. The one tune by Joe that did reflect Weather Report's previous style was "Adios"—Joe seemed to be saying good-bye to the band's old sound.

There were some important personnel changes on *Sweetnighter*: Joe brought in Herschell Dwellingham on drums, and tried out multi-instrumentalist Andrew White on bass, an instrument he'd played to great funky effect with the Fifth Dimension and Stevie Wonder. But Wayne first noticed a response from a younger audience when drummer Greg Errico joined the band for the tour following *Sweetnighter*'s release. Errico had serious credibility with the rock audience from playing with Sly and the Family Stone. "The internationally minded people got into the band first, but the younger people started coming when Greg Errico played. Greg had this driving beat, and people saw him and said, 'That's the guy with Sly!' Greg was with us only a short while. But that was when we started to notice that thirteen- and fifteen-year-olds would be coming to see us, sometimes with their parents, and the audience started building."

Miroslav was most severely affected by the band's stylistic shift. No matter how much he tried to be modern and funky, his bass lines were tethered to the old country, to European improvisation. And though Miroslav was a founding member of the group, he was never as principal a player as his renowned elder co-leaders. On the summer tour of Japan in 1973, for example, Weather Report was honored for *Sweetnighter,* but only Wayne and Joe were presented with gold records. Miroslav was miffed and considered quitting the group. The incident blew over. When the band returned to the U.S., Joe convinced Miroslav to move to Los Angeles, where he and Wayne both lived.

Then in October 1973, Wayne and Joe happened upon bassist Alphonso Johnson. "I was playing with the Chuck Mangione Quartet at the Academy of Music in Philadelphia, a big place like an opera house," Alphonso said. "We were opening for Weather Report, and I was playing for my hometown crowd. Wayne Shorter happened to be standing on the side of the stage, checking the band out. At that moment, I was doing a bass solo, and all my high school buddies were there, and my family was there, all making a lot of noise, and it made an impression on Wayne." Alphonso was asked to go out to L.A. for what he assumed was a Weather Report audition, but when he arrived, he was the only bassist there. His "audition" was playing on the band's next recording, *Mysterious Traveller,* which they tracked over the winter and spring of 1974. Alphonso brought in an original composition, "Cucumber Slumber," and on this tune and others he grooved with natural persuasion. He knew how to hold down the bottom of the band, he knew the whole jazz tradition, and he even understood Wayne's poetic instruction. "Wayne never came out and said, 'Play this or play that,'" Alphonso said. "If Wayne said anything, I knew to listen and listen carefully. If we were playing a song and Wayne said something like 'Sometimes springtime can be deceiving and winter can be the time to blossom,' I would think about it and go, okay, in the pretty parts of the song it's not so important to be aggressive and during the driving parts it's important to step out more."

Perhaps more dynamic band members came later, but Alphonso's recruitment was the most critical personnel change for Weather Report. It finalized the band's shift from a free-improv sensibility to a staunch groove-driven stance, setting the stage for its popular success. Miroslav was very upset about being let go, but recognized that his talents were not suited to the changing group. "Number one, I couldn't play the black funk, and number two, I was not supposed to," he said. "I am an innovator and a pioneer and an advanced musician, and I am right on the edge of developing new music. How can you put me in a black funk band trying to make some money? It's not me." Miroslav was embittered by what he saw as Joe's subterfuge: "I really didn't feel like moving to California. But Joe said, 'Well, the whole band is here.' So I went. Two months later, I get a call from Joe that Joe and Wayne don't want to work with me anymore." Miroslav's dismissal came back to haunt Wayne and Joe. Miroslav was part owner of the Weather Report name. When he threatened legal action over royalties and the use of the band name a few years later, Wayne and Joe were forced to pay him a monthly sum for a period of years.

While Miroslav was a casualty of the band's stylistic shift, Wayne survived these changes. He was the saxophonist, the band's proof it was still a jazz group. And Wayne's shrewdness and generosity protected him—as always, he just played what was right for the music. Wayne's versatility as a player would be confirmed throughout the seventies in a number of surprising projects. But with a survivor's instinct, he began to take refuge in an idealistic vision of the band during the recording of *Mysterious Traveller*. "As I hear it, working on it, it's beginning to mean many more things than the other three [records]," he said at the time. "It's more kaleidoscopic. In many ways, there's more of a tendency to share something in this album, rather than to show something. There's a kind of allness, a spirit of sharing, in this one which includes everybody in the group."

When *Mysterious Traveller* was released in 1974, there was a combined review of the record and *Moto Grosso Feio*, Wayne's Blue Note recording from 1970 that also was released in 1974. The review acknowledged Wayne's fading leadership of the band but affirmed his abilities: "These albums showcase the steady growth of Wayne Shorter into the most authoritative soprano sax force since Coltrane. . . . As part of Weather Report, his playing has often been overshadowed by the formidable keyboard presence of Zawinul, yet he, more than anyone else in the unit, is responsible for the band's individual personality. . . . Zawinul seems to be steering Weather Report into a landscape of his own imagination, something that may not ultimately be compatible with Shorter's lyrical abilities. One thing is indisputable: both men show no sign of creative stagnation and, because of this, Weather Report remains one of the most seminal small ensembles of the day."

11

Native Dancers and
Fairy-Tale Friends

FOR MANY MUSICIANS, Brazil is a fantasy world of rhythms. Wayne first flirted with them on his early Blue Note recordings. At that time, the bossa nova craze was in full swing. In 1962 jazz saxophonist Stan Getz released *Jazz Samba* to popular crossover success, inspiring otherwise jazz-indifferent and sedate suburbanites to dance around their pools in beach towels. Many jazz musicians were encouraged to capitalize on the popular trend with their own recordings of cool bossa jazz. Wayne always had a Stan Getz influence—like Getz, he liked to play ballads up in the tenor saxophone's high register. But Wayne avoided any imitative bossa stylings: The Brazilian rhythms on "El Gaucho," for example, from his 1965 recording *Adam's Apple,* were abstracted into his own jazz mix. When Wayne met his Portuguese wife, Ana Maria, in 1966, he naturally began some intensive home schooling in Portuguese and Brazilian culture. His song titles like "Feio" and "Surucucu" paid homage to Lusophone cultures, and in 1969, he included Maria Booker's version of the Jobim tune "Dindi" on *Super Nova,* adding the exotic singing sound of Airto's *cuica* drum and other percussion.

Still, no one was prepared for the deeply affecting sound of Wayne's *Native Dancer* recording. It was unlike any Brazilian music most Americans had ever heard. The record's first few notes introduced a voice, one that had to be the most potent falsetto on the planet. This voice was not an acquired taste. You either loved it or hated it—it was sublimely otherworldly or just eerily disembodied. The voice belonged to Brazilian pop singer and composer Milton Nascimento, and *Native Dancer* was Wayne's 1974 collaboration with the singer. The record was Wayne's love song to Brazil: to *alegria,* or "joyful fun"; and to *saudade,* that untranslatable Portuguese term for peaceful melancholy, for the presence of absence. On *Native Dancer,* Wayne married jazz to Milton's melodies in a kind of holy union that made other Brazilian jazz efforts of the time seem like one-night stands. This was the sound of a relaxed and happy Wayne Shorter in confident command of the studio, which was all too rare in the seventies. It was his last solo recording until 1985.

Milton had been a revelation for American jazz musicians. In September 1968, Herbie and Gigi Hancock went to Rio on their honeymoon, and Herbie called the only person he knew there, a young piano player named Eumir Deodato. When Eumir called back, he told Herbie he was in the recording studio with a "great young artist" and a few other musicians. Herbie excitedly invited them all over to his hotel. The great young artist was Milton Nascimento, whose star was on the rise following his 1967 appearance on the televised International Song Festival, an event that launched the careers of many Brazilian pop musicians. But when Eumir told Milton he was organizing an informal showcase for Herbie Hancock, Milton was loath to play. "I thought, the guy's here for his honeymoon, not for a concert, and I didn't feel like showing him anything anyway, because I was shy," Milton said. "I knew Herbie and Wayne and all those musicians because they played with the Miles Davis Quintet. For me, Miles was above everything and everyone, Miles was a god, and anyone who was close to him would be at the same level. I felt that I could die just by being touched by one of those musicians."

Milton's curiosity to meet Herbie overcame his nervousness, and he took his guitar over to Herbie's hotel. Milton cut a striking figure. A dark-skinned black man, he usually wore white overalls and a white floppy hat—comfortable, friendly attire that clashed with the calm gravity of his gaze and serious strength of his features. Accompanied by his own guitar, Milton started to play one of his hits, "Travessia." Herbie was stunned by his voice: "I went whoa . . . and told him to wait a minute while I ran and got my tape recorder." (In 1968 relatively few musicians had serviceable portable tape recorders, but Herbie, known among musicians as the King of Gadgets, did.) "I recorded several of those songs that became standards in Brazil. It was awesome stuff. And just to hear Milton, just his guitar and voice, the stuff was really fantastic. And I was wondering, how did he get this harmonic concept? And melodically, the songs were gorgeous. I didn't know what the words meant, but then when I asked to have them translated, it was so beautiful."

The mysterious harmonic concept came from Milton's home state of Minas Gerais, or "general mines," a region named for its gold and gemstone mining. Separated from the coast by a mountain range, the state's isolation preserved Portuguese cultural traditions such as Catholicism that were absorbed into native culture elsewhere in Brazil. Minas was also cowboy country, a land of vast, rolling coffee plantations. The region's pragmatism and religiousness were a far cry from the festive sensuality of coastal cities like Rio de Janeiro and Bahia—as different in cultural climate as Appalachia is from New York City.

Milton was born in Rio in 1942 and moved to Tres Pontas, Minas Gerais, when he was two, adopted by the white couple who'd employed his mother as a cook. The town's name was Milton's first lesson in poetic license. People who'd never been there imagined that Tres Pontas, or "Three

Points," referred to a trio of large mountains that surrounded the town. There were actually only three small hills to the north of Tres Pontas that were barely distinguishable from other peaks on the horizon. Milton learned other lessons in symbolism and faith as a practicing Catholic, and sang the church's chant-like hymns in his falsetto. Those church-music harmonies affected him as profoundly as the bossa nova rhythms he avidly listened to on João Gilberto's records.

Milton's adoptive mother, Lilia, was a musician who played with the composer Heitor Villa-Lobos. His father, Josino, was an electrician who ran a radio station on the side. Milton sang popular songs by request on the air, but at twelve he became worried about losing his charming falsetto to puberty. Then one day the radio transmitted a kind of revelation back to him. "I associated emotion with a female voice, so I was afraid I would lose my heart when I couldn't sing with a female voice anymore," Milton said. "Then one time I was playing next to my father's office when I heard a singer come on the radio. It was Ray Charles, a man, and he was singing with heart! Then I knew that no matter what happened to my voice, I would never lose my heart." Milton didn't lose his falsetto but did gain a bass voice, which only gave him a greater range of expression.

Milton moved to Minas's capital, Belo Horizonte, playing bass in a jazz band and taking up with a group of musicians who called themselves Clube da Esquina, or the "Street-Corner Gang." His big break came in the 1967 International Song Festival, when he also released his first album, *Travessia*. By then it was clear to everyone that he was no ordinary singer. Robertinho Silva, who played drums with the singer for more than thirty years, said Milton's strong identification with Minas made him unique: "Unlike most musicians, Milton had an influence from the Gregorian chants of Minas as well as from bossa nova, and he played bass in a jazz dance band. So Milton was totally different at that time." Like Joao Gilberto and other bossa nova artists, Milton played the guitar in rhythmic counterpoint to his voice. But his sweeping lyricism and peculiar sense of harmony differentiated him from bossa artists, and from peers like Caetano Veloso and Gilberto Gil who were busy pioneering the wild rock/bossa collage of the *tropicalia* style. Milton brought a jazz sensibility to folk and church melodies, and while he did reveal the influence of the Beatles' psychedelic sound, it was subtle and tempered by melancholy. Milton was his own thing. Later, when Milton toured Europe, a Copenhagen festival poster listed him as one of its performers. The poster gave a stylistic label for each act—jazz, rock, fusion, etc. Beside Milton's name it simply said "Milton."

A few English-speaking fans first heard Milton on *Courage,* which he recorded with producer Creed Taylor for CTI Records in 1968. The record didn't do much to expand his popular audience in the U.S., though musicians did take notice. "It was great for me because the U.S. musicians liked this album very much," Milton said. "One talked to another, then another and then another, and jazz musicians were especially interested, because the jazz musicians at the time were the most open to everything. Word spread very quickly." Herbie Hancock and Tony Williams both played on *Courage,* but Wayne said someone else actually stirred up his interest in Milton: a "hip little Chinese girl" named Darlene Chan, a young festival promoter in California. "I had just been to Brazil and fell in love with Milton," Darlene said. "I was amazed that Wayne didn't know about Milton, because with Wayne he's 'there' even if he's not there. Milton just blew me away, and I immediately had the thought that they were of like minds. I just knew that Wayne should hear him, because Wayne's mind is so unfettered by prejudice, and Milton was unfettered in a similar way musically."

"I was moved by how Milton had moved away from bossa nova and away from the typical Brazilian pop format," Wayne said. "He was not like [bossa nova artist Tom] Jobim—he's got more of an Indian or Amazonian or African element. And he told me that from his early childhood whenever he wanted to express the sound of his voice, he used to go out in the countryside around his hometown and sing until it sounded right to him."

Milton's sound was transcendent to Wayne: "Coltrane and Miles said if you have a sound, the sound will take you places further than the instrument demands. A lot of people have a one-dimensional sound. I don't hear much unique sound from the vocal quarter. For example, all the high-talking singers in Motown could drown you in altitude." "Milton's falsetto was gorgeous in high altitudes, and he also had a rich palette of tonal color in the bass register. The singer said he was always happiest near the ocean. Growing up far from the sea in Minas, it was as if he conjured its immensity and motion with his own voice. If Motown singers "drown you in altitude," as Wayne said, surfing along a wave's summit, Milton dove down octaves below the surface and used his bass to power his way to the top, lifting you up to glide along on the crest of his falsetto. There was a good reason for Wayne's attraction: He used his soprano saxophone to similar effect.

Wayne covered Milton's "Vera Cruz" on *Moto Grosso Feio,* an album he recorded for Blue Note in August 1970. Wayne's melodic side emerged when he set in on Milton's tune, as if it were simply too beautiful to mess around with. By 1972, when Weather Report traveled to Brazil to play Rio's Municipal Theater, Wayne's appreciation of Milton's music had deepened considerably. Ana Maria read a local newspaper announcement of some Milton shows that were happening on the same nights as Weather Report's performances. Wayne and Joe were so eager to hear the Brazilian singer that they rushed through their own show. "They cut their Weather Report concert short," Milton said. "They kept a car running right outside the stage, so that they could run out, grab the car, and head over to my concert to see at least half of it."

In the liner notes to a CD reissue of Milton's *Travessia,* singer Caetano Veloso discussed Weather Report's interest in Milton's show: "Milton suggested a fusion that . . . merged with the 'fusion' inaugurated by Miles Davis. It was interesting to note that this Brazilian fusion bewildered and thrilled the very same followers of the American 'fusion.' Milton was performing at a theatre alongside the Lagoa Rodrigo de Freitas in 1972, just after I had arrived from Bahia, and I was as impressed with what I saw and heard as were the Weather Report's musicians, who were visiting Rio at that same time. Maybe for different reasons—and with different conse-quences—but at least with the same intensity."

Ana Maria encouraged Wayne to record with Milton, and that oppor-tunity came when Wayne heard that Flora Purim was bringing Milton to the U.S. in 1974. He and Flora shared travel expenses for Milton and two of his closest musical associates, keyboardist Wagner Tiso and drummer Robertinho Silva. After rehearsals with Flora in New York, the Brazilians performed with her at the Montreux Jazz Festival in early July 1974, where they recorded *500 Miles High* for Arista Records. When they returned to the U.S., they went to Wayne's house in Malibu, where they lived and worked for two weeks, recording *Native Dancer* on September 12, 1974.

Wayne was insistent about bringing together the right personnel for this record with Milton. Along with himself and Herbie Hancock, there were the Brazilians: Milton, Wagner, and Robertinho. There were also two players from the pop scene, Dave McDaniel, a bassist with Joe Cocker, and Jay Graydon, a guitarist, producer, and songwriter. There was Dave Amaro, Flora's guitarist, on a couple tunes, and Airto on most of them. The engineer was Rob Fabroni, who had worked with The Band and other rock groups. And finally, Jim Price, a multi-instrumentalist who had worked with the Rolling Stones, produced the record. "This grouping of people showed how Wayne perceived my music," Milton said. "There was a little of everything here and there, but all in the right places. Aside from being beautiful, this record opened a new way for me to put together pop, blues, jazz, everything. Wayne is amazing 'cause besides being an excellent musician, he has perception in the heart and in the mind that's above average."

The Brazilian musicians were clearly awed by the novelty of recording with one of their jazz heroes in America. Wayne knew he had to demystify their inflated notions about the session; if they went into the studio with that reverence, the music might be stiff. So Wayne eased everyone into the recording with a retreat and hang at his home. Ana Maria, the Portuguese-speaker, translated as necessary. Sometimes the musicians found other ways to get meaning across. "Wayne and I understood each other, even though I didn't speak English," Robertinho said. "We would stay up all night in his kitchen talking about whatever, and Ana Maria would come in and laugh so hard, 'cause she didn't understand a single word of what we were talking about. She'd say, 'How can you guys be talking?'"

Though his house was full of Brazilian musicians, Wayne was emphatic about not making a stylistically pure "Brazilian" record. "I didn't try to impose components on Milton and those guys," Wayne said. "There were no barriers, no demarcation lines. In reality there is no 'Brazilian Thing.' If I had heard something from Poland, like a hip polka, I would have called them and said let's do something together. Something like Chopin's mazurkas, where the polka is so far removed, but not that far removed from what he did. Music is like a piece of clay. You get inside it, make a cubbyhole, and then punch your way out."

In the opening bars of "Ponta de Areia," Milton's voice sounded like an ocean breeze gracing the hinterlands of Minas. "Ponta de Areia" referred to the final stop on the train line that connected Minas with Brazil's shoreline. Though the melody had the singsong quality of a nursery school rhyme, its odd 9/8 meter could be hard to follow. "When we first arrived in New York, there was a birthday party for some musician there," Milton said. "They wanted to hear me play something, so I went to the piano and started playing 'Ponta de Areia.' Some musicians grabbed their instruments, but none of them could follow the rhythm. Wayne walked into the party. I talked to him in a way I never do. I said, 'This song I'm playing, I want it on the record. It's *got* to be the first one. Otherwise I'm not in.' My mind must have been flying to the moon!"

Wayne smilingly watched everyone struggling with the song and said to Milton, "You're very tricky, 'cause it sounds like a children's song but no one else can follow you." Wayne did start off the album with the song. "It was about a train that was everyone's friend, and a train station that someone tried to get rid of," he said. "Most of the Tin Pan Alley songwriting style was infantile, except for some of the stuff that Sinatra did. But Milton didn't just write songs about romance, that 'You and me baby' stuff."

Along with his regular lyricists, Fernando Brandt and Marcio Borges, Milton wrote poetic rhapsodies on his homeland's history and sing-along homilies for a better future. If Sting got together with the poet Pablo Neruda, they might come up with something like Milton's lyrics.

"What can I say?" was Milton's terse description for "Lilia," a song named for his adoptive mother. "What can I say?" seemed like an irreverent response to a pesky demand for explanation, but the comment actually had some serious bearing on his music. Milton sang "Lilia" with wordless vocals, which was for him a style born of necessity and perfected under pressure. Under Brazil's military dictatorship in the sixties and seventies, the ruling regime monitored pop music, censoring anything seemingly rebellious. Musicians couldn't say much that was acceptable to the censors. Milton's compatriots Gilberto Gil and Caetano Veloso were exiled to London because of their controversial music. Airto Moreira and Flora Purim escaped the artistic restrictions by moving to the U.S. But Milton felt a responsibility to work within the repressive climate. "I had to be in Brazil; it's my country and I had a job to do," Milton said. "I didn't want to leave, no matter what happened."

When Milton recorded *Milagro dos Peixes* in 1973, the censors denied clearance on several of its songs. His record company asked him to write new lyrics. But Milton didn't want to play the military's editing game, which had no clear rules or logic. "The censors didn't really know which ones were protest songs and which ones were not," Airto explained. "Sometimes they'd say, 'No you can't sing that,' and it wasn't even a protest song, it was a love song." So Milton protested by singing without words, using his voice in an instrumental role. Fans got the message and the record was a hit. (The censors then became suspicious of Milton's voice itself. "At the time, I did lots of stuff with Nana Vasconcelos," Milton said. "Stuff without lyrics, just sounds and voices and birds, and censors would ask, 'What does this voice or bird mean?' It was funny.")

Milton's voice had always been expressive, but after using wordless vocals it became supremely so. On *Native Dancer*'s "Lilia," a single note trembled with all his doubts as a black kid in an all-white town; then a melodic leap triumphed with love for his mother's protection. On "Tarde," he seemed to lean into a pitch as long as an entire afternoon, until its tone finally gave way to perpetual twilight. Even more dramatic expression came in his musical interaction with Wayne. "After Wayne soloed, when Milton would come back in, you couldn't even tell it was a voice," Herbie said. "Because when Wayne played, it sang, and Milton's singing has an instrumental quality." Beyond their telepathic trade-off of tones and timbres, the two men shared the same spiritual passion in their sound.

Wayne was so enchanted by Milton, his "brother," that he wanted to use him throughout the record. Milton tracked vocals for each song, but then advised Jim Price not to include his voice on all the tracks. So Wayne's three original tunes on *Native Dancer* were instrumentals, though the spirit of Milton's soaring lyricism suffused Wayne's solos, which were some of the most romantic and purely emotional of his career. One tuneful instrumental was "Diana," a ballad Wayne wrote for the newborn daughter of Flora and Airto. Wayne paid tribute to his wife with a more pensive ballad, "Ana Maria." The song didn't embody her personality so much as it chronicled her shifting moods. Milton later recorded the tune on an album of his own. "The poetry that Ana represented to him came across beautifully in that song," Milton said. "Ana was a perfect companion for Wayne. She brought him many things, she was a link for him to get to know many things, 'cause she was involved with so many people." The relaxed intimacy of the session inspired Wayne to play the melody with loving affection on soprano. But the rhythm section intermittently rose up and struck back at his horn lines, personifying another aspect of Wayne's wife: "One of the best things for Wayne was how Ana would kick his ass," Joe Zawinul said. Ana Maria's presence went well beyond this eponymous ballad. Wayne said she was the "tenth player" on the record, her contribution "equal in desire and performance."

On "Beauty and the Beast," Herbie delved into street funk rhythms on piano that captured all the urban optimism of his 1969 album *Fat Albert Rotunda*. The final tune on the album was Herbie's "Joanna's Theme," from his soundtrack to *Death Wish* starring Charles Bronson, a song that was a rare tender touch in the film's bleak story of revenge. Herbie was in a romantic mood, too, accompanying Wayne's soprano with lush arpeggios.

"When the album was near to completion, we all knew authenticity and honesty had won," Wayne wrote in the liner notes. Reviews, however, were sharply divided. *Native Dancer* was "rhythmically monotonous Gallic balladry" with "generally mellifluous, often naive meditations," as *Coda* and *Jazz Journal International* respectively judged it. *Down Beat*, on the other hand, called it "an entirely accessible, thoroughly satisfying LP that continuously discloses harmonious surprises and bursts of sweet wildness."

Whatever its critical reception, *Native Dancer* raised Milton's profile, especially in Europe, and he went on to become one of the most popular Brazilian musicians in the world. And in Brazil, the American saxophonist with the sympathetic sound intrigued Milton's fans. "For Wayne to record Milton's music the way he did, so deeply and with jazzy roots but that kind of Afro-Brazilian bluesy stuff, it was very well done," Airto said. "It got the attention of the Brazilians 'cause he hit right there at the target and everyone said, 'Wow, what is this and who is this?'" For many Brazilians, the record was an entrée to jazz: They sought out Wayne's Weather Report records, then bought his records with Miles, and then checked out his Blue Note catalog of the sixties. *Native Dancer* had an extraordinary effect on some people, Wayne said: "I got a letter from a surgeon who said he listens to all kinds of music—ballet, opera—and that my stuff with Milton has inspired him to be a better surgeon in the operating room, better husband to his wife, father to his kids, citizen in the world."

For years after they recorded together, whenever Wayne and Milton were performing anywhere in the same vicinity, one would make a guest appearance at the other's show. In Milton, Wayne found a musician who gave voice to his own flights of fancy, and a friend who was as stubborn as he was in refusing to give up on imagination. Wayne later played on several of Milton's recordings, many of which bore the unmistakable influence of *Native Dancer.* On *Milton,* Wayne joined the singer on one of his most unabashedly idealistic "castle in the sky" tunes, "Fairy Tale Song." Milton's English lyrics included lines like these: "Where are all your friends from the old days, Tinkerbell and Peter Pan? / Where is all the hope Snow White tried to give you? / Show me all the games you know from the stories / So that I can play."

Milton likes to tell a story about a time when Wayne was at the singer's oceanfront home in Rio for a party. Everyone drank to high gaiety, except Wayne ("No drinking? That doesn't sound like me at all," Wayne joked. "Maybe I was on antibiotics"). Wayne's sobriety didn't prevent him from suddenly deciding he was a storybook character. He stood on a window ledge, yelling, "I'm Peter Pan, I can fly!" and then jumped out the window, landing on the balcony a few feet below. Milton later converted that balcony into a small outdoor amphitheater and dedicated it to Wayne with a commemorative plaque. "When I think about the gifts that music brought me, Wayne is one of the most important ones," Milton said.

Elegant People in
Heavy Weather

THOUGH WAYNE'S 1975 *Native Dancer* recording had great personal meaning and value for him, it was just a single, one-month project. Wayne's main gig was Weather Report, and he and Joe were its foundation, sustaining the band as a kind of cottage industry throughout the seventies. The group's other personnel shifted, with especially an assorted cast of characters cycling through the drum chair in the mid-seventies. For bassist Alphonso Johnson, this game of musical chairs was the most memorable thing about working with Weather Report. "We would be on tour and we would land in a city," he said. "I would be at the airport watching Joe at the gate greeting the new drummer who was coming in that day while Wayne was at the baggage check saying good-bye to the drummer who'd played the previous night, saying, 'Well it was good,' or whatever Wayne said in his Wayne way. That was the tour, and there were several tours like that." This was frustrating for Alphonso, who was demoted to playing timekeeper onstage, since the drummers never stuck around long enough to settle into the role. Alphonso knew that these players were simply too intimidated to do their best playing: "Most of the drummers, God bless their souls, were so petrified of playing with Joe and Wayne that they never even got a chance to play what they normally did—the thing that got them there in the first place." Drummer Chester Thompson finally did click with the band, but by then Alphonso was burned out, and gave Joe and Wayne his notice.

That's when a twenty-five-year-old bassist from Florida named Jaco Pastorius entered into Weather Report's epic story. The braggadocio of his self-introduction to Joe gave the band a hint of his extreme personality: "My name is John Francis Pastorius the Third, and I'm the greatest bass player in the world." In some ways, Jaco *was* the greatest electric-bass player in the world—certainly the most spectacular one—and he came to dominate Weather Report with his brilliance. In Weather Report's traditional way, they auditioned Jaco in the studio, using him on a couple tracks on *Black Market*. The bassist then made his live debut with the band on April 1, 1976, in Ann Arbor, Michigan.

Jaco impacted the band like an earthquake. Weather Report began playing his compositions as quickly as Blakey and Miles had played Wayne's—that first concert included "Continuum" and "Come On, Come Over" from Jaco's first solo album, as well as his "Barbary Coast" from *Black Market*. As a performer, Jaco was as audacious as he was gifted. "Jaco had the long hair and the bandanna tied around his head, and he was always jumping off the stage," Wayne said. "He had a very pronounced way of playing, and there was an immediate presence of tone on his bass, which looked like a guitar. He had everything to give the audience that rock association." Jaco was a force of nature on the electric bass, the Jimi Hendrix of the instrument. Weather Report toured with Jaco, drummer Alex Acuña, and percussionist Manolo Badrena throughout the spring and summer of 1976 before going into the studio to make another record.

This record, *Heavy Weather,* was the band's biggest critical and commercial success, with catchy, grooving music that nevertheless stretched the musicians artistically. Wayne's "Palladium" was a tune dedicated to the Fifty-second Street club where he played in a band opposite Tito Puente in the fifties, stealing the show with his early composition "Midget Mambo." The Palladium was next door to Birdland, and it was Joe's tune by this name that was Weather Report's breakout hit. "Birdland" was the opening track on *Heavy Weather,* and it was a revelation for many music lovers and young players coming of age in the seventies, with Jaco's introductory bass harmonics, state-of-the-art production, and a true fusion of Wayne, Joe, and Jaco as equal contributors to the performance. Much jazz-rock was based on simple musical structures like vamps, but Joe and Wayne both devised compositional forms of considerable sophistication. Critics noticed that Joe's "Birdland" incorporated a history of jazz styles in its celebratory groove, but rock fans were blissfully unconcerned with the details, and the record went gold. Weather Report had previously played 2,500-seat halls. Either Jaco or *Heavy Weather* alone would have popularized the band, but the combination was explosive. *Heavy Weather* gave them a hit, and Jaco's stage presence gave them the flamboyance of an arena band. They began playing festivals and stadiums, finally achieving the success they'd been building toward for several years.

But in the interim, Wayne had begun practicing Buddhism, and music had increasingly taken second place for him. With Weather Report's popular rise in 1976–77, Wayne was thrust into the most prominent and demanding musical job of his life. At age forty-four, his durability was tested like never before. Jaco would sometimes tease Wayne about his whitening hair: "You been painting the ceiling of Iska's bedroom again?" he'd ask. By the mid-seventies, jazz was a young-man's game—the most commercially successful jazz musicians catered to a youthful audience. The Mahavishnu Orchestra had thrived on the flaming virtuosity of John McLaughlin's guitar; Herbie's Headhunters flourished on feel-good funk; Freddie Hubbard's

Red Clay had hooked an audience with funky vamps. The fusion scene wasn't the best environment for a bop-schooled musician approaching middle age. But in many ways, Wayne was lucky: Some jazz musicians of the previous bebop generation, like Bird or Bud Powell, hadn't even lived past their mid-forties.

Beyond his playing and composing skills, Jaco was an expert in studio production, especially nimble at the mixing board. On *Heavy Weather,* Jaco earned co-producer credit with Joe, while Wayne received credit as an assistant producer. "One time they stayed in the studio for forty-two hours, and I said, 'I'll see you guys later,'" Wayne said. "To them, what could be more important than getting ahead? They were like, Michelangelo wouldn't do that, leave his art behind. Sometimes I'd leave the studio to be a moderator at Buddhist meetings. We'd talk about dedication in Buddhism, and I was thinking there's another kind of dedication going on here, to something other than art." As it turned out, the "life versus art" conflict in Wayne's favorite movie, *The Red Shoes,* was more than a fictional romantic trope. He was now aware of the conflict on a daily basis.

Fans assumed that Jaco drove a wedge between Wayne and Joe and relegated Wayne to a background role. Wayne said he was actually making another choice, "a life choice that transcended profession, position, or station." His withdrawal was a self-exile: "Everyone talked and wrote about the onslaught of my partners, Jaco and Joe, but that's wrong. It was something I was going through myself. Other aspects of my life were developing. I was going through a metamorphosis, like the pain of being born. Parts of myself that had been stunted for a long time started to grow, and they met resistance. If value is being created in your life, you meet a lot of resistance. A lot of resistance came in the form of 'Hey, you're not taking care of your music, you're not the one-hundred-percent musician you're supposed to be.' But I let everything go, I didn't try to do some forced music, which would have been catastrophic, to commit that kind of suicide."

It's easier for a camel to pass through the eye of a needle than for a man to reach enlightenment in a band on the road. Touring made Wayne's Buddhist practice irregular—he'd steal a few moments for morning and evening chanting while staring at a blank wall in a hotel room, or riding on a train or bus, turning the preferably private ritual into a public exhibition. Joe viewed the practice with some disbelief. He sometimes stood outside Wayne's hotel room door listening to his chanting. When Wayne came out, Joe would say, "Nam-myoho-renge-kyo . . . It sounds like you're saying, 'I know, I don't know, I know, I don't know.' Why don't you decide?" Sometimes, Joe was derisive. "I used to make fun of it, which wasn't right," Joe said. "'So fucking what, you chant?' I'd say, but I was just fooling around. I'd actually tell Wayne, you chant as much as you want."

Wayne strove to reconcile his Buddhist practice with his musical life, but it wasn't always easy to find a Middle Way on tour. Jaco and Joe were competitive and athletic, engaged in contests of strength offstage and on—the music itself was a battleground for them. "People said they heard a volume battle between the synthesizers and the bass," Wayne said. "A lot of times they were playing the same bass lines in the arrangement. You might say that people were looking at Jaco and then over at Joe, like it was a tennis match—who's going to be the loudest? Who exuded the most presence with the volume carpet that they had at their command? They had accessibility to the knobs. Who's going to take his hand off the knobs first?"

Instruments have distinct personalities that can influence the musical roles in a band. With its broad chordal and rhythmic capacity, the piano can account for all the parts in a band. As keyboardist, Joe naturally had omniscient command of Weather Report; his fondness for synthesized effects only enlarged his sphere of influence. Conventionally, the bass solidly holds down the bottom of the band, hence the stereotype of bassists as good-natured and plodding. Jaco rejected that role, playing soaring, dynamic melodies on the traditionally sturdy, low-riding instrument and commanding territory that had previously been the province of the saxophone.

Wayne always thought like a composer and orchestrator when he improvised, so he tried to accommodate Jaco's flexible bass personality with an instrument update himself. He sometimes played the Lyricon, a breath-controlled synthesizer that looked like an electronic saxophone, a wind instrument reborn as a wind machine. "One time I had a Lyricon, and that had a range," Wayne said. "I could do a bass or flute with that. I used it sometimes to free Jaco up, so he didn't have to be down doing *boom boom, boom* [sings walking bass line]. I'd do a bass line with the Lyricon, so Jaco could be up going *do, do do* [sings fluid melodic run]. But then Jaco came out and played a little tiny bass, less than a foot long. Like *la la la* [sings a fiddle-like line befitting a circus band]. So I think Jaco was a combination of a lot of talent and showmanship. 'Cause he liked James Brown, he liked getting the audience involved and all that."

Wayne's musical mediation didn't have much effect, because the group's battles weren't really about music. They were about ego—and about arming oneself with the latest technological charms. In the seventies, new musical equipment was showing up almost monthly, so if Joe tested out a Robert Moog synthesizer prototype, or Wayne tried out a Lyricon, then Jaco would toy with a midget bass, whatever its musical effect.

Drummer Peter Erskine joined Weather Report in 1978, and the group became stable for several years. Peter had been in Stan Kenton's and Maynard Ferguson's big bands and was also conversant in jazz-rock rhythms. "He was acquainted with straight-ahead jazz as well as so-called fusion that called for a driving beat," Wayne said. "The communication that Peter and Jaco locked into at different times kind of helped us chill and thrill the audiences. And also Peter was healthy, young, strong, with a solid physique. We'd play three-hour concerts, and he was always ready to do it, ready to go. Also, Peter listened whenever we had talks. He was not an obstinate person who said, 'You can't show me nothin', 'cause I was with Stan Kenton.' He didn't ask, 'What should I play?'" Above all, the bandleaders demanded savoir faire in their young sidemen. "When I first joined the band, I was fearless," Peter said. "For all the laudables or bad things you could say about the drumming, at least you could say that I wasn't looking too much for permission." But Peter didn't "make his bones" in the band until he was agitated into a confrontation with Joe onstage one night.

"Because of the volume of the band, and the fact that the band was doing a show—we had all these hot lights—at the end of the night I'd be exhausted," Peter said. "So I said to Joe, when I'm maxed out I'll shoot you a look, and then you'll know I'm shot. So he was like, yeah, yeah, okay. The next time we played, I ramped it up at the end. Then I gave the signal to Joe, but he just looks at me kind of nonplussed, sort of half smiles, digs into his keyboards and turns up the volume louder, and we have to do this whole long cycle again—we can't get out of the tune for another minute or two. And so now I'm hitting the drums with an incredible amount of anger, imagining that the cymbals or drums were Joe's head. And finally Joe turns around triumphantly and says, 'Now we'll end it.' And I said, 'Nuh uh, no we won't.' I just start smacking the snare drum as hard as I could. I look up, and Joe has jumped up on the drum riser, perched on the very edge with half his shoes under my bass drum and an incredibly excited face. He yells, "Yeah, yeah, yeah, yeah!" punching his fist into the air like it's the coolest thing ever. And so it just finally ends and I stopped. I was emotionally depleted. Joe came over and goes, 'Thank you, man,' shaking my hand. The band talked about it later, saying, 'Peter got the spirit, he got the ghost.' And they all thought that it was a really cool thing, that finally I stopped being the sideman." With brawny muster, young Peter thus bludgeoned his way into the back of the cave.

Wayne struggled to find an elegant role in these onstage antics at the same time that he struggled to integrate Buddhist philosophy into his everyday life. "I came to a point where I didn't want to see anybody and didn't want to go out anywhere," he said. "I'd be out at a restaurant having dinner with people and go into a men's room and just stand there looking in the mirror for a long time—sometimes *half an hour*—and then time myself to walk out around people." Wayne's impatience with casual conversation and escape from his dinner companions were "based on a distorted view of Buddhist principles," he said. He didn't fully understand how they related to the actual world, and so the world seemed somehow contaminated to him. "I had to find out that the mundane world is where the principles of this Buddhism come from," he said. "You know the lotus flower that grows in the swamp? The swamp is the mundane world, the negative, and the negative tells you what the positive is." The lotus flower, which blossoms in a muddy swamp, symbolizes the growth of Buddha nature from the desires and problems of everyday life.

Most people are aware that Buddhism involves compassion, and yet the concept is often misunderstood. The word's Western meaning comes from its Latin root, which means "feeling with." For most English-speakers, compassion connotes a sensitive vibe, a kind of sympathetic emotional state—feeling sorry for your fellow man or at least trying to avoid gloating over someone else's bad luck. The Nichiren Buddhist concept of compassion is much more involved. It comes from the Japanese term *jihi*. *Ji* means "giving pleasure and happiness"; *hi* means "removing pain and suffering." Developing compassion in this sense was a long and active process for Wayne. First he had to investigate the roots of unhappiness, to understand its causes. Only after he'd understood suffering could he cultivate happiness in its place. "When you practice Nichiren Buddhism, you go through a lot of different phases," Herbie said. "It can get heavy—things can occur to you that have a stark clarity in your mind, that never occurred before, and they become issues that you have to deal with."

Wayne's bandmates weren't necessarily aware of the heavy changes he was going through. Well before he began his Buddhist practice, he'd developed a reputation as an eccentric, and his bandmates saw his spirituality simply as another strange and harmless aspect of his genius. Part of his "human revolution" was about recovering his fifteen-year-old persona, and Wayne's childlike enthusiasm for film and books was anything but stodgy. Once he went to a wrap party for *Virus,* a Japanese film with American actors and a score by Teo Macero. Afterward he was excited about the film—for Wayne, this meant suddenly looking sideways at someone, smiling, and calling out "*Virus!*" with impish glee. When a novelization of the film came out, he looked for the book on tour in Japan, and finally found a copy in Sapporo. At that night's show he playfully stuck the paperback under his coat and repeatedly pulled it out to show everyone. Joe just nodded knowingly, but Peter made the mistake of pointing out that the book was in Japanese. "How are you gonna read it?" he asked. Wayne looked at Peter disappointedly, like "You will *never get it.*" Wayne brought this single-mindedness to all his passions and interests. One day while the rest of the band went sightseeing in Rome, Wayne dedicated himself to searching for a particular handbag for Ana Maria. He didn't find it, despite the fact that his spare time for several days was spent combing the shops in each town, seeking out the holy-grail purse.

Wayne's odd routines provided a safe port for Joe. "Whenever we went to hotels, the first thing Wayne would do was call room service," Joe said. "So as soon as I put my bags down, I'd rush to call them first, or I knew the phone would be locked up for fifteen minutes with Wayne's order. In the big hotels, the nice ones, he'd have the oven shipped up with the candles, the thing they have to keep the food warm, a real elaborate setup, 'cause he'd *never* leave his room. The incense smell would be so strong you could always find his room. I'd get hungry sometimes in the middle of the night, and I'd go to his room 'cause he'd be up, reading and watching a movie. At three o'clock in the morning he'd always have nice fresh steak, potatoes. He kept me alive. He was always a lot of fun, and it was a very great friendship."

Wayne stopped drinking for a full year with Miles, in 1967, but as he struggled with the tension between his spirituality and responsibilities in the real world, his drinking problem reemerged. Wayne and Joe always fueled their rapport by "bending the elbow" together, usually with cognac. "I remember one time going to the bar, waiting for them to come down before we went to the gig," Alphonso said. "Wayne ordered *three double shots* of cognac. And then just sat there. He was looking at them, twisting the glasses around, and as soon as Joe showed up, Joe ordered two, and then Wayne went *glop, glop, glop,* and just knocked them back. It was amazing how much they could drink and then play and stay up all night."

"We started drinking before the show," Joe said. "After the sound check, we'd have a little something, we'd eat well, no problem. I don't think we ever once went on the bandstand sober. But that was our life, that was Weather Report, one of the greatest music bands in history." Joe and Wayne regaled younger musicians with war stories of how they would knock back five or six boilermakers in the cab on the way to their house-band gigs in the fifties, and still manage to play 128 tunes from memory.

The trouble was that Wayne went on drinking after the show. "After the gig, Wayne used to load up before the bar closed," Joe said. "He'd have a cognac in a water glass, up to *there* [points to brim of glass]. I'd pour it out and say, 'Wayne, do something else. Go to sleep. This is no good.' His eyes were all crossed."

In a rare interview with writer David Breskin for *Musician* magazine in 1981, Ana Maria spoke about the cause of Wayne's drinking: "Wayne always told me that being on the road is the loneliest thing; 'It's lonely out there,' he'd say. I guess drinking filled up that hole." Wayne felt worse knowing that Ana Maria was left with the burden of Iska's care while he was out on the road. As Iska had grown a little older, they'd realized the cause and extent of her brain damage, which relieved their uncertainty. But there was no escaping the sadness of raising a child with Iska's problems. "By the time my daughter was seven, she went to school with a helmet on and rode on a special school bus," Wayne said later. "She was different. She was profoundly brain-damaged, but the pathologist said she's very bright, she can receive but she can't send. She hears you, is reading your eyes, and is growing up. They put things in front of her, square pegs, geometric forms, colors. One time, they took her down a hall in the school, not through a maze exactly, but to the place where the cafeteria was. They had her find her way back to the classroom. She knew where it was. Even when she was all fixed up in a new dress, she had to walk with her hands 'cause she was always ready to fall, but she was *cute*."

In the same interview with Breskin, Wayne talked candidly about Iska's effect on his life. "It takes a human revolution when you got to do something because your daughter's got brain damage and you can't do anything, you feel like you can't do anything about it. . . . I mean, you can't ignore the notion of karma. Why are we together, Iska and I? Why are we linked together? Iska was normal for three months, until she got that shot; I said *never mind* the shot, her life came in this condition to change ours, to open our eyes. It's very funny, but it's like . . . Iska kicking my butt, and at the same time, she's contributing a helluva message to us, every moment we look at her. She's fortifying us, she's helping us become indestructibly happy—even in the face of droughts and external catastrophes."

So for Wayne, the height of Weather Report's success was a time of major growing pains with few artistic gains. In that 1981 interview, he admitted that he went through a long compositional drought in this period: "I was struggling, trying to write—starting about four and a half years ago—trying to break through, wondering who else is like this, in the world, struggling and struggling. It was very painful trying to write, for the first time. I've heard about painters who would stop in the middle of the canvas and say, 'That's all . . . I have nothing more to paint.' That's how I felt. I was worried I'd gone dry, permanently, I'd wonder." For twenty-five years, he had scribbled out tunes as prolifically and unselfconsciously as a child absorbed in a coloring book. And then nothing came. Though Wayne's loss of inspiration worried him, he had to trust that the drought would ultimately yield something better. "You have to believe that something's happening to make you produce something more worthy, more humanistic than what you've been writing before," Wayne said. "You have to ask yourself, *Do you want to find out what's hidden? Can you take it?* 'Cause it's a situation where you're gonna have to go on vacation while we do this operation, and your real self comes out."

Miles Davis had been enormously innovative in the fifties and sixties, but was even more uninspired than Wayne in the late seventies. Fans gossiped about how far the mighty trumpet hero had fallen—word spread of a misanthrope confined to a messy palace of an apartment with drugs as his only escape. Given Miles's decline, it seemed especially unfair to Joe that the media persisted in crediting the trumpeter for Weather Report's success, and for spawning the entire fusion phenomenon. Wayne was happy to give Miles credit for the trend he'd launched with records like *In a Silent Way* and *Bitches Brew*: "Miles was the source for it all, for me and Joe going on to do Weather Report, for John McLaughlin's Mahavishnu Orchestra, and for Chick Corea and Return to Forever. We were all in the studio with Miles as he was going in that direction, and then we took off from there." But Joe's irritation with the "offspring of Miles business" reached its limit when the band received a 1-star rating from *Down Beat* for its 1978 record *Mr. Gone*. Commandeered by Joe, Weather Report took a public stand against their "children of Miles" labeling in the summer of 1978. "There was a big press conference before our concert in Rome, we were doing the Olympic indoor stadium," Peter said. "The band said, 'No questions about Miles. The first question about Miles, we'll walk out.' So promoters, you know . . . the first question that's asked at this press conference is about Miles. Joe, Wayne, and Jaco just kind of all look at each other, just like that TV show *What's My Line?* All three of them stood up and then they exited. They thought that that would be making a statement."

In public, Wayne joined Weather Report in this Miles boycott—why sit there answering the same tired old questions when he could be back in his hotel room? But in private, Wayne remained close to Miles throughout his "dark period." When they spoke on the phone, Wayne confided in him about his difficulty writing music. Miles would say, "Yeah, man, I know what you mean; if there ain't no more, there ain't no more." Miles seemed relieved to have some company in misery. Wayne attributed Miles's lack of onstage motivation to his sidemen. "Miles would call a lot and he'd say, 'If you don't have anything to say, why play?' But I knew he didn't have the company he wanted to be in, too. He didn't want to go out there and be the lead horse on the stagecoach, pulling all the guys along. I always wondered, *Who entertains Miles?* Coltrane, for sure, and he really enjoyed Bill Evans, and then there was the thing he did with us. But who entertained Miles in later years?"

In 1978, drummer Jack DeJohnette released a tune called "Where or Wayne?" on his *New Directions* recording. Critics and fans read the title as a commentary on Wayne's self-effacement, but Jack said it was simply a tribute: "It was like, 'Where *or* Wayne?' like you'd say 'Where or When?' It was just a tune dedicated to Wayne, and was inspired by his tune 'Masqualero,' actually. It was a musical tribute to Wayne. I've also written them for Ahmad Jamal, Miles, Eric Dolphy, Ellington, 'cause I like penning musical tributes to people I like." These facts didn't stop the tide of opinion that Joe and Jaco's dominance had marginalized Wayne's role in the group. When the band released *Mr. Gone* in 1978, the record had only one composition by Wayne. Like "Where or Wayne?" some saw the record's title as a statement on Wayne's absence. Actually, Wayne *was* responsible for the "Mr. Gone" title. He burst forth with it in a bit of spontaneous poetry. When Joe brought in the tune for rehearsal and Jaco started in on the bass line, Wayne marveled at the strangeness of the line, exclaiming, "That's gone! That's so gone, it's '*Mr.* Gone'!" In the bebop days, "gone" was slang for "out of this world."

Even the least reactionary critics were perplexed by Wayne's disappearing act. Bob Blumenthal reviewed a show for *Rolling Stone* in late 1978: "Shorter, who played ferocious tenor sax on the [concert] opening "Black Market," continues to maintain a low profile. For those who recall his prolific output with the Jazz Messengers, with Miles Davis and on his own Blue Note albums, Shorter's reticence is an endless disappointment. . . . If Shorter's priorities seem odd, we can only assume that when he chooses to play and write more, he will. Part of the problem may be that he has done it so often before. 'You know I'm forty-five years old,' he says, as if he still can't believe it himself. 'In five years I'll be fifty! Fifty!' "

Wayne weathered the criticism, protected by the deep sense of artistic purpose he had developed long before. Bud Powell had sought *him* out in his Paris hotel room one night. He had a package of Charlie Parker's musical goods that had been bequeathed to *him*. His collaboration with Milton Nascimento had confirmed that his musicianship transcended national borders. And most important, Wayne had already proven himself with Miles. "Miles had the most charisma of anyone, even when he just stood still there and played," he said. "What was coming out of him was so happening, and the way he looked so good in his clothes . . . standing next to him, you wanted to go to the gym. It was a challenge to compete with Miles in front of people so that you actually felt good about how you looked and what you were producing." Wayne remembered when they played at the Village Gate in 1969. He had looked so sharp that jazz neophytes in the audience couldn't distinguish him from Miles. "That was the pinnacle of my show-business stuff," Wayne said. "The acid test, playing alongside Miles, staying cool with the audience, so anything after that didn't bother me . . . after that, I could never care about whether I was 'projecting' onstage or whether I was dedicated enough."

And Wayne did take some solos at shows. His tenor sound was alive and well in his solo performance of "Thanks for the Memory" on *8:30,* the band's 1978 live album. This solo alone would have been a clean bill of health for most players, but the accomplishment was obscured in the haze of his Mr. Gone mystique. Though Wayne was in crisis as a composer, he actually had a healthy confidence as a player, no matter how much or little he played. "There was no need to be in any rush to be visible," he said. "It was value-less to always play as if I were One of the Founding Fathers of Weather Report, one of the 'often sounding' founding fathers they wanted me to be. So when I was not stepping out in front, soloing, I was doing orchestration, thinking, *Man, if I had twenty cellos, this is what it would sound like here.* It was almost like tai chi going on."

Herbie found shrewdness and generosity in his friend's musical background dance. "I heard people saying, 'Wayne's not playing a lot,'" Herbie said. "So I checked it out, but when I listened, I didn't hear it the same way. What I heard was that if he played more, it wouldn't fit. Joe Zawinul had a way of doing things that could be pretty busy, so if Wayne was busy, too, that would be a lot of busyness. Besides, Jaco was playing the saxophone part, in a way—he's got all the countermelodies, so Wayne did more of the long-tone things, the things that have space, which made the other guys come out better." Herbie could be a master of discretion himself, supporting soloists with just the right piano chord voicings so that their phrases came out in starker relief.

For Herbie, it came down to ego. "Wayne had an ego, but kept it in check," he said. "He did what he thought was necessary under the circumstances. The great thing about jazz is that it's about sharing. Wayne and I know it's all about the service." But as Wayne's Lyricon experiments proved, charity didn't go far in Weather Report. It had worked in Miles's quintet, where everyone recognized a good turn and was ready to follow the best musical idea, but it didn't mean much in a fusion band on an ego trip. Herbie himself conceded to the grand gesture of a big funky sound in his Headhunters group, which was a phenomenal success. But however much Wayne's humility guaranteed invisibility and his kindness was taken for weakness, he stuck with subtlety—as he said, "Anything else would have been suicide."

Herbie also had some onstage evidence that Wayne's musicianship was intact. Herbie reconvened Miles's sixties quintet for an acoustic show as part of his three-concert retrospective showcase at the 1976 JVC Festival. Joining the old group of Herbie, Wayne, Ron Carter, and Tony Williams was Freddie Hubbard in place of Miles. The band's music was close enough to the sacred sound of the sixties to please jazz purists, but in some ways the group was actually a fusion band in an acoustic setting. They used group improvisation, intertwined solos, big drumming, and repeated keyboard riffs—some of the strengths of fusion that could get lost in its electronic wash of sound.

Herbie's JVC showcase was billed and recorded as VSOP, as in "Very Special One-Time Performance," touting the rareness of his career retrospective. VSOP also referred to the superior variety of cognac for which Wayne and Herbie shared a copious appreciation. The clean, cultivated flavor of VSOP made it a fitting label for the classic style of the acoustic quintet. The following year, the quintet toured as VSOP with sponsorship from a Courvoisier distributor. "What do you call something that gets finer with age?" Herbie said, suggesting that he and the other musicians—the young lions of the previous decade—had benefited from age and experience, maturing like fine cognac into a deeper subtlety and elegance. Most fusion, on the other hand, was brewed up and sold off as quickly as bathtub gin. So though only eight years had passed since the breakup of

Miles's quintet, VSOP was greeted with a nostalgia usually reserved for artists in their golden years. Wayne talked to writer Conrad Silvert in May 1977, just before the band hit the road: "When we go out on the VSOP tour, generations who never saw us perform in the sixties will get a chance to see what we look like playing together," he said. "It's like seeing if an actor can play more than one Shakespearean role."

The VSOP tour also meant that combined with his Weather Report work, Wayne spent forty-two consecutive weeks on the road during 1977. "The reward was being able to do it," Wayne said. "Meaning I didn't make excuses for not being able to do it." He said he also needed the money: "The financial reward at that time was right on time." Contrary to popular belief, even after Weather Report's success with *Heavy Weather,* the band was not exactly rolling in riches. With no tour support from Columbia, Wayne and Joe were forced to put a lot of their earnings back into the band, covering the costs of a seventeen-man road crew. Their managers, Joe Ruffalo and Bob Cavallo, eventually negotiated for the band to receive a monthly stipend from Columbia Records, arguing the group should be treated like a "state band" rather than a "profit center."

In VSOP, Wayne gave some electrifying performances and enjoyed spending time with his old friends. But for him, there was no contentment in reliving old times. "It's like when they were tearing down the old Met," Wayne said. "Somebody asked an opera singer, 'Are you going to miss it?' He shot back, 'No!'"

"No matter who it was I was playing with, I was learning to see something through, to see the benefit of something that's pleasant, just as I see the benefit of something that is averse to that," he said. Not all VSOP members shared Wayne's philosophical approach, and there were a few flare-ups on the road. "When we did the VSOP tour, it was the best band I ever worked in," Freddie said. "Everybody was good. But sometimes I'd get mad at Tony for playing too loud." Miles had always indulged Tony's thunderous sound. During sound checks, engineers occasionally asked if they should reduce his volume; Miles would threateningly advise them, "Leave the drummer alone." But Freddie was so irritated by Tony's force that he once kicked Tony's drums off the stage—for a musician, this was tantamount to slapping his only child.

When Freddie and the group had a fatal falling out a couple years later, Herbie invited the young trumpeter Wynton Marsalis to play with them. Wayne dropped out of the group to spend more time at home with Iska, but Herbie, Ron, and Tony went to play on part of Wynton's debut recording, which Herbie also produced. VSOP's acoustic setting presented an alternative style to young musicians like Wynton who were not interested in following electric trends. It was around this time that Wynton showed up by surprise at Wayne's house and humbly asked if they could listen to *Live at the Plugged Nickel* together. "Wayne and I talked about other things, 'cause I had an autism in my family and his daughter had trouble, too," Wynton said. "But I wanted to hear that record with him. A lot of times if you listen to music with musicians—it doesn't matter if it's music they played on—it can give you insight into what it is. Once I listened with Dizzy to a recording he made with Charlie Parker. He'd make comments, like yeah, we were doin' this or doin' that. It's easy to learn a lot more about something that way; I didn't know all my music history yet when I first went over to see Wayne." Wynton quickly gained self-confidence and grew into a force to be reckoned with. With his success in the mid-eighties, he launched a neo-conservative trend in jazz that affected Wayne and everyone in the business.

13.

Wild Flowers

ONE DAY in the summer of 1976, Wayne came home from tour to find soul diva Tina Turner scrubbing his kitchen floor. Tina was a Nichiren Buddhist. She lived with Wayne and Ana Maria during the critical period when she was separating from her husband, Ike.

Tina was introduced to the practice through Ike, inadvertently. "Know anything about chantin'?" he asked Tina, then introduced her to a woman named Valerie Bishop. In Tina's description of her first encounter with Buddhism, in her memoirs, she seemed as impressed by the progressive interracial makeup of the "L.A. chanters" as by the practice itself. "There was a group of mixed-marriage couples in L.A.—Herbie Hancock's wife, Gigi, who was German; Wayne Shorter's wife, Ana, who was Portuguese;

and also my friend Maria Booker was married to a black musician. Valerie was one of those. And she was also a chanter."

Tina began chanting and quickly developed greater self-esteem, which made her less susceptible to Ike's physical and emotional abuse. Ike recognized the empowering effect the chanting practice was having on Tina, and so he discouraged it, which only confirmed its value to Tina. When their relationship reached a point of violent disintegration, she went to stay with Maria, but was in serious danger of being discovered there by Ike. So the week after the Fourth of July, Tina moved in with the Shorters. "She was cooking and cleaning and washing and everything," Wayne said. "She had nothing, during those four months she stayed with us. I was going in and out, on tour and recording. She was so quiet, you didn't even know she was there. Tina and Ana Maria were doing *daimoku,* chanting sometimes four hours without stopping. They were doing some intense things."

It didn't take Ike long to figure out where Tina was staying. Wayne went to the studio one evening, leaving Tina and Ana Maria at home. The two women were chanting in the Gohonzon room when Ana had a sudden intuition that someone unfriendly might be coming near the house. She turned on the lawn sprinklers. That way, anyone who tried to enter the house in any manner besides the traditional one—through the front door—might be deterred by the water.

A few minutes later, someone knocked on the front door. Tina went to get her .45 and returned to the Gohonzon room, which was a little like receiving Holy Communion armed with an ax. Ana warned, "No, no you can't bring a gun to the Gohonzon." Tina answered, "Ana, between the two of these things, I'm gonna be safe." Robbie, an ex-Ikette, was at the front door, sent there to do Ike's bidding. When Robbie called out for Tina, Ana Maria stood behind the locked door and did her best impression of a Portuguese maid: "Sorreee . . . es no one home."

"Ana Maria went to acting school," Wayne explained. "And she'd learned how to use the functions of the universe to protect herself. She channeled them like a magnet. She showed me how to do it, too."

Tina carefully peeked out a window. "Right across the street from the house was the Rolls-Royce," she wrote. "And there was Ike, in his jumpsuit and his big belt—looking real bad, right? And there were three or four straggly cars parked behind him, filled with every kind of low-life guy you can imagine—wearing the bad hats and the belts and all that stuff, too. They looked like a bunch of Mexican banditos—all comin' to get little Tina!" Ana and Tina called the police, who sent Ike away. When Wayne got home from the studio and heard the story, his relief in their safety was tinged with disappointment that he'd missed all the action. His own wife as a superheroine, using her uncanny intuition and sharp wits to take on Ike and his evil entourage!

Wayne found some inspiration in seeing another artist struggle with something in life beyond her career. "Maybe for the first time, in our house Tina was left to herself with no one looking over her shoulder, no one giving her orders. There was no Ike, no dictator," Wayne said. "She was in a place where she was making all the decisions for herself and making causes to support her new role. Tina was actually learning to make causes that she never made before to attain the effects that she never had before and among those were the cause and effect to stand alone, which has nothing to do with singing." Tina's career comeback took ten years, but she eventually went on to success as a solo artist in the eighties with the Grammy Award–winning *Private Dancer,* and her life story was made into a film, *What's Love Got to Do with It.* "Tina was getting her fortune together, chanting to make it on her own," Wayne said. "Her fortune grew, and she attributed all the success to her practice."

Tina also attracted some curious people to Buddhist meetings. "Some people came just to see Tina," Wayne said. "Nina Simone came to two meetings. The guy from *West Side Story,* the leader of the Latin dancers, George Chakiris, he came, too. He was in a movie about Hawaii, too, a good guy, and he played in a movie called *Kings of the Sun,* about sacrifice and the Incas and Aztecs. George played the king in that one." Wayne clearly loved film, and Tina's presence in their home initiated him further into the Los Angeles movie-district scene and Hollywood lifestyle. Wayne and Ana became friends with Kareem Abdul-Jabbar, who served as best man at singer Gil Scott-Heron's wedding, which took place at the Shorters' home. They also became friendly with Jack Nicholson, who liked the way Wayne talked: "Rightly put," Jack would say to him. He invited Ana to the set of his movie *Borderline,* to see if she wanted a role in the film. Ana stayed there a week but ultimately "decided that she didn't want to be an actress, because real life was the real script," Wayne said.

Though Wayne didn't compose so much in the late seventies, Los Angeles did afford the opportunity of studio work on film soundtracks. He eventually went on to play on several soundtracks: *Round Midnight* (1986), for which he wrote a Grammy Award–winning composition, "Call Street Blues"; *Glengarry Glen Ross* (1992); *The Fugitive* (1993); and *Losing Isaiah* (1995). More immediate, Wayne had many offers to work with pop musicians. Jazz players usually avoided pop music like the plague, but living in L.A. naturalized Wayne to the pop scene, and made the prospect of working in it less transgressive. Also, the times had changed. If John Coltrane had played with the Beatles in 1964, he would have rocked the very foundation of the jazz world with scandal. The rise of fusion and progressive rock changed jazz in the seventies, blurring its division from pop music. Still, Wayne knew he would take some flack for pop appearances. He responded to potential critics with a rather obtuse analogy. "When I saw Marlon Brando playing in *Superman,* I thought, *The critics are going to go off, and wonder what Marlon Brando is doing in* Superman," Wayne said. "Even if it was only fifteen minutes. That's when I really dug him for that. I said okay, even if he got fifteen million dollars, a million a minute, that's a reason, but also I think he really wanted to do something different. Sometimes you want a change." While Wayne's jazz composition suffered a drought as he was challenged with some adverse conditions in his life, his natural ability as a player allowed him to adapt easily to the pop terrain, and his solos on pop records flourished like wild flowers in his career.

Wayne was particularly receptive to pop material with oblique lyrics, irregular harmonies, and meticulous studio production. No band had those qualities more than Steely Dan. Combining rock with R&B, Tin Pan Alley, and jazz, Steely Dan created a new kind of pop music in the seventies. The band's core members, Donald Fagen and Walter Becker, grew up in New York, taking in the jazz scene, and their childhood musical heroes were giants like Coltrane, Miles, Ellington, and Charlie Parker. Sharp-eared fans noticed that on the 1974 recording *Pretzel Logic,* Donald and Walter drew inspiration for the opening piano riff on "Rikki Don't Lose That Number" from Horace Silver's "Song for My Father." This was a pop band that didn't shy away from modal boogies, like "Bodhisattva," or from a tribute to Bird, "Parker's Band." Steely Dan's reputation convinced Wayne to work with them. "I knew that Steely Dan was a different kind of pop," Wayne said. "And they had the 'Die Behind the Wheel' and all those kinds of lyrics."

In 1976, Walter and Donald began to conceive *Aja,* a record with an even more ambitious use of jazz. "Wayne was our first choice to play," Walter said. "Conceptually his playing was so much more interesting than other bebop-schooled players. His work with Weather Report showed he was obviously familiar with the idea of what pop records and crossover were. That wasn't always the case with jazz musicians—lots of them didn't overdub well, because they were not familiar with the pop form." Jazz musicians could become so geared to improvising over complex chords and jazz progressions that they could have a hard time finding something profound and moving to say over simpler harmonies and chord changes. Walter and Don had Wayne's style specifically in mind for the instrumental section of "Aja," the record's title track. Their studio manager, Dick La-Palm, a veteran of Chess Records, knew Wayne and offered to contact him. When Wayne didn't respond for a while, they considered using "a musician from the 'sounds like Wayne' camp," Walter said. "We caught ourselves and said, 'We have to get Wayne.'"

When Wayne went into the studio, the song was nearly complete, except for a few overdubbed synth pads that came later, so Wayne had a full sense of the song—an eight-minute Latin-tinged suite. Jazz players are famous for relating their solos to the lyrics of tunes, to the emotional content of the words. Wayne did play to the homonymic meaning of the tune's title, "Aja," with a certain chant-like quality resonant of the Orient. But mostly he related to the music itself. "He was very thoughtful and probing about the musical possibilities," Walter said. "Wayne said as a jazz musician there could be a stage where you see a certain harmonic thing going on and react to that in a preprogrammed way. There could be a certain boilerplate aspect of the bebop language, a way of looking at chromatic passages. He was very intent on not doing that, of forging a novel approach to the piece. He was influenced by the contour of sections other than the section that he actually played over."

There wasn't much bebop language in the section over which Wayne played, which was mostly built on a very static, single-chord vamp, though it was a rich chord. Even with this limited vocabulary, Wayne managed to tell a blockbuster story in just one minute. Explosive drumming by Steve Gadd goaded Wayne's lines, much as Tony Williams had in Miles's group. Wayne's solo was majestic and stately, tracing a mountainous arc with cleverly displaced references back to the vocal melody. It was suitable for bronzing. Steely Dan was famous for its "heavily massaged solos." After an instrumentalist laid down several takes of a solo, they usually kneaded them into submission with meticulous editing. But Wayne's solo was recorded in just two takes. On his first and second pass, he gave them the cohesion and drama they usually labored to produce in the studio, spontaneously constructing his solo so carefully that they were able to use the beginning of one take and the end of a second.

The record's expert production and aspirations toward "perfection" made it a favorite of audiophiles—if you were a stereohead in the seventies, you owned this record—but it was also a hit with a wider audience. *Aja* reached number three on the *Billboard* album chart within the first three weeks of its release, trailing Fleetwood Mac's *Rumors* and Billy Joel's *The Stranger,* and also produced some hit singles: "Peg" hit 11, "Deacon Blues" made it to 19 and "Josie" to 26. "Aja" introduced a wide audience to Wayne's playing, and for years afterward, people approached him and said they'd first heard him on this record.

"Aja" was Wayne's only work with Steely Dan. That same year, Wayne began a more long-term and substantial association with another pop artist, singer and songwriter Joni Mitchell. By 1976, Joni had influenced songwriting as much as James Taylor or Bob Dylan, and had surpassed them in her ability to relate the meaning of words and music. Joni was a jazz fan, who said her opening vocal line on the 1971 title track "Blue" was influenced by Miles's muted trumpet tone. Joni elaborated on her early formation of a musical connection to Wayne. "I had polio when I was nine, and I lost my ability to stand and walk. I made a little prayer, saying, 'I'm not a cripple, give me back my legs.' So I got my legs back, and I had to join the church choir. Nobody wanted to sing the descant part. I said, 'I'll do it, that's the pretty melody,' the part with odd intervals, fourths and fifths. Most kids couldn't really hear them. They were lucky to hang in with triads. Wayne always reminded me of a descant player, like 'Nefertiti'—that melody is like a descant. Those strange intervals, and great leaps." Joni began as an angelic-sounding acoustic folksinger, but that was deceptive, because as early as *Blue* she wrote chord progressions that took strange paths: The song "All I Want" didn't resolve at its ending so much as it ran up to the edge of a cliff. In 1974, Joni began experimenting with jazz on her top-selling record *Court and Spark.* By the time she released *The Hissing of Summer Lawns,* in 1975, there was critical backlash against her experiments—a sign for Wayne that she must be doing something right.

Wayne respected Joni's music. "They don't even have a name for her stuff anymore," he once said. Wayne's favorite description of jazz is "no category," a variation on Duke Ellington's definition, "beyond category," so he admired Joni for venturing into uncharted territory in the pop world. He was even more impressed by her renegade status within the music industry. "It was her fight against the establishment of things that really got me," Wayne said. "Her lyrics are poetry, but they also take on the corporate establishment. By the time Joni was twenty-one, she was signed by a recording company and did 'Both Sides Now.' And one of the executives, the head of the company, he peeped what she was really meaning in the lyrics. You know, that recording companies will find somebody young, milk what they can out of them, and then throw them away. So this executive, he walked up to her after she'd finished recording it, and he said, 'You *know*, don't you?' Joni said, 'I thought everybody knew!' People sitting next to her said, 'Know what?'" Joni said the idea of seeing "both sides" of life probably struck a chord in Wayne because of his Buddhist practice. "At twenty-one, I already was beginning to conceive of the concept that perhaps life is somewhat of an illusion," Joni said. "Which is kind of a Buddhist idea. Wayne and I are both Buddhists."

Wayne and Joni were introduced through Jaco Pastorius, who played his bass to stunning harmonic effect on her 1976 album *Hejira*. Jaco invited Joni to a Weather Report recording session, and Joni and Wayne met briefly. She got a more lasting impression of Wayne at another meeting. "Jaco was late for a session with me, and Weather Report was getting ready to go on tour," she said. "So I grabbed my engineer, Henry Lewy, and we went to get that bad boy Jaco. Weather Report was on a break, and Wayne was onstage holding his soprano in the crook of one arm, and noodling around on the piano with the other hand. Jaco and Zawinul were playing Frisbee, and Peter Erskine was standing off to the side. He was the new guy in the group and was looking very New Guy in the Group–ish. Zawinul and Jaco were tossing this Frisbee so proudly and erect, like they were balanced on a high wire, just throwing it so excellently. They threw it toward Peter Erskine, who was so terrified that he looked like it was a missile coming at him from outer space, and he missed it. Then they looked at Wayne, and I thought *Uh-oh!* 'cause his back was to them and he was holding his horn. The Frisbee came toward him, and just at the last minute he reached out behind his back and caught it with his free hand. That was my lasting image of Wayne, as this Zen master of economy, of efficiency in motion. That was my first introduction to his supreme marksmanship—he later told me about his sharpshooting days in the army."

Wayne first joined Joni in a London studio in 1976 for work on *Don Juan's Reckless Daughter*. When Joni arrived at Basing Street, Wayne had already listened to "Paprika Plains," the first tune on which he was going to play. He walked over to Joni and said, "Okay, Joni, this is like you're in Hyde Park after it rains and it's cleared and there's a nanny with a baby in the boat on the pond, and her hand's just nudging the boat, just nudging it." Joni said she was thrilled to find someone who spoke her language, metaphor: "He's a very pictorial thinker, Wayne. What he described to me is exactly what he played." "Paprika Plains" was a sixteen-minute episodic orchestral suite, and its lyrics had a long, dreamy flashback section. Wayne's soprano solo came in the song's final minutes, gently prodding the story back into the present.

They went to a London café after the recording. When they sat down, Wayne decided to break the ice. He turned to Joni and said, in the voice of Walter Brennan, "I've been bitten by a water moccasin forty-seven times and I ain't dead yet!" This was one of Wayne's favorite bits from the film *Swamp Water*, starring Brennan as an accused murderer who escaped to a swamp where he was bitten by water moccasins so many times that he built up immunity to their venom. Wayne was testing Joni, in a sense. She didn't catch the specific reference but did pick up on the emotional tone of his impersonation. "Maybe that water moccasin thing is what he says when he's intimidated by something, I don't know," Joni said. "He tends to flash back on these many, many movie scenes. It's almost like he's seen so many movies that when he has a feeling, up into his little pictorial brain pops a movie image that depicts that feeling. Well, if you haven't seen that movie, you may be in the dark sometimes, sometimes not. Sometimes you're seeing the movie for the first time, he's enabling you to see it. I saw right away that he was a very unusual character."

When Wayne went in to record his solos on subsequent records like *Dog Eat Dog* and *Mingus,* the foundational harmony was already tracked on guitar or keyboards, as were Joni's vocals and a couple other soloists. "Her husband, Larry Klein, had letter chords written down, the sequence of how it went," Wayne said. "Joni didn't play the guitar in an academic or clinical approach. It was like she was going where her vocabulary guitar-wise took her. And there was variation on things. They put the music in front of me, and then I'd start playing and close my eyes instead of looking at a B or D7 chord, because it wasn't actually those chords anyway. It was an inversion of something, and the chord would sound like it was from Asia. Some other chords sounded minorish, or besides minor you could say melancholy, sentimental, questioning. Some harmonic chords you'd hear in Stravinsky, Bartók, those kind of chords." Most musicians didn't have the dimension of mind to explore the intricacy of her musical structures this way, Joni said. "The chords aren't moving in a way that anybody's used to—the ones I put Wayne on are a little eccentric anyway. Most musicians come in and think they're going to play down for some chick pop musician, and then they come in and look at the chords and say, 'Oh this is really strange.' But Wayne never did."

By the time Wayne hit the studio for Joni's *Chalk Mark in a Rain Storm* in 1988, they communicated on sheer playroom imagination. When Wayne went in to track "A Bird That Whistles," Joni's version of the traditional blues song "Corrina, Corrina," she simply asked him, "Can you be the bird?" That was all the encouragement Wayne needed to replicate a convincing whistling birdcall on his saxophone. After they did the "bird," Wayne packed up his horn and said, "Okay, now sculpt!" He was giving Joni his approval of her editing process: She fashions his solos from ten or eleven takes. Miles once told Wayne that he felt like a "big bucket" when he played with a vocalist, as if his splashes of trumpet washed a singer's voice away. "You have to be an artful dodger to play with a singer," Wayne said. Jazz instrumentalists are so accustomed to highly interactive playing that it can be limiting to considerately daub and stroke around a singer's lines.

But with Joni's method of editing Wayne's solos together from multiple takes, he doesn't have to worry about that. "Basically I have Wayne come in with his crayons and scribble all over my canvas, and then I paint over the ones I don't want, to get my space back," Joni said. "I just give him his lead and let him run all over the track." For the final product, Joni likes to use Wayne's phrases that are most sympathetic to her voice. "There are places where I can tell he's touched by the tone in my vocal, 'cause he'll notice and respond to it, on one of the eleven takes. He'll never notice it again, because he'll be noticing something different in that spot on the next take. And then, of course, you can't just use all the bits that you like and expect it to work as a whole; you have to make it sound like a total performance." "Dry Cleaner from Des Moines" on *Mingus* has only a few notes by Wayne, but evokes an entire scene. Joni edits him into these vivid sketches based on the "pictograms" she finds in his phrases. "I don't think everyone is able to pick up on the pictograms," she said. "Maybe they're just for me, because for a lot of people they just sound like *dot dot dash*. But those *dot dot dashes* are drawing an image to me."

Joni put Wayne's musicianship in some perspective. "Most players, even the jazz guys, they come in," she said, "look at what's written out, listen, come up with an idea, then give you five or six performances of that same idea. But they only get one idea. Whereas Wayne gets an idea, carries it through half of the piece, abandons it for a second idea, carries it through part of the piece awhile more, abandons it for another idea, abandons it for yet another idea, and then starts crawling along braiding together the parts, jumping from one to another just like embroidery. There's no one like him on my music. There's nobody who's so exciting to work with."

Elis

Elis Regina was the reigning Brazilian pop singer of the seventies, as renowned for her charismatic interpretations of popular songs as Sinatra was at one time in the U.S. She could be volatile onstage, and fans lovingly nicknamed her "The Hurricane." Wayne was attracted to her music for the same reason he was drawn to experimental pop musicians in America. "I was interested in Elis because she was popular but had the facility of an instrumentalist, as if she were a flutist, violinist, or bassoon player," Wayne said. "She was a complete musician." Elis loved composers, and brought Ivan Lins, João Bosco, and Wayne's friend Milton Nascimento to national prominence with her renditions of their work. Wayne met her in the early eighties. "I saw her when we were both performing at the same festival in Japan, and she was wearing a sailor suit," he said. "When she saw me, she got down on her hands and knees, saying, 'I kiss your feet,' in Portuguese, and I said, 'Get up, you're Elis Regina!'"

As she and Wayne talked, they discovered they were both cinephiles. She invited Wayne and Ana to stay in her home in Rio. Elis cooked them breakfast every day while Wayne chanted or went out for a jog—the scenery on Rio's beaches was a little more compelling than that of his usual jogging route, two hundred circles around his backyard at home in Los Angeles. Wayne returned the hospitality. Elis stayed with Wayne and Ana in L.A. for six weeks, and they began to work on a record together, but tragically, Elis died of a prescription drug overdose in 1982. "She told me when she was a young girl and heard Nat King Cole playing the piano and singing, the way he played the songs on the piano told her something," Wayne said. "The piano was her inspiration, that's why she married a piano player [Cesar Camargo Mariano]. Elis didn't want to be a singer who knew nothing about music. Elis Regina was one of the most special people on the planet. Because she was one of the few women who—along with Ella Fitzgerald and Sarah Vaughan and Billie Holiday—transcended the superficial presentation of something called a performance in a night." Elis gave the world another musician, a daughter, Maria Rita, who eventually went on to phenomenal success as a pop singer—she was the Norah Jones of Brazil in 2003.

When It Was Now

Wayne's picturesque sound and solo craftsmanship made his playing a jewel in the crown for pop musicians in the U.S. and beyond. He turned down many recording offers, and never went on tour with Joni. "In a way, to play with a pop-oriented group helps them transcend the label 'pop,'" Wayne said. "You choose very carefully who you're going to do something like that with. And some of the older musicians won't even play with anybody pop." Tenor saxophonist Sonny Rollins famously consented to play with the Rolling Stones on *Tattoo You* in 1981. Sonny said he didn't go on tour with them for similar reasons: "I didn't want to be the jazz guy playing rock." Sonny and Wayne became better acquainted in the late seventies and early eighties in Japan, when they both appeared in the Live Under the Sky festivals there. During Weather Report shows, Joe would often conspiratorially tell Wayne, "Sonny's backstage checking you out." Sonny stayed on in Japan studying Zen Buddhism, and he and Wayne sometimes traveled on trains together, discussing how to stay physically healthy and spiritually strong as they aged.

By the start of the eighties, Japanese and European tours were Weather Report's bread and butter. And like Jerry Garcia and the Grateful Dead in later years, the group's venerable stature propelled it along on tours overseas. And Joe seemed to pull Wayne along, though Wayne said they were respectful of each other's autonomy: "Joe and I left each other alone, in a way. People look for leaders. 'Who's doing the producing, who's producing this record? Who's the source, where's the input?' . . . like when the Beatles came along, and people said, 'Is John Lennon doing the input?' like it was designed to break them up. Whoever's doing the leading, the most writing, is not an indication of who's affecting the life of the band, or life in general." In 1980, Weather Report released *Night Passage,* with only one of Wayne's compositions, and his only contribution to 1982's *Weather Report* (the band's second eponymous album) was "When It Was Now." In 1982, Jaco and Peter left. (Wayne played some festive soprano solos on Jaco's *Word of Mouth* recording.) Omar Hakim, a twenty-three-year-old drummer, and Victor Bailey, a twenty-two-year-old bassist, replaced them. Within a month, this new group recorded *Procession.* It was not one of Weather Report's best albums, but was still an outstanding example of jazz-rock, a sign of how completely Weather Report dominated the field in later years, long after the Mahavishnu Orchestra and Chick Corea's Return to Forever had disbanded. There was a great deal of energy from Omar and Victor when this new Weather Report grouping came together, and Wayne stepped up to solo a little more. But for the most part, Weather Report was now Joe's story.

Wayne no longer had the same struggle he'd had in the late seventies. "I knew that this human revolution thing would take a while, I couldn't rush it. Then I got to a place where I didn't worry about music at all anymore. I became more confident about the inner resources I was building, the stuff that can't be seen." Wayne admitted that he initially misused his Buddhist practice as a means of escape from routine realities—like when he'd leave a dinner party to go gaze in a bathroom mirror. Wayne still checked out his reflection, but now a passing glance was enough: "I'd look in the mirror and say, 'What's your real name? What is anybody's real name?' That sparked, 'What are you supposed to do? What are you supposed to do *also*?' By playing music, I am doing less than a fraction. Music is a drop in the ocean of life."

As Wayne's practice strengthened, it gave him philosophical protection against extremely sad circumstances. Having a child like Iska meant never hearing his daughter call him "Daddy" or Ana Maria "Mom." While Wayne was out on the road, Ana Maria struggled with Iska's care, making exhausting trips to the emergency room when she had seizures, and nursing her punctured tongue afterward. Sometimes when Wayne got home, Ana was so stressed out that she would go away for days on drinking binges of her own, leaving Iska with him. "I had to believe that even when the family thing was crumbling, when it was getting the darkest, I must be breaking through," Wayne said. "When you think that there's no place else to go and you're getting near the end and panicking, that's when the adversity that has accumulated is panicking, too, because it knows it's losing its hold on you."

During these trying times in the early eighties, Wayne began to practice Buddhism in a more profound sense. "It means you are living your life reaching for a higher and higher life force in everything you do, everything." Wayne said. He came to see the practice not as a means to avoid suffering, but rather as a way of cultivating happiness from sadness, finding ways to turn "poison into medicine" in all areas of his life. "I realized that being 'spiritual' in a heavy way doesn't make you profound. What made me profound was sitting and feeding Iska, or spending time with Miyako, my other daughter. Everything started to become an adventure, from moment to moment. You'll see a man out shopping with a woman, and he doesn't want to be there, so he stands with his arms crossed, impatiently stepping back and forth from foot to foot. I started to see the adventure in simple things like shopping that women do, the adventure of doing things that had nothing to do with music." Stuck with housekeeping and the home care of his brain-damaged daughter, Wayne got creative, improvising a way to find meaning in the routine. He drew on lessons learned along the way in music: Miles, for example, was always able to turn his sidemen's mistakes into musical themes.

Wayne was concerned about his mother, Louise, who lived alone in Newark. The city had become unsafe, and she was getting old. His fears were confirmed one day when, on her way home from the grocery store, Louise was mugged in the foyer of her building. While she somehow managed to scare off her attackers, she was left with scattered groceries and shattered nerves. Wayne ordered Louise to come live with him, and she moved to L.A. in 1982. Louise and Tina Turner became fast friends. "They were both Sagittarius, so they talked together real quickly," Wayne said. "And Herbie's mother came out from Chicago. Our mothers would go together to see two or three movies in one day! They'd pack their lunch and just go from theater to theater. They said, 'We're going to do what *we* feel like doing now.'" Wayne was happy to see his mother following her whims; he'd been around enough to know how rare it was that she had encouraged him to do the same.

Wayne was glad to have his mother's help with Iska, whose health worsened throughout 1982 and 1983. Her seizures grew more frequent and wore her fragile body down even further. On October 25, 1983, shortly after her fourteenth birthday, Iska had a grand mal seizure and died. Wayne wasn't home at the time; he'd gone on a quick tour of Europe with a makeshift band. Wayne was hard-pressed to find meaning in his daughter's death, though he did find solace in his Buddhist practice. "Iska didn't have false illusions," he said. "She cut through all that. When she passed away, our practice was saying that she completed her mission. Her mission was to lead her mother and father to the ultimate law of life. She made that decision before she was born. She returned to her original throne of Buddhahood when she passed away, and left this threefold world, this school of reality and illusion, this hard-ass school."

Wayne and Ana Maria considered litigating against the medical malpractice that basically ended Iska's life just as it was starting. But they knew it wouldn't bring her back. Someone offered to take legal action for them. "After she died, a lawyer came to us, and said he wanted to take on the cause of Iska's brain damage, the tetanus thing—there were adverse substances in the serum," Wayne said. "The lawyer had three thousand cases he was working on, and he volunteered to work on our case. He tracked down where she got the first vaccination and looked for the manufacturer's ID of the booster shot. They checked with the doctor, but after eight years they can destroy records. It was part of his process of covering things up. The lawyer won anyway, and we later got a settlement."

This Is This

Just as Iska's birth and medical accident precipitated Wayne's departure from Miles's group, her death hastened the end of Weather Report. The group had its last tour in 1984 and released *Sportin' Life* in March 1985. Joe called the record an "international resort album," an apt description, considering percussionist Mino Cinelu's cosmopolitan rhythms on the record. But Joe's depiction was not an entirely flattering one. In the beginning, Weather Report's fusion experiments had the feeling of fresh adventure and global discoveries, like a musical version of Jules Verne's novel *Around the World in Eighty Days*. By the end, they seemed more like jet-setters on a jaunt around a chain of Club Meds—the exoticism felt a little too comfortable, padded with synthesizers instead of soaring off into the unknown with them. Wayne and Joe thought they'd fulfilled their contractual obligation to Columbia Records. They hadn't, so Joe hurriedly put together a final record with the straightforward title *This Is This*. Wayne was working on a new solo project, so there were no compositional contributions from him, and little playing.

Any world-weariness on Weather Report's final records didn't take away from the overall achievement of the group. Even with the decreased market value and critical disfavor of the fusion style in the eighties, and despite Wayne's fading presence in the later years, his musical association with Joe endured fourteen years and spawned fifteen records.

This Is This was released with a photo of Joe and Wayne in a left-handed handshake on the record sleeve, inviting speculation from fans about the leaders' cross-purposes. The photo was simply reversed in printing, though fans could be forgiven for their gossip: Joe and Wayne did have one of the most complicated bandleader relationships in musical history. They were good cop and bad cop, road warriors, hard-nosed realist and dreamy romantic, commanding officers of a changing detail, priest and pimp, drinking buddies, enabler and codependent. Their many sidemen generally agreed, however, that they were complementary opposites. One regular feature of Weather Report's shows was a Joe and Wayne duet, commonly on "In a Silent Way" or an Ellington tune. With the full band, Joe was unassailable behind his flotilla of keyboards, but he let his guard down when it was only he and Wayne. He adoringly watched and listened to Wayne as he played, waiting for any creative sparks. Anyone who noticed how avidly they played for each other during these duets could perceive their deep respect for each other's musicianship. "Wayne—I said this before and I'll say it again—is my favorite musician I ever played with," Joe said. "All in all. And I played with great ones—Coleman Hawkins, Miles. It doesn't even matter that Wayne played saxophone, I'm not even talking about the saxophone, just pure musicianship."

For Wayne, any conflict within the band was part of a natural growth process. "There was always a lot of speculation about anything that could have been juicy or contentious in Weather Report," he said. "You can slump that stuff into the growth category. Your ideas about music some-times are ahead of your growth as a human being. I think that's when heated discussions come about. Like someone might want something now, a certain way, *now*. And another person might want another thing, *now*. It takes a process of growth to say, 'Let's get it all in. Let's do it all.' In other words, no one pretends that in Weather Report we were all 'com-pletely processed perfect human beings, mentally and physically, having a one-hundred-percent benevolence and altruistic intentions for fellow be-ings within the group and around the globe.'"

Wayne had invested a major part of his career in the group: "When you do something for fourteen years—and those fourteen years are considered prime time—when it's over you don't want to think, *I wish I'd done . . .*" Wayne didn't have any regrets, and was proud of his and Joe's accomplish-ments. He went so far as to trumpet them, something he almost never did: "With Weather Report we won things. Actually, we changed things for the business!"

14.

Joy Ryder

DURING THE LATTER YEARS of Weather Report, Wayne had thought his compositional well might have run dry. When he started writing for himself again, however, he found that it definitely had not. "There was a difference in being alone," Wayne said. "It was like I was a kid working with clay again. I said, *That's where I am again now, and I've got to make all the things I can, and get back to that whole world perspective.* So my music was multi-output, and I varied or reiterated lines in different ways to celebrate the discovery of eternal energy. With that energy, you never become depleted. You become depleted when you deny yourself that true endeavor." When Wayne unleashed all the multiple melodies in his mind, he tapped an inexhaustible supply of inspiration. He had reams of compositions to prove it, a metaphorical "piano bench overflowing with stories." He needed lots of music. When Weather Report disbanded, Columbia Records exercised the "leaving member option" in Wayne's contract, which committed him to recording three albums for the label.

Wayne was drawn to the legend of Atlantis, one of history's unsolved mysteries. The passage of time hasn't reduced popular interest in the fabled continent, which made it a fitting title for Wayne's first record for Columbia—it had been eleven years since his last solo record, *Native Dancer,* and his submerged solo career remained an intriguing mystery to his fans. Released in October 1985, *Atlantis* was both electric and acoustic, with electric bass, percussion, piano, reeds, and a chorus of seven women and children. There was a statement by Wayne on the sleeve of the record: "The making of *Atlantis* allowed me to exercise the principle of artistic license as a means to 'break away' from known formulas of presenting the 'song' to the world. Some of the selections herein are miniature movies that may never be made into stories on film. The challenge here was to use the limited elements on hand and spin the 'creative wheel' so as to produce something as grand as a Lucas or Spielberg production."

This was no traditional jazz record. It was something like a soundtrack for an animated, feature-length children's adventure set in Atlantis, and Wayne said the record's "story line" did follow "in close truth the legend of Atlantis." But the first track, "Endangered Species," was a fusion funk number unlike the rest of the record. It served what Wayne called a "tactical function," like Sirens using their irresistible voices to lure sailors to their deaths. Wayne jokingly imagined the listener's response to this first tune after moving on to the second: "I thought this was a discotheque when I walked in!" Wayne thought that listeners would then dive into the rest of the record's mostly acoustic netherworld with him, like he'd eagerly gone underwater with the character Tom in the book *The Water Babies.* Unfortunately, some listeners just crashed up on the rocky shores of the first tune and didn't experience the rest of the story.

If you did listen below the surface, to the rest of the record, there wasn't much improvisation. With the exception of his own horn solos, Wayne wrote out each part, pasting them together with an artist's mosaic or bricolage in mind. As Wayne said, he "varied or reiterated lines"—most tracks had at least five intertwined melodies, and any one of those lines could serve as the primary one. The compositions used counterpoint to high drama, especially between the bass and melody lines. "When I heard *Atlantis,* I was blown away," bassist John Patitucci said. "The compositional thing is so ridiculously beautiful. Wayne is one of the few people who can write bass lines, who understands that a bass line can be not just rhythmic but melodic and contrapuntal. Like Bach or other great composers from years ago, some of them had a great skill at writing bass lines." Wayne said the final piece, "On the Eve of Departure," represented "a spaceship taking the survivors to safety." One of its sections hovered around a grounded D7 to G7 chord alternation, with infinite variations launching off the vamp. Wayne's harmony was some strong medicine, so he added melody like the proverbial spoonful of sugar—the smooth leading voices of the reeds or the chorus sweetened the mix and reconciled the ear to his odd, complex harmonies. Wayne's previous work with musical partners was monochromatic, compared with this richly layered perspective.

Wayne also tracked the growth of extramusical interests on the record. " 'The Three Marias' was inspired by the arrest of three ladies in Lisboa," he said. "They were arrested for writing obscene literature. There were three—one was a journalist, one was a dramatist, and the third was a poetess. They had one thing in common, the first name—Maria. There was a play running around Europe by that name, and a book, too. The judge dismissed the case and they won. A giant step for Portugal."

At long last, Wayne was making a giant step of his own, his big move. He was no longer the silent partner. In interviews he analogously brought up his friend Tina Turner, identifying with her need to go solo after working with Ike, and also mentioned that he was "rooting for Mary Wilson from the Supremes." On November 5, 1985, Wayne made his New York debut as a leader at the Blue Note club, a premiere *The New York Times* called "the year's most significant jazz event." After Wayne had gone gen-

tly into that good night during his final Weather Report years, the anticipation for his resurgent record and gig was almost lustful. The band was
Tom Canning on keyboards, Gary Willis on electric bass, and Tom
Brechtlein on drums. They played a few tunes from *Atlantis* along with a
couple from his last album as a leader, *Native Dancer*—Wayne wanted the
repertoire to bridge the decade since he'd last recorded. So, had a giant of
jazz reemerged? Most critics didn't think so. Many wanted to hear him
come charging out of the gate after Weather Report with the swinging,
acoustic jazz he played before the jazz-rock era. And *Atlantis* was definitely
not a record that could be evaluated according to traditional standards of
jazz virtuosity. As Robert Palmer noted in *The New York Times,* "It is not
the sort of album one should listen to a few times and then knowledgeably
evaluate, as critics are routinely asked to do. It is an album to learn from
and live with."

Wayne was judged as a jazz musician, and his success was mitigated by
a prevailing neo-traditionalism in the music. Wynton Marsalis made a virtuosic debut as an acoustic jazz trumpeter in 1982, and his first self-titled
recording sold 100,000 copies, a huge number for a jazz record. In 1983,
he became the only instrumentalist to win Grammy Awards in both jazz
and classical categories in the same year. Wynton was, however, a controversial twenty-five-year-old figure. Fans revere jazz musicians not least of all
for their outsider status. According to unwritten jazz law, a fan is supposed
to extend himself into a musician's own existential state in order to "get"
the music, which makes fans outsiders, too. What is jazz? "If you have to
ask, you'll never know," Louis Armstrong said. Wynton broke the rules by
giving away the answer. He angered people with his pompous definitions
of jazz, and was especially notorious for his establishment-friendly attitude. But he was also successful.

Joseph Campbell pointed out how mythology is empowered by the image of death. Wynton used the notion that jazz had died with the fusion
sellout and free-jazz excesses of the seventies to support the idea of himself
as the music's savior in the eighties. For Wynton, electric instruments and
pop influences diluted jazz's creative force, but he empowered the music

with a holy return to the down-home sound of his native New Orleans and the sleek rhythmic and harmonic sophistication of the bebop and hard-bop eras. Though Wynton didn't attack Wayne directly, his story line put Wayne in the position of a jazz Judas, because he'd helped define those celebrated earlier eras in jazz, then went on to pioneer jazz-rock with Weather Report.

Wayne hated factionalism in art. It made no more sense to him than the idea of owning or betraying the past. And he still saw the boy in Wynton who'd come over to his house starry-eyed, clutching a copy of *Live at the Plugged Nickel.* "That means, to me . . . at that time he was in a position to grasp the profundity of what was going on then at those Plugged Nickel dates," Wayne said. "Somewhere after that, between when he left my house and now, that grasping process is on vacation—quite a long vacation." For Wayne, the questing, creative spirit that guided Miles's quintet at the Plugged Nickel was the same one that later inspired him to experiment with pop music and electric instruments.

"Sometimes the world becomes a great big advertisement," Wayne said. "You can't live up to it, and others can. When I was younger, I had dreams where there was lots of traffic, a big light up ahead, and the dream was to get up there." He didn't feel like that anymore. He didn't buy into any destination or expected goal for his career, and didn't have to live up to anything other than the long-term goals related to his Buddhist practice. "Any music you heard on *Atlantis* was just a shell of the metamorphosis going on inside me," Wayne said, and then he returned to the traffic metaphor of his early dreams: "Music was the vehicle, the car for other changes."

Wayne wasn't just making excuses for failure, or "bruising," as Lester Young would say. He *was* changing. In 1986, Wayne's mother, Louise, passed away of old age. After the harsh abruptness of his father's death in a car crash, and the long trial and premature end of his daughter Iska's life, Wayne's grief over his mother's peaceful death was relatively mild. But unhappily, he and Ana Maria were having marital problems. Though Ana was enormously supportive of Wayne's career, she had a drinking problem of her own, one considerably worse than Wayne's, so there was some ugliness in their marriage. Wayne went to local Al-Anon meetings in Los Angeles for group support. Finally, they agreed on a separation, which lasted a year and had a feeling of finality. "I wasn't divorced, I was separated but treating it as a divorce," Wayne said. Still, Wayne and Ana Maria remained connected through their Buddhist network in Los Angeles. "I'd hear about her being at meeting, and she'd hear about me," Wayne said.

When Ana Maria specifically heard about Wayne's new girlfriend, a French woman, she was eager to reconcile her differences with him. "One time, I came back from Europe and I called her and said, 'I'm coming to get you!'" Wayne said. "She was staying at a girlfriend's house, and when I got there, she was standing outside with her suitcase waiting for me. I said we're not doing this shit again. And then we had years of great life together. We both had a realization that we'd find a way to create value together no matter what. We were making causes to confirm the mission that we had together with our daughter. When you practice this Buddhism for others, that's when the mountains crumble, all obstacles become mutable. Even in the midst of your own struggle, you can go into a Buddhist meeting and see people who are struggling. People walk in looking like a two-by-four hit 'em, like the dog died, the floods killed their crops, and all that. They're practicing for themselves. Then you'll go to meeting where people are practicing for others, and you'll see some Oscar winners."

In the early eighties, Wayne started to learn how to find the joy and meaning in simple things like feeding his daughter. Now that he was practicing Buddhism for others, it put him in a position to lead by example. "I felt like the best way to show adventure was to just be it myself," Wayne said. "But not in a 'Look, Ma, no hands!' way. Your adventure is often not advertised. Results happen to show what is transforming inside you." As a bandleader, it would take Wayne fifteen years to find a group of musicians who shared both his sense of adventure and artistic sophistication.

On his *Atlantis* tour in the summer of 1986, Wayne came across keyboardist Jim Beard—or rather, Jim came across him. At first sight, Wayne didn't seem like much of an adventurer. "There were flight cases backstage, and Wayne was crouched down in between them with a big beer and cigarette," Jim said. "He was hiding there like a kid—he had a look of mischievous innocence, sneaking his beer and cigarette. You almost got the sense of somebody skipping class in school." Wayne and Jim rode back to the hotel together after the show, and Wayne's conversation took Jim by surprise. "I was only twenty-five," Jim said, "and when Wayne started talking about things relating to life, not music, it really blew my mind." A few weeks later, Wayne flew Jim out to L.A. to play on his next record, *Phantom Navigator*, and then asked him to join his band.

In early November 1986, Wayne performed at the Blue Note in New York with Jim on keyboards, his old Weather Report bandmate Alphonso Johnson on bass, and a musician from the Gil Evans Orchestra, Kenwood Dennard, on drums. The group started the show with one of Wayne's few late Weather Report tunes, "Plaza Real," and then segued into "Beauty and the Beast." Wayne wasn't pleased with the band's performance, though he tried to lay the blame on himself. After the tune was finished, he announced from the stage, "That last one was called 'Beauty and the Beast.' A little more beast than beauty. Startin' with *me*. Some people should know *better*." He then introduced the band, emphasizing its temporary nature by calling it a "Christmas Band" and adding, "Nothin' lasts forever, except for forever . . ." Wayne was visibly unhappy, and Jim had the feeling it was because of the shredding style of the drummer. "At the end of the night, it looked like a sawmill around Kenwood's kit, like a beaver had been there," Jim said. "He played so loud, played loud as shit. One time, Wayne stood at the end of the stage and he looked like someone was pounding spikes through his feet."

Within a few weeks, Wayne remedied the problem. He kept Jim on keyboards, hired Marilyn Mazur on percussion, and then held auditions in New York for a drummer and bassist (Alphonso was returning to his regular spot in Carlos Santana's band) at the end of the year. Twenty-one-year-old prodigy Terri Lyne Carrington was one of fourteen drummer candidates. As the granddaughter of jazz drummer Matt Carrington, Terri had a jump start on the competition from birth. By the time Terri was twenty-one, she already had experience playing with Stan Getz and Clark

Terry. Still, she was very nervous about her audition with Wayne. That morning Terri got some excellent advice from her friend, saxophonist Greg Osby: "Whatever you do, don't overplay," he said. Terri had already decided not to go the road of some women drummers, who play audaciously and aggressively to counter any essentialist association with a "feminine" sound.

Terri got the gig, and Wayne gave her three reasons why. When Wayne auditioned the drummers, he played saxophone with each one, first facing him or her and then slowly turning around so that his back was to the drum set. "Wayne said I was the first one who didn't make him feel he was being stabbed in the back when I played," Terri said. "He said he felt safe when he turned his back on me. And then he said he got a feeling in his stomach that he used to get when he drank cognac. A warm feeling, a rush. And finally he said that when I played after thirteen other drummers, I was the only one who didn't sound like the rest of them. I had my own sound, even though we all played on the same drum set." Wayne's motto was subtlety first, then feeling, and finally individuality.

Terri was surprised she won out, but guessed that Wayne valued promise rather than perfection. "He saw in me the potential that I had," Terri said. "It's not like I played anything spectacular. I only got better over the years of playing with him. But he has a deep understanding. He knew I could do the job and grow within it, and I think that's something that great artists see within other people. They like helping someone come into their own." Wayne saw something else in Terri: He and Ana Maria told her she resembled their late daughter, Iska. Terri's time on the road with Wayne was spiritually as well as musically beneficial. The Shorters introduced her to Buddhism, which was not without its practical advantages for Wayne. Terri had a tendency to be grumpy about the inadequacies of her hotel rooms. One time, Wayne told her, "Maybe you should chant to eradicate your complaining nature."

Terri was part of what they jokingly called Wayne's "Unisex" band: There were two men, Jim and Carl James, who won the bass audition; and two women, Terri and Marilyn. The group hit the road just after Wayne's

Phantom Navigator recording was released. *Phantom Navigator* continued the musical odyssey of *Atlantis,* with complex counterpoint worthy of Bach, and strong leading melodies. If you heard "Remote Control" while shopping in a clothing store, for example, you might just hear a happy dance tune, unaware of the dense harmonic elements churning underneath—though the track's intermittent synthesized monster roars might stop you in your tracks. "Condition Red" was a study in theme and variation, with four-bar progressions repeated in different combinations, and the humorous highlight of Wayne's own voice scatting over the top. Wayne took the title for another tune, "Mahogany Bird," from a piece of original artwork. "I have a drawing of a little girl sitting on a bird riding through space wearing a helmet," he said. "I used it for the cover of another record later [*Joy Ryder*]. I just borrowed the title from the painting. See, it doesn't mean that the bird's going to be mahogany. What does mahogany really mean? Define the deeper meaning of color, wood, texture, and everything else. A bird could be a process of living purposefully against all odds. People can make obstacles for themselves, and throw handicaps in front of themselves. A lot of handicaps are invisible to people."

Many listeners thought the synthesizer-heavy production on *Phantom Navigator* seemed like an obstacle to Wayne's music, crippling the beauty of the composition. Ideally, production will bring forth what's inside an artist's head in as clear and comprehensive a form as possible. In some ways, the record's production did project a complete musical reel of Wayne's imagination. He said that the record was based on *Other Worlds,* the comic book he'd created as a fifteen-year-old. The synthetic monster roars on "Remote Control" popped out of nowhere, as they would in one of Wayne's beloved comic-book stories. But the fanciful aspects of his vision didn't always connect for listeners as they did for him.

Whether or not the savage beasts of Wayne's imagination needed soothing or smoothing, the record's programmed drumbeats troubled many listeners. As Miles noted, what made Wayne's compositions special was the way he notated on the beat, as Charlie Parker did. On *Phantom Navigator,* Wayne's rhythmic ingenuity could get lost in the driving 4/4 backbeat, and some critics couldn't hear the music at all. As Jack DeJohnette noted: "I love those compositions on those Columbia records. Because they had backbeats in them, the critics missed the chemistry going on, the creative workings that Wayne uses in his orchestration palette. He's a great composer for small groups, but especially for orchestra stuff. He wrote a lot of different chords that move mysteriously, but yet they're very beautiful, and so . . . I think his stuff is really deep." Joni Mitchell said she wished Wayne had a better producer at times: "Sometimes when producers push jazz in a fusion direction, they end up with a track that sounds like it's waiting for a singer. It isn't as successful to put four-on-the-floor with jazz. Playing a rock beat, an R-and-B beat against jazz . . . well, sometimes it puts fence posts through the music."

This music begged to be heard in a live, open setting, but Wayne's "Unisex" band had some trouble with it on tour. The band played composed scores, and it was hard to do right by such ornate music onstage. When the musicians did break away to improvise, it was over sections based on just one or two chords, or vamps. "It was a challenge to improvise on those vamps," Jim said. "You had to find something interesting to say on D minor for ten minutes." Wayne asked musicians to perform the equivalent of writing a story with only verbs. He didn't have any trouble with this task himself: He'd first kindled his creativity in Newark's bleak Ironbound District, after all, and as solos like the one on "Aja" showed, Wayne was nothing but inventive over vamps. Even if he had only a couple chords at his disposal, other raw materials were only as limited as his imagination. He could build solos with humor, mystery, suspense, melancholy, classical music themes, false cadences, melodic displacements, the microcosmic, macrocosmic—and then with repeated variations on all of the above. Wayne even stretched his solo storytelling over multiple nights.

Wayne tried to ignite creativity in his sidemen and -women with cinematic images or moods, like "The ship's pulling into the harbor," or "We're all working the late shift in the steel mill tonight." And he chided them only in the most oblique ways: "Sometimes the rabbit runs down the hole, and sometimes the rabbit falls down the hole," he'd say. As a Buddhist,

Wayne wanted to validate every musician's potential. "Genius is a statement that says that anything is possible, but only when acted upon assiduously," he said. "That covers everyone's genius, everyone's potential." Wayne assumed that anyone could realize a certain potential with applied effort: "A lot of musicians don't ear train. They don't listen to something out of the blue, to see if they can hear what's going on and if they can be a part of it, even something complex and classical. They may want to stay in a comfort zone with what they earn and what they learn." Most musicians also hadn't committed large sections of film soundtracks to memory by age nine, as he had. Wayne's great flaw as a bandleader was his strength as a mentor: his inability to see that everyone didn't have his genius.

So the tour was musically inconsistent yet fun. Ana Maria was along for the ride, and they did a leg of the tour with Miles, who had a lively group that included Kenny Garrett on saxophone. Wayne's old bandmates saw a change in him. "In those years in Weather Report, he just stood there," Curtis Fuller said. "He didn't want to talk and was very withdrawn. Years later, in the late eighties, we both played at Japanese festivals, and Wayne's dressing room was right next to mine. We finally caught up then, and he was happier, telling stories and laughing, like he'd learned how to balance his holier-than-thou attitude with his old fun self."

One time on tour, the band was on an airplane beginning its final approach to Hong Kong. To anyone who would listen, Wayne suddenly announced, "See that cloud? There's a spaceship behind it!" Even in random moments, Wayne was on a mission to set the group's collective imagination free. In 1988 he released *Joy Ryder,* his third album in four years, which included a tune called "Daredevil," dedicated to a blind comic-book superhero whose other senses became superhuman when he lost his sight—a character who definitely challenged conventional ideas of adventure. Other titles, like "Someplace Called 'Where,'" joined "When It Was Now" in the category of Wayne's linguistic LSD trips. Wayne liked titles and words that stimulated thought about what it really means to be human. "That's the greatest honor, to be manifest as a human being, to arrive, to cognate as a human being," he said. "You can give yourself an incomprehensible concept or word, like 'always.' That's a little rattle for us, to say what 'always' really is. If we were always here, always human entities, we promised to take care of each other. Then when we come in this form, we can try to remember the promise we made to each other." This was nothing like the comforting promise of romantic constancy that songwriter Irving Berlin had in mind with his classic ballad "Always." For Wayne, "always" was a kind of eternity you found only by ignoring the obvious.

15.

"Get your cape out of the cleaner's and fly, Superman!"

AFTER RELEASING *Joy Ryder,* Wayne considered heading out on the road with his band again, but he had a more compelling offer: a tour with Carlos Santana. Wayne agreed to a five-week run of dates with the rock legend during the summer festival season of 1988. Musically, the collaboration provided certain challenges for both musicians, but ironically, it was during this period—when many of Wayne's old fans had written him off—that he continued to emerge from the withdrawn stance he'd perfected in Weather Report. He moved into a mature stage of his career, and laid the foundation for his eventual comeback.

Like all of Wayne's friends, Carlos Santana has a favorite bit of "Wayne-speak." On tour, he and Wayne were offstage watching the other players. Wayne turned to Carlos and said, "You know, I think we're going to go on a solo tour, just me and my soprano saxophone. And I'm going to play the straight man." Wayne did sometimes feel like the straight man to his own saxophone, which faithfully turned out a series of one-liners, with or without him. Wayne had been on the road almost constantly for thirty years: 1959–64 with Blakey, 1964–69 with Miles, 1970–85 with Weather Report, and then with his own band. And while Wayne welcomed the Santana tour's change of pace, he also harbored some ambivalence. Would he be perceived as riding Carlos's coattails? Would people think he was turning tricks for a pop band?

Though most would identify Carlos Santana as a rock musician, he himself identified with jazz early in his career. Carlos made his first outing in jazz with John McLaughlin, leader of the Mahavishnu Orchestra and former Miles Davis sideman. Carlos and John initiated their friendship with a shared appreciation for jazz, and for Wayne's music in particular. "When I first talked to John McLaughlin," Carlos said, "the first thing I said was 'I love what you played with Wayne on *Super Nova*,' and we became friends. We both knew that we adored Wayne and Bill Evans and Coltrane, and that was it." By 1972, the two guitarists also shared a spiritual leader in guru Sri Chinmoy, who bestowed upon John the name Mahavishnu, and upon Carlos a less elegant-sounding but nevertheless serving designation, Devadip. The musicians combined their spiritual leanings and love for jazz on *Love Devotion Surrender*, with earnest covers of Coltrane's "A Love Supreme" and "Naima." The record reached the Top 20 and went gold, introducing legions of Santana's rock fans to jazz.

Carlos and Wayne first met in 1973 when Weather Report opened for the Santana band in Texas. Carlos felt guilty when his fans yelled out "Santana" during Wayne's solo, and he apologized to Wayne. But when it came to befriending Wayne, Carlos was initially as tentative as Herbie had been. "Wayne was into his own orbit in Weather Report," Carlos explained. "And I didn't have words or facility to talk to him. It's the same thing with Wayne or Miles or Coltrane, you don't just stroll up and say, 'Hey man.' If you're sensitive in your heart and have some dignity, you don't approach them like that. So I admired him from a distance."

Carlos did finally talk to Wayne and created an opportunity to collaborate with him in 1980. The enterprising guitarist lured Miles's entire classic quintet—except for Miles—into the studio to record *The Swing of Delight*. Carlos still identified himself as a disciple of Sri Chinmoy, and the record included three of the guru's compositions, along with four of Carlos's own, one of Wayne's, and a cover of the love theme from *Spartacus*. Despite Chinmoy's presence on the project, Carlos's devotion to his master was waning. Carlos was especially aggravated by Chinmoy's public criticism of tennis star Billie Jean King's lesbianism, and Carlos's wife, Debbie, was pressuring him to leave Chinmoy. When the group recorded the love theme from *Spartacus,* Wayne saw Carlos's avid interest in the tune's enslavement theme as a sign of his desire to split with Chinmoy. "Carlos was really into *Spartacus,* and thinking about what was given up, sacrificed by slaves. He played that melody himself," Wayne said. "That's when he was thinking about starting to depart from that Mahavishnu thing with John McLaughlin. John was beginning a departure from it, too. Carlos was starting to question it, 'cause when someone starts to tell you, 'You can't get from A to P except through me,' that's when you watch it. A little while later, John left Chinmoy and was celebrating by buying drinks at a bar."

In 1985, when Weather Report was disbanding, Joe and Wayne asked Carlos to join the band in the studio for its curtain-call recording, *This Is This.* Carlos hammered out some guitar effects on several tunes, including "The Man with the Copper Fingers." By this time Carlos had renounced Sri Chinmoy, and the guitarist had come to revere certain jazz musicians as medicine men, attributing supernatural powers to their music. "Wayne's notes are like acupuncture," he said. "His music rearranges your molecular structure immediately; your eyes change, become more at peace. He compels people to feel totality. Coltrane and Miles and Wayne were the ones who made me aware that you don't have to die to feel absoluteness and totality."

Carlos asked Wayne to go on tour, and finally, three years later, Wayne agreed to the summer 1988 tour. In a spirit of cooperation, both Carlos and Wayne brought personnel to the band: a couple of keyboardists, Patrice Rushen and Chester Thompson; two percussionists, Jose Chepito Areas and Armando Pereza; and a traditional rhythm section, with bassist Alphonso Johnson and drummer Ndugu Chancler, both Weather Report alumni. This grouping added up to a full-bodied combination of Latin percussion, progressive rock, and jazz improvisation, but also resulted in a group divided by allegiance and aesthetic. Alphonso had worked with both Carlos and Wayne, so he had a singularly broad perspective on the band. "It always felt like there were two camps," Alphonso said. "Wayne had Patrice and Ndugu, and then the other camp was Carlos, Chester, Armando, and Chepito. It was like there were two bands onstage. We just accepted that that's what it was and played. Not that the two bands hated each other, they were just noticeably different. I was somewhere in the middle, just trying to bridge the gap, because I had history with both of them."

Wayne decided to capitalize on the group's differences. "Wouldn't it be interesting to explore the *uncommonness* of people?" he commented to journalist Jim Macnie during the tour. Still, the band's factionalism could make its performances disjointed, and on occasion its sounds even clashed, producing a big thundercloud of turbulence. When Wayne felt this musical tension building up behind him during a solo, he'd transform it into humor with some comic asides. He lightened the mood by quoting "When You Wish Upon a Star" or other morsels of cheesy old songs. Hal Miller, a writer and a friend of Carlos's, accompanied the group on tour and remembered these humorous references. "Wayne loved to work in snatches of melody from 'I Love You Baby' and 'South of the Border,'" Hal said. "He always got everyone laughing." Wayne also put some early listening experience to good use: These songs were standard fare on Martin Block's popular 1940s radio program, *Make Believe Ballroom*.

Jazz musicians are often quote-happy, but their references are usually not so blatantly comic. Onstage with Santana, Wayne's hyper-pop commentaries were hilarious and bizarre, sticking out like gargoyles on the narrative arch of his solos. Wayne's pièce de résistance was the theme from *Star Wars,* which he used in truly critical moments. "I use that theme at the moment of potential disaster or triumph, when we might have victory over something," Wayne said. "It represents *Keep your shoulder to the wheel, don't let life's pitfalls discourage you. If you take two steps back, take eight forward.* I like those themes that say, 'Get your cape out of the cleaners and fly, Superman!'" As author Greg Martin has pointed out, the *Star Wars* character Obi-Wan Kenobi was a kind of Buddhist superhero himself, adept with the mystic power of "The Force" in a way that recalled the legendary power of the "Buddha life force."

It was a good sign that Wayne was playing the quoting games he had played back in his Messengers days. "Wayne didn't do the quoting thing as much, if at all, in Weather Report," Alphonso said. "He was much more serious. By the Santana tour, he was open, more jovial, and seemed to have both the serious side and the humorous side. The funny thing about playing with Wayne in these different situations was seeing that later he was a very different person: in his spiritual life, in his personal life, the way he functioned onstage—he'd dysfunctioned in Weather Report. All through Wayne's life there was tragedy, and by the tour with Santana, he had finally learned how to use it. After that, the way he internalized things came out through his musical expression."

Following performances in Montreux, Pori, Munich, and Paris, the tour swung south into Spain. After a late-July date in Valencia, the band headed to its next one in Barcelona. Driving up the orange grove-lined stretch of Spanish coast on a sunny morning, Carlos was in a good mood, so he popped some Coltrane into the tape deck. As strains from his favorite tune, "A Love Supreme," began to swirl around the bus, the other musicians tried to catch Carlos's eye, and then glared at him. When Wayne stepped off the bus at the next rest stop, someone asked Carlos how he could be so insensitive to Wayne: Didn't Carlos know that Wayne must suffer from a Coltrane inferiority complex? "Would I be intimidated if he played some Hendrix?" Carlos asked. "We don't think like that, coming from blues and rock-and-roll."

Drummer Chepito Areas saw an opportunity he couldn't resist; he'd test Wayne and expose exactly how he felt about being the "not quite Coltrane" of the tenor saxophone. When Wayne came back to the bus, Chepito pulled himself up to his full five feet of height and said, tauntingly, "Wayne took the Trane." Without missing a beat, Wayne replied, "In Spain insane." Chepito had been *read*. He started crying and said, "You're too deep for me."

Wayne had reconciled with Coltrane's legacy decades before, in Miles's group, and that musical background intimidated Chepito, as it did many of the group's rock musicians. "Every day was a challenge to be in that band," Carlos said. "I can't speak the language of jazz, of Charlie Parker. So all I can do is try to find the universal note, and have the willingness to have an open mind to confer with my inner light. People can practice till their fingers fall off, but if you want to have a sound, you should meditate and chant to feel a oneness with your life." Wayne did like Carlos's sound, and also appreciated his willingness to learn from the experience. "Every day, I'd look forward to just learning Wayne's songs," Carlos said. "I really wanted to honor the time with him. Everybody else in the group was writing then, but I felt like I was learning how to write by listening to Wayne's recomposition onstage."

That recomposition turned up an opportunity for some inspired work between Wayne and Carlos. Wayne's "Sanctuary" was a standard on the Santana–Shorter set list. In the late sixties, Miles's electric band had trademarked the tune with a memorably moody version. Together, Miles and Wayne gave the melody a rubato treatment, playing it in open, floating time, yet managing an eerily precise unison, as if they were of one mind. Then Wayne would produce an echo effect by falling slightly out of line behind Miles. The Santana-Shorter band made some transformations to "Sanctuary," but remained true to its earlier interpretation, abstaining from a regular rhythm or groove and preserving the piece's spacey atmosphere. By the time the tour reached Barcelona, Carlos wondered how the tune would respond to a little more rhythmic kick. He imagined a "boogie" version done in a John Lee Hooker style. Ever enamored of the blues guitarist, Carlos was especially high on him just then—at a show in London a couple weeks before, Hooker had joined the Santana–Shorter band on a couple tunes. "At the sound check, I asked Wayne if he'd be open to the idea," Carlos said. "The rest of the band looked at me like I'd just committed a sacrilege. They couldn't believe that I was asking the greatest living jazz composer to mess with one of his own tunes that way."

That night, thousands of Spaniards packed into an open-air plaza, bathed in the light of a full moon that seemed as strong as the spotlights shining onstage. The band worked down its set list to "Sanctuary," and launched into the tune with Carlos's groove-driven boogie. The rhythmic innovation seemed to combine with the moonlight to occasion an exceptional solo from Wayne. "It was like he went into channeling," Carlos said. "It was like watching kids open fire hydrants in the summer in Harlem. As he played, he started taking over for all the other instruments. He was playing the keyboardist's chords, the bass line, all kinds of rhythms. One by one, everyone dropped out, 'cause he was playing it all. But then he started shape-shifting. I swear. He played Lester Young and Ben Webster, and his face took on the aspect of all those musicians. His face changed into Bird and finally Coltrane, and then he put one knee down on the floor like a bullfighter. He was frozen, his veins were popping out, and time stopped."

On the way back to the hotel from the gig, the band rode in silence. Finally, Carlos broke it. "Wayne, what was that stuff about?" Carlos asked. "You were doing everything, playing all that stuff. On your solos tonight," he prompted. "Oh, well, during the show I looked out in the crowd, under that big moon," Wayne said. "I realized that Ben Webster and Coleman Hawkins and all those other guys were dead and couldn't ever play there, so I had to play for all of them."

Wayne adopted the boogie style for his own band's later performances of "Sanctuary." In the end, Wayne and Carlos found more common ground in politics and spirituality than in music. Their marathon conversations on tour fostered an enduring friendship. "Carlos doesn't bother with much static," Wayne said. "You know, extraneous stuff." In a roundabout way, Wayne added that Carlos was like a brother to him: "With Carlos onstage, it felt like when me and Alan used to make up stuff as kids at night."

Wayne's only brother died of a ruptured aorta at age fifty-six in 1987, so he was on Wayne's mind during the tour. "Before Alan passed, he was engaged to get married to Herbie Hancock's cousin. She used to babysit Herbie. Ruth Ann, Herbie said she was a fox. All the other women were chased away by Alan. They ran. They couldn't take it. But he couldn't do it with Ruth Ann. When he tried to go outside, avant-garde, it didn't bother her at all. So he didn't do it with her. And she said that for the first time in his life they went on a picnic. He was always fencing with the status quo, with the ideas people had and all that. But he didn't do anything like that at the picnic. His mind stopped working for a while, and he went to sleep for four hours in the park on her lap. She said she knew then that he was home. She was receptive to him. Ruth Ann was in the ambulance to the hospital with him when he died. It was in the morning. He was always talking about something. Lectures about philosophy or something. She said that in the ambulance on the way to the hospital, he was still arguing a point. Trying to make a point. Saying, 'You dig?' I can see him with his finger. Wagging it. Talking about the universe or how people are afraid to take chances or be individuals, have imagination. He'd say, 'The imaginative powers of the U.S. are in dire straits! Undeveloped to the point of lunacy!'"

16.

High Life

WHEN WAYNE GOT HOME from a tour in 1988, Ana Maria was waiting at his arriving gate at the airport, which she almost never did. And she wasn't alone. "She was standing there with this woman who had dark eyes, and announced to me, 'This is Carolina,' like this is really special," Wayne said. "I was thinking this must be a special friendship with them. Carolina was looking right into my eyes. People have shifty eyes, which can be embarrassment, shyness, or manipulation. All I thought was you couldn't bullshit Ana Maria. I was seeing the same thing on Carolina's face. And it revealed itself to me more and more as time went on." Ana's friend Carolina Dos Santos was a gorgeous and generous Brazilian dancer and actress who had moved to the U.S. to work in Brazilian Carnival events that

Maria Lucien produced at the Hollywood Bowl. "My background was Portuguese, but I didn't know my Portuguese grandfather," Carolina explained. "I wanted to know more about that country, that whole side of my heritage, and Ana was Portuguese." Carolina quickly became an invaluable friend to Ana Maria: "Because of being a daughter of an alcoholic father and a strict and angry stepfather, I had so much compassion for people battling that disease. Ana was struggling with all those demons, she'd have all those battles, and she would call me at four in the morning and ask me to go rescue her. She didn't want Wayne to have to do that." With Carolina's support, both Wayne and Ana finally overcame their drinking problems in the late eighties.

Wayne made a considerable amount of money on the Santana-Shorter tour—Carlos generously covered much of the tour's expenses himself. With this money, Wayne was able to take a break from steady touring. He built a studio addition to his house and continued composing music, though he was in no hurry to make a record. "Looking at life, you stop worrying about whether or not you're missing the next boat or train or bus," Wayne said. "That thing people are thinking, 'You better hurry, your time is running out and you better get a recording out there before the final hour!' I didn't need to make a superficial statement, because my awareness of eternity became stronger. Not that I had all the time in the world." Mostly, Wayne painted. "I do painting every forty years," he'd tell friends, since he'd last painted as a teenager. The rooms were soon filled with futuristic portraits of his wife and daughter. He also did a portrait of Carolina. "Why is he painting you?" Maria Lucien asked her. "He usually only paints his family."

Legend

On July 10, 1991, Wayne went to Paris for a concert with Miles Davis. Miles convened seventeen of his former musical associates at La Grande Halle de la Villette: Steve Grossman, Jackie McLean, Herbie Hancock,

Chick Corea, John McLaughlin, and many others. At this concert, Miles did something that was rare for him: He looked back. The retrospective show included "Dig," a tune he'd recorded with Jackie McLean forty years before. Wayne joined the trumpeter for "In a Silent Way" and "Footprints." On August 25, Miles played a concert at the Hollywood Bowl, the venue where Wayne had first played with him decades before. It was Wayne's fifty-eighth birthday, so Ana got a limo and took Wayne to the show with a large group of their friends, including Joni Mitchell, Danny Glover, and Jimmy Rowles. Wayne and some of his friends went backstage to see Miles in his dressing room. "Miles had lost so much weight between July the tenth and August the twenty-fifth," Wayne said. "Just enough to make it too much. But he also had an illumination around his skin; his face and everything, emanating from within to without. He looked very smooth, almost like he was going back to a baby."

When everyone left the dressing room, Miles asked Wayne and Ana Maria to stay behind. Miles went over and stood directly in front of Wayne, placed his hands on Wayne's shoulders, and brought up something he almost never did: music. Miles asked him if he still had a piece around called "Legend." Wayne had it, as he did all his scores. Miles said they ought to do it again, and Wayne said he would work on it. Then Miles gave Wayne some career advice, suggesting that among other things, he bring out the more romantic side of his playing. "You know, you need to be exposed," he said, looking Wayne in the eyes.

During their conversation, Miles sensed someone tiptoeing into the room. He turned around and saw Joni standing there. "I'll see *you* after the show," Miles said gruffly. Joni laughed, saluted him, and walked out, but she'd caught the gist of the conversation. When it was showtime, Wayne headed back to his seat in the theater. Onstage, Miles started in on one of his tunes, something with a contemporary harmony, and just as Wayne reached his seat, the trumpeter skillfully superimposed the melody of "Happy Birthday" over the tune for Wayne.

This backstage conversation took on special significance when Miles passed away a few weeks later and Miles's nephew found the score of "Legend" under the trumpeter's bed. Joni elaborated on the meaning of Miles's final tête-à-tête with Wayne. "It was like Miles knew he was going," Joni said. "And with him gone, Miles would have known that Wayne was the great voice left. And that Wayne should do all in his power to bring that into the forefront. Because history doesn't in very many cases reevaluate artists. For musicians, even if you wrote your most brilliant stuff at the end of your career, your popular stuff is what gets recycled and your growth goes unnoticed. As in the case of Mozart, who always pandered, he was so showy and competent. Once he fell from favor, he did his best work. But it's not performed as much, because it wasn't popular when he was alive. Somehow or other you can't count on historic corrections after you go. That's what Miles was saying." Joni understood Miles to mean that Wayne should promote his more recent compositions, or the work from the latter years of his life would be forgotten.

"When Miles said 'You need to be exposed,' he had a lot of confidence in his eyes," Wayne said. "He wanted me to know that he knew that I knew that. In a funny way he was trying to tell me that I was special. He never said anything like that in person before. He'd say, 'Wayne, you're crazy,' which meant, like, 'I like you.' I had a feeling that he was saying something for the last time and he knew that I had a battle in front of me. The battle was against the whole of the corporate world, and the marketing system, against the simple thing that's easy to market. He knew that I had to take it on myself to find a way to be exposed. And I had to do it legitimately, not using any controversy or skullduggery to get exposed. So after that conversation, I acted in that way, I took steps that led that way. I thought, *I'm going to think like an astronaut; I want to go to Saturn now, but I'll have to design the ship myself.* The idea of being exposed to a large audience would have to happen slowly, almost in the way that a prophet may be exposed to a few people, then progress through exposure to true believers who are ready to hear it, to the people with courage. It's a long process."

The following year, Wayne went on a "Tribute to Miles" tour with the Miles Quintet, with Wallace Roney sitting in for Miles. With the exception of Tony's "Elegy," the group played music they'd performed or recorded back in the 1960s—tunes like "So What," "RJ," "Little One," "Pinocchio," "Eighty One," and "All Blues." In his later years, Miles sometimes mentioned the quintet. "We covered a lot of ground, didn't we?" he'd say to Wayne.

Shortly after Miles died, Wayne ran down his mentor's voodoo in an interview: "To sum up Miles, I like to call him right now an original Batman. He was a crusader for justice and for value. He'd be Miles Dewey Davis III by day, the son of Dr. Davis, and at night in the nightclubs, he's in his lizard-skin suits with the dark shades and he's doing his Batman—fighting for truth and justice. But Batman had to be a dual personality, too, like he knew the criminal mind. So Miles, whatever he did that was not criminal but like short-tempered or he cursed everybody out, and when he was younger he'd hit somebody, or like they say Miles treated some woman really bad, or something like that . . . I would say that Bruce Wayne, the guy that played Batman, he was capable of doing that, too. That's why he was such a good Batman. . . . A pure person does not know what defenses to use against the vampire!"

A Great Music Experience

Wayne took a couple more years off from regular touring, staying home to compose, only emerging for odd gigs here and there. In 1994, Elektra Records executive Bob Krasnow signed Wayne for a sizeable advance—at least ten times what he'd earned with Columbia Records. In May, Wayne and Ana Maria headed to Japan for the Great Music Experience, a three-day music festival and UNESCO cultural event produced for global TV broadcast, with former Beatles producer George Martin as sound producer and musical consultant. The concert was held in Nara City, the country's ancient capital, on a stage set before the eighth-century Todaiji—at ten stories tall, this temple is the largest wooden structure in the world. Wayne went over as a solo act, joining two hundred musicians, including Joni Mitchell, Bob Dylan, INXS, the Chieftains, Ry Cooder, Jon Bon Jovi, Japanese pop and folk musicians, and film composer Michael Kamen, who conducted the Tokyo New Philharmonic Orchestra.

For ten days leading up to the show, the musicians mingled and brainstormed ways to combine their acts. Wayne had a powerful moment of communication with one of the show's more anonymous performers. "There were some Buddhist monk ladies in the show," Wayne said. "During a dinner break, they were looking over at us. There was one that was kind of new. She'd been listening to records before she became a monk, and she gave me a nod of acknowledgment, like, *I know you.*" The temple was quietly beautiful, and though music hadn't been played there much since the fourteenth century, the site's silent breezes and contemplation pools had a resonance of their own. The temple was set within a park inhabited by small deer, and Wayne, Ana, and Joni spent an afternoon playing with them. They bought biscuits and offered them to the animals. The deer seemed to bow as they took the biscuits in their mouths.

Festival organizers aimed for a "We Are the World"–style uplifting group sentiment, with a grandiose production similar to "The Wall" concert in Berlin. The show's mixed, global cast did enable a great musical experience, but also gave rise to cross-cultural comedy of errors. Wayne was asked to play "Footprints" in a duet with trumpeter Toshinori Kondo, a musical situation worlds apart from the one he'd played in thirty years before when the Messengers first traveled to Japan. Kondo envisioned himself as a kind of Miles of Japan, though his onstage bearing was closer to a Vegas nightclub act. With slicked-back hair, he animatedly played a plugged-in pink horn, speaking little English other than his idol's favorite word, "fuck." When Kondo and Wayne rehearsed "Footprints," the trumpeter did his best Jimi Hendrix impression, with some wild blowing and bleeding synthesized abstraction. Wayne wanted to be respectful of the experience, so he had to find a way to make the duet work.

At the show that night, Wayne solved the musical problem with stylistic time travel back to the very beginning of the twentieth century. Against Kondo's abstraction, Wayne laid down a kind of Dixieland rhythm on his tenor saxophone. He made "Footprints" swing deeply, like a New Orleans funeral march. Wayne's strong rhythmic thrust and Kondo's wailing sound combined into an impression of Japanese ceremonial music, a tribute to the concert's temple setting. The crowd went crazy. Joni listened to the performance offstage. "It was magnificent," she said. "What impeccable judgment from Wayne. The music needed some kind of grounding, and Wayne's solution was to go back almost to the origin of jazz, to the brothel, the beginnings." When Wayne came offstage, Joni and Ana told him how great it had sounded. He made light of the feat. "I know I'm certifiable now; they can take me away," he joked.

The Great Music Experience show was also one of the few times that Wayne and Joni performed together live. Joni had some challenges of her own at the event, she said. "The stage crew broke my guitar, and first gave me a replacement Stratocaster that hung down to my knees, then loaned me Jon Bon Jovi's guitar, which hung high around my neck, actually smashing my breasts. For 'The Magdalene Laundries,' a song that was critical of the Irish Catholic Church's treatment of women, I played with the Irish Chieftains. Having the group play on a song with such a controversial topic drew lots of questions from the Irish press. And then to top everything else off, they put me in a dressing room with Bob Dylan."

Joni was calm and centered when she and Wayne performed together. His soprano saxophone wove delicate lines around her voice on "Hejira" and "Sex Kills," and Joni's entrances after Wayne's solos expertly reflected his tone. But Wayne struggled to find openings on "The Magdalene Laundries," when the Chieftains crowded onto the stage with them, and on "The Crazy Cries of Love," which featured Ryu Hongjun on traditional Japanese flute. Hongjun's flute melodies matched the mood of Joni's vocals, but filled up her rests and pauses so completely that Wayne was left to play the artful dodger, and sometimes, the artful abstainer.

High Life

When Wayne returned to Los Angeles, he continued composing for several months—he still hadn't delivered a recording to Elektra. In the fall of 1994, he got a call from keyboardist Rachel Z, whom he had met at the North Sea Jazz Festival when she played there with the group Steps Ahead. Rachel asked Wayne to play on her next record. He declined, but invited her to work with him: Rachel was adept with Digital Performer, an audio-editing program for Macintosh that would help him arrange his compositions. In December, Rachel went out to Los Angeles, Wayne put her up in a hotel, and they went to work. Wayne's first order of business was bringing Rachel up to speed on his creative process. They watched movies like *On the Waterfront, Logan's Run, Wolfen,* and *Count Dracula*—Wayne told her that Coltrane had gotten some musical ideas from horror movies. Wayne also gave Rachel a few books to read, like *The Three Marias,* so that she'd understand the inspiration for his compositions.

On February 19, there was an earthquake west of Eureka measuring 6.6 on the Richter scale. It didn't hit Los Angeles as hard as the Northridge earthquake had a few months before, but was jarring enough to be frightening, especially to a native New Yorker like Rachel. Rachel moved in with the Shorters, and she and Wayne worked on his music in earnest. "The music was like a huge piano score for a piano player that had fifteen fingers," Rachel said. "I loved the music, really, really loved it. Every day was such a joy to hear what he was going to do with the harmony, 'cause the chords were so incredible. They were twelve-note chords, really complex." Each day, Rachel played several pages of music into the computer, arranging it for orchestra, with Wayne specifying exactly which line should be an oboe or a clarinet. "I grew up doing opera and with the symphony and had that knowledge, so I knew what he wanted in an orchestral sound," Rachel said. "But I didn't orchestrate it, I just followed his instructions."

With some wrangling from his lawyer, Wayne was released from his Elektra contract, and he signed with Verve Records in April 1995. He and

Rachel had already been working for six months when Wayne brought in bassist Marcus Miller to produce the recording, "just to kind of organize things," Wayne said. Wayne didn't have to spend much time initiating Marcus into his creative world—Marcus had worked with Miles, who showed him how anything from boxing to TV to food could feed into the compositional process. Miles also passed along his high esteem for Wayne to Marcus. The first time Marcus went over to Miles's house, in 1981, he saw an impeccably neat, handwritten score lying on Miles's piano. Marcus asked him what it was. In an affectedly casual tone, Miles answered, "Oh, just somethin' new Wayne sent me."

"I could tell Miles was droppin' that on me so cavalierly, just to blow my mind," Marcus said. "Like he was so damn hip he could just let an original piece of Wayne Shorter's music sit on the piano without looking at it." When Marcus was writing music for Miles's recordings like *Tutu* and *Amandla,* Miles would encourage him to capitalize on his creative period, and then add that he'd told Wayne the same thing back in the sixties. For Miles, Wayne's composition was the benchmark, an indication of how high young composers like Marcus might aspire.

Still, Marcus was unprepared for the sheer magnitude of music he found when he went to Wayne's house. "The thing I discovered when I began to work with Wayne was that he was like a wellspring of creativity," Marcus said. "It was unbelievable. All those classic songs that we heard from Wayne when he worked with Miles and everything, I came to realize that that's just like the tip of the iceberg for him. A lot of stuff he wrote for Weather Report was one page of a nine-page composition, where Zawinul said, 'We really only need this.' And I realized that when left to his own devices, there's a lot of music that will come out of him. When I got to his house and heard the *High Life* music, that's when it really hit me."

As a producer, Marcus was supposed to help organize Wayne's musical output, which proved to be a Sisyphean task: Wayne never stopped composing. One day, they were going over a twelve-page composition, and Wayne told Marcus he hadn't written the piece's bridge yet. "Man, this thing is complete, the way it is, Wayne," Marcus said. "Don't mess with it." Wayne seemed to agree, but when Marcus returned the next day, Wayne had written another seven pages of music. "I just wrote a little new section," Wayne said. This wasn't a traditional bridge, which connects the choruses of a song. This was a bridge that could span the Atlantic Ocean. Marcus knew Wayne's ambitious music would be a lot for listeners to digest —most people are unaccustomed to hearing such vast dissonance and bracing harmonies.

Rachel had tracked model orchestral parts on synthesizer, but Wayne wanted the sound and organic phrasing of a real orchestra. He took thirty members of the Los Angeles Philharmonic into the studio. While they were rehearsing, a violinist raised his hand and said, "On bar seventy-six, I'm on an A-natural, and the gentleman sitting next to me is on an A-flat. Is that correct?" Marcus and Wayne laughed. Marcus said, "Oh yeah, just play it strong, with some conviction. You're part of the section you're in and can't hear the whole group, so it might sound weird. But trust me, the whole thing sounds great." The players were dubious. The music was baffling, as was Wayne's musical instruction—mostly cinematic references like, "Remember Marlon Brando's walk in *On the Waterfront*? Let's go for it!" The orchestra players felt a little like musical servants in the court of a mad king.

During the playbacks, a French-horn player wandered into the control room and finally heard a recording of the full ensemble. He said, "Oh! This music is just way over my head." The man had to reconsider his assumptions about Wayne when he heard that the music made sense, just not to him. "The difference between a genius and a crazy cat is usually not much," Marcus observed. "This guy had to get into the control room and hear the whole thing to see that Wayne was on the genius side, rather than the crazy side."

After the orchestral parts and some live percussion had been tracked, Marcus added his own bass and machine-produced hip-hop backbeats, which along with Rachel's keyboards gave the recording a stylized, grooving electro-symphonic sound. The final touch was Wayne's own tenor and soprano solos. Wayne spoke about his episodic compositions with Joe

Woodard for *JazzTimes*: "In some places, there's an intention to get over the A-B-A song form. The best example might be the song called 'High Life.' It sounds kind of lush when it starts. Then another section appears and another kind of romantic section appears and then there's a kind of 'head 'em up and move 'em out' section. And then there is an arrival, a galaxy with lights. The phrase 'high life' also means up high, higher than any reference point, 'high' meaning far away, taking a chance to go somewhere where no one . . ." He let the *Star Trek* reference dangle. For Wayne, the music told stories and had a lot of character: "There's a melody that appears in places throughout the album. That appears in 'Children of the Night,' it appears in 'High Life,' and in another way, it appears in 'Pandora Awakens.' To me, that's antiphonal writing. You see that in opera, when a certain character appears."

When the record was released in October 1995, most reviewers didn't hear these stories. *Musician* magazine did, hailing the music as "atmospheric essays which evolve and mutate before our ears, with strings and horn parts lining the way." Mostly, reviewers were too repelled by the electronic stylings and/or harmonic density to hear much of anything in the music. Wayne received the harshest criticism of his career from *New York Times* critic Peter Watrous, who called the record a "pastel failure." He acknowledged that Wayne "may be the most important living jazz musician," then went on to use *High Life* as a gateway to criticizing the electric "curse" Miles Davis had given to a generation of musicians. He praised Wayne's early work, then wrote, "He has spent the last quarter century flashing bits of his grand talent, then finding the nearest drain down which to dump the rest."

One glancing statement held Wayne responsible for spawning the smooth-jazz phenomenon, claiming his fluid soprano sax—which he'd started playing to be heard over electric music—begat Kenny G, the best-selling smooth-jazz saxophonist. This was perhaps the most poorly laid of Watrous's criticisms. Deceptively simple innovators often spawn merely simple imitators who lack the depth and beauty of the innovators. According to this logic, Watrous should have blamed Miles's beautiful minimalism for the vacuity of Muzak, Coltrane's keening drive for long, belabored free-jazz solos, and Monk's twist-and-turn piano dances for spastic, disjointed keyboard solos. Watrous's most personal strike at Wayne was a claim that the record's electronic sound was intentionally mercantile, but would prove to be a "commercial mistake," because he'd sold so few copies of his electric Columbia recordings in the eighties.

The article was so subjective that fellow musicians rallied in Wayne's defense, and the bad press advanced Wayne's position in jazz as a misunderstood genius. Trumpeter Dave Douglas began work on a tribute record to Wayne. And on the day of the article's publication, a Sunday, Wayne got a call from Tom Carter, director of the Thelonious Monk Institute of Jazz, in Washington, D.C. Tom relayed a request from President Bill Clinton that Wayne take part in the institute's educational workshop in Thailand, as well as a State Department concert honoring the king of Thailand on the fiftieth anniversary of his coronation. A saxophonist himself, Clinton was a big fan of Wayne's, and they'd met a couple times, when Wayne performed in Little Rock at the kickoff event following Clinton's nomination in 1992, and then at his televised inaugural ball in 1993, when Wayne appeared as the second-to-last act of the evening, after Michael Jackson and before Barbra Streisand. Clinton had read the *Times* article and wanted to make some kind of affirming gesture to Wayne. Wayne later got a call from Vice President Al Gore's staff, asking for advice on selecting a soprano saxophone stand, a surprise gift for Clinton.

Wayne didn't want to be the Job of the Jazz World, and he had long before given up on any understanding from critics. "Critics hide in the bushes waiting for a stagecoach to come along so they can ambush it," he said, and invented a new category for his music. "I don't like duty music. I want to make duty-free music." He was bothered, however, when he took the music out on tour with a group of musicians who wouldn't learn it. His band included Will Calhoun from Living Colour on drums, Tracy Wormworth on bass, who'd played with the B-52s and was later on *The Rosie O'Donnell Show,* Adam Holtzmann and Rachel Z on keyboards, David Gilmore on guitar, and Frank Colon on percussion, when he could get away from his regular gig with Manhattan Transfer. After the band's first show in San Francisco, Wayne was panned in the local paper the next day. He had to agree—the sound was bad, and the band didn't know the material.

Wayne hired a new person to be both sound engineer and tour manager, a sprightly, competent, and extremely upbeat man named Rob Griffin. Rob improved the sound quality but couldn't do anything about the fact that Wayne's sprawling, ambitious arrangements sounded cumbersome in this instrumental setting. Even Rachel Z, who loved Wayne's *High Life* material, encouraged him to play some of his earlier compositions from the Blue Note era, too—a full two hours living the *High Life* was just too much to take. The next night, at the Showbox Theater in Seattle, the band again wallowed in the music, reading charts off the floor of the stage. In one of his solos, Wayne quoted "The Death March," with grim humor. It was a piercing statement; his sidemen's faces drained of color. Wayne's road hand, Eddy Strickler, attested to the tour's difficulties. "I watched that band struggle mightily through hellacious tours around Europe and the U.S.," he said. Now even the musicians who had defended *High Life* were perplexed. Neither the music nor the band was working onstage. Why didn't Wayne just put together a small group of suitable musicians and play some of his old Blue Note stuff that everyone loved?

In a November 1995 interview with writer John Garelick for the *Boston Phoenix,* he explained: "You know the actor John Garfield?" he asked, referring to the 1940s movie star. "In one movie he walked up to this train station, the ticket booth, and the guy says, 'Yes, where are you going?' And he says, 'I want a ticket to nowhere.' I thought: *That's it.* The freedom to do that. I want a ticket to nowhere." This was in part an escapist fantasy, but Wayne's determination was clear: No matter what the cost, he wanted to take the path less traveled in his musical career.

17

Super Nova

AFTER THE TROUBLED 1995 *High Life* tour, Wayne began reassembling his band. In March of 1996 he went to Bangkok, joining up there with Herbie Hancock, who was completing a three-week tour of India and Thailand with seven students from the Monk Institute. Wayne was relieved to have a break from leading his band, happy to instruct student musicians in the rudiments of jazz. "Wayne sometimes tells oblique stories and speaks in ways that can be complex," institute director Tom Carter said. "But in teaching situations with younger students, Wayne speaks clearly and concisely so that they can follow his experiences and instruction directly. He comes in very organized, with every lesson plan plotted out, like a college professor. His generosity to the Monk Institute compares to no one." It was a fun and exotic trip. Ana Maria came along, as did Herbie's wife, Gigi, and the couples toured local Buddhist temples and went on an elephant safari. The institute's workshop culminated in the fiftieth anniversary celebration at the Royal Palace for the coronation of the king of Thailand, who was a jazz musician himself. (Saxophonist Benny Carter later commented on the king's musical skills: "He's no Bill Clinton!")

In the spring of 1996, Wayne and Ana's friend Carolina moved into their house on Dona Amelia Street in Los Angeles, and she stayed on there while they were in Thailand. Ana often said that she and Carolina were so close that they must have been sisters or mother and daughter in a previous life, so it felt natural to invite her to stay with them. "Opening our house to a Brazilian friend, people told us we were going to have a constant *ding-ding-a-ding,* lively party stuff," Wayne said. "But we didn't hear Carolina." Carolina was working three part-time jobs at the time, so she was usually away from the early morning until late at night. "When she came into the house, it was so quiet you didn't even hear the key metal against the lock," Wayne said. When they got home from Thailand, Carolina thought about returning to Brazil, where she had a business opportunity to run a fitness center chain, but Ana convinced her to stay in Los Angeles, and in their home. "I don't know why, but you just have to," Ana said, with inexplicable conviction.

With a new band, Wayne headed out on a summer tour of Europe in June. Ana Maria invited their niece Dalila, Maria Lucien's daughter, on a trip to Rome. The trip was a high school graduation gift to the girl, who was a budding artist. Ana and Dalila planned to meet up with Wayne on tour in Italy, and then visit Roman museums together. The women left on July 17, and were supposed to take a direct flight from New York to Rome, but the flight was canceled. Ana managed to get first-class seats on TWA Flight 800 to Paris with a connection to their final destination. Ana quickly called her sister Maria from the airport, excitedly telling her about their first-class upgrade on a rerouted flight to Paris.

That evening, as they were boarding the plane in New York, the Wayne

Shorter Band had returned to its hotel following a show in Nice, France. This tour was going much better than the previous one. Wayne had a svelte group, with Rodney Holmes on drums, who had been with Joe Zawinul; Jim Beard on keyboards; Alphonso Johnson on electric bass; and Dave Gilmore on electric guitar, the only holdover from his previous group. Other musicians were talking up the new band, whose set list included some of Wayne's popular 1960s tunes such as "El Gaucho," "Chief Crazy Horse," and "Footprints"—Wayne had finally consented to revisit the past, as long as he could do it on his own terms. At the band's North Sea Jazz Festival appearance a couple nights before Nice, Carlos Santana, Herbie, Dr. John, and a dozen other musicians gathered around the sound board, enraptured by the show. John McLaughlin drove over from his house in Monaco to see the gig in Nice.

Nice would be the last show on the tour. The plane carrying Ana Maria and Dalila got only as far as the coast of Long Island, when it exploded, crashing into the water below and killing all 230 people aboard. Wayne's travel agent, Kristen Birner, knew about recent flight cancellations to Europe and was concerned that Ana and Dalila may have been switched to the crashed flight. Kristen called Scott Southard and said that she wasn't sure, but thought that the women might have taken Flight 800. Scott Southard alerted Rob Griffin to the situation, and both of them tried to get verification from the airline as well, but TWA was not releasing Flight 800's passenger list, by order of the National Transportation and Safety Board.

Wayne had high blood pressure, so Rob called in a doctor to be there when he told Wayne about Ana's presumptive death. Rob waited until he saw the light go on inside Wayne's room, and was sure that he was awake. Rob called him. "What's wrong? Tell me what's wrong," Wayne demanded. Rob and the doctor went into Wayne's room, and Rob gave him the news. Wayne collapsed into Rob, but then quickly recovered a calm serenity that was "almost scary," his bandmates said. Wayne was determined to exhaust all possibilities before he accepted that Ana Maria had definitely been on the flight to Paris. Rob called bassist Matthew Garrison's mother, who lived in Rome, and asked her to go to the airport to meet Ana and Dalila there. Their luggage arrived, but they never did—the women switched to Flight 800 so late that there hadn't been time to transfer their baggage to the correct plane. Still, Wayne stubbornly refused to believe they'd been on Flight 800. Rob called Tom Carter's wife, Cheri, who worked in the Clinton administration, and asked her to persuade the White House to release the flight's seating chart. The directive went out, and Cheri faxed the seating chart to Rob in Nice. Ana and Dalila were in seats 3A and 3B.

Herbie called Wayne from his tour in nearby Marseilles, and they chanted together on the phone. Wayne was resilient, immediately resisting the attack on his faith that the tragedy represented. "I know these are my demons, and they think that they can get me with this," he told Herbie. "I made a vow. Bring them all on now. This isn't getting me now." Wayne's tour was quickly canceled. Alphonso accompanied Wayne on the plane home to the U.S. and was entrusted with the responsibility of keeping him from drinking—he'd been clean for seven years, but everyone knew how tempting it would be for him to drink himself into numbness at a time like this. TWA officials met and guided them through each leg of the trip, and again the White House intervened, requesting that Wayne's final flight from New York to Los Angeles be held until he could board it.

For the better part of twenty-six years, Wayne had unconditionally devoted himself to his charismatic, beautiful, and sometimes demanding wife. And Ana was his greatest defender. Once, when they didn't have enough money for the security deposit on a rental apartment, she somehow procured the place with an argument that her husband was "a brilliant composer who needed a nice place to live." In the final decade of their marriage, both Wayne and Ana had overcome drinking problems, which brought them closer together. "It's not true," he said, that when a couple is together a long time, "the light wanes, the darkness sets in, and so much changes that you don't know each other. The opposite was happening." Wayne's loss was compounded by the fact that Ana had vanished in the plane's explosion, so there were no bodily remains, nothing to grieve over. When he got home, he combed the house for signs of his wife. She had worn Fracas perfume, a scent that especially became her. He couldn't find a trace of the scent anywhere, or any traces of her at all. This absence felt mysterious, like Ana had not just packed for a trip but had wiped the place clean of her most personal effects before she left.

When family and friends visited, Wayne was clearly in grief, yet it was subdued. "Some people don't know how to act in the face of death," Joni said. "They milk the drama or they solicit self-pity, but Wayne was never pitiful about the thing. He dealt with it, as far as I could see, with such grace." Wayne was so self-composed that he might have seemed unfeeling. He had experience with grief after having lost his daughter Iska, and twenty-three years of Buddhist practice had given him the faith to deal with Ana's passing in an exceptional way. Nichiren Buddhists don't believe death is the end of life. In the Judeo-Christian ethos, a soul or spirit governs your body and mind and continues to exist after death, but you leave behind an absence of yourself on earth. Instead of this ethereal soul, Nichiren Buddhism espouses the notion of a true self, which continues to exist whether you're alive or dead. It's not reincarnation, exactly, but more of an eternal continuation of self.

Buddhists work to overcome their fear of death through realizing this true self. Wayne was soothed by the knowledge that Ana had been fearless about death. "Ana was in a place of extreme, unshakable confidence in her life condition," he said. "And the people around her—me, her family—we knew she had decided not to live her life in fear. She didn't grow up that way. Since she was ready to face whatever came, her life condition transcended that." Tina Turner called Wayne to offer her condolences. "She did it, didn't she?" Tina said. "She left in the greatest array of light. She went with the whole spectrum." Tina was acknowledging the Buddhist belief that death is the moment when the true self emerges. In Ana's defining moment of self, the plane went up in a blaze. With Wayne's unique perspective on death, the very explosion of the plane was a consolation to him. Friends came over to offer other comfort. Terri Lyne Carrington stopped in with chicken, some hot wings. Wayne asked her to bring some more the next day, and everyone took it as a positive sign.

Wayne had a tour of Japan planned for August. He was loath to go, but knew Ana would have wanted him to move ahead with his life and with his music—she had championed his career like no one else. So a month after the accident, he went to Japan for a three-week tour. Rodney Holmes's birthday was on August twenty-fourth, Wayne's was the twenty-fifth, and Jim's was the twenty-sixth, so the Japanese clubs treated them to champagne backstage, and the band had some fun despite the circumstances. There was a lot of feeling in Wayne's playing, and he pushed himself physically to extreme levels. One night in Tokyo, Wayne played a long, muscular solo, after which the band settled into a groove. He went over to lean on the piano, sweat pouring down his face, and he said to Jim, "Do you . . . ever . . . get . . . tired . . . of playing . . . *music*?" Wayne was asking and answering the question himself, saying yes and no at the same time. Carolina went along on tour to look after Wayne, providing moral support. Wayne's grief didn't entirely distract him from the fact that though this band was much better than his other groups, it still didn't realize his musical vision. "We kept thinking there must be people out there, even if they're young people who are not there yet, who have the spirit and are coming up," Carolina said.

Herbie had the spirit. Musically, he was the closest thing Wayne had to true north. Wayne especially needed dependable direction and musical sympathy. In March 1997 they recorded a duet album together, *1+1,* then went on tour that summer. One of Wayne's new compositions, "Aung San Suu Kyi," was dedicated to the Burmese Nobel laureate. It had the sound of an instant jazz standard and won a Grammy for Best Instrumental Composition. He'd had its gamelan-like melody floating around in his head for a while—he used it briefly on an earlier tune, "Atlantis."

"Me and Herbie and the whole line of musicians who came through Miles learned not to stray too far from the fine point, and that fine point was the same as back with Beethoven, Ravel, Satie, Tchaikovsky," Wayne said. Appropriately, their onstage duets were classically influenced conversations, but they strayed freely according to a sixth sense. One night they were playing "A Memory of Enchantment," and Wayne noticed that Herbie had moved away from usual jazz technique, in which a pianist plays the melody with the right hand and "comps," or plays chords, with the left. Instead, Herbie played a tremolo, a rapid alternation of two notes, in both hands. There were no recognized chords, the tremolos were just moving around, creating the impression of . . . Picasso or Salvador Dalí. Wayne let his soprano lines melt into Herbie's surreal frame of sound, and in return, Herbie acknowledged the hallucinatory effect with a leaping "Dance of the Sugar Plum Fairy" line in his left hand. Their musical dialogues brought new meaning to the phrase "Go with the flow."

This music could come off as rarefied twin language, making sense only to them, like the conversation of two brothers sharing a stoned afternoon in the basement rec room. Their passages denied expectations of usual musical techniques such as crescendo and decrescendo, and tension and release. Some listeners were content to settle into the surreal experience, but others, especially traditional jazz fans, sat waiting for the real music to begin. Many critics found the music merely lugubrious.

Herbie said the music was in fact an elegy for Ana Maria, though he heard hope in it. "When we did *1+1,* it was almost like her presence was there," Herbie said. "Not as a person sitting there, but in the body of the music. Something about the way the music flowed and the sensitivity that was there reminded me so much of her. And at same time, there was an openness towards the new day that will emerge as it always does." As the tour continued, Wayne often played upsurges of clear, bold intervals—thirds, fifths, and octaves—the sounds of triumph, as if he was determined to prevail despite his personal loss. By the time Wayne returned home from the tour, he had made a decision, as he told Carolina. "Because of our human interconnectedness, we affect everybody else with our thoughts, actions, and deeds," he said. "Because we affect lives of those who are here, the best way to honor Ana's life is to become the happiest man alive."

Many people had thought that Wayne, at sixty-five, would give up on life and on music in his grief. This decision to become the happiest man alive was the product and culmination of his Buddhist practice. Wayne had lost a child, his parents, his brother, and his wife of twenty-six years, but through his practice he found the courage to embrace life again.

Ana Maria's sister Maria Lucien noticed how much Wayne was relying on Carolina for friendship, emotional support, and practical help—with Wayne's creative mindset, he sometimes needed someone to help him with the basic business of living. "Maybe that's why Ana kept asking Carolina to stay in Los Angeles when she got on that plane," Maria told Wayne. "Maybe there's no one else in this whole wide world who could be with you." Ana's request that Carolina stay in Los Angeles began to take on mystical significance for Wayne. "When Ana told Carolina, 'Stay here until I get back,' it was just an outer plea," Wayne said. "The inner plea was a real directive, one that transcends all language." It became more and more plausible to Wayne that Ana "had been preparing another woman to take over."

"We'll end up together," Wayne said offhandedly to Carolina one day. Carolina was moved by Wayne's amorous proposition, but worried about the implications. Though all their friends knew Carolina was an ethical and even conservative woman, she was afraid outsiders might see her as an opportunist, taking advantage of Ana's trust by snatching up Wayne for herself after Ana died. Maria Lucien kept up a steady stream of innuendos around Carolina and Wayne. She'd wander around the house suggestively singing Tom Jobim's "So Tinha de Ser com Voce"—"It Had to Be with You." Ana Maria's own sister, the person who should have been most protective of her late sister's marriage, was authorizing the new romance. Ultimately, both Wayne and Carolina felt that their relationship had been condoned by Ana Maria and even "written in the stars." They were married on February 2, 1999. At age sixty-six, Wayne was a newlywed for the third time, married to a woman twenty-six years younger than he.

Meanwhile, Jazz at Lincoln Center commissioned Wayne to compose and perform some symphonic pieces for its spring program. It was an opportunity for Wayne to finally realize a performance of his broad arrangements in a large setting. He wrote a new composition for small jazz group and chamber orchestra called "Dramatis Personae," a title he borrowed from theater, which refers to the characters of a play. Robert Sadin conducted the performance, and had a special appreciation of Wayne's painterly and cinematic musical descriptions at rehearsals. "When rehearsing, Wayne rarely speaks about music in a technical way," Robert said. "He prefers to describe the mood, or the image, or the motion he envisions. When you read Debussy's writings, he also resists technical exposition. He and Wayne share a beautiful sense of the evocation of language . . . and of sound! I don't presume to 'explain' why Wayne does this, but I do know how strongly he wants his musicians or collaborators to draw on all of their personal resources and experiences when they play. A technical explanation, however accurate, might reach the musician but not the whole person."

At the April 1998 Lincoln Center performance, Wayne played the first half with a small shifting group that included Ryan Kisor on trumpet, Jim Beard and Eric Reed on piano, David Gilmore on guitar, Christian McBride on bass, Herlin Riley on drums, and Mino Cinelu on percussion—a mix of Lincoln Center regulars and his own regular band members. In the second half, this smaller ensemble was joined by a chamber orchestra, debuting "Dramatis Personae" and revisiting some older compositions: "Angola," from his Blakey days; "Orbits," from his years with Miles; and "High Life," from his most recent solo recording. Wayne had realized that his tunes had no expiration date. "That's my premise," he told journalist Ed Bradley during rehearsals. "That no song is really finished. Or no symphony is really finished. You can do *da-da-da, da-da-da, BAM!* but the word *finish* is artificial. So I can take a song I've written a long time ago and it's, it's not finished." Robert Sadin also gave Bradley his take on Wayne's revisitation of older material: "Wayne's compositions are living organisms which change over the years. He never goes back to repeat things by rote. Wayne just can't—it's not even a question of won't—he can't do that. The music grows within him. So when he returns to play any of the older material, it has to evolve, as he evolves."

The performance was a qualified success. With the orchestra playing complex, composed music behind an improvising jazz group up front, it didn't always click. The gulf between classical music and jazz narrowed considerably in the eighties and nineties, when many jazz musicians studied classical music. There was, however, still a big difference in the way classical musicians were trained and jazz musicians played. Jazz musicians are weaned on rhythmic subtlety, while classical musicians learn more complex rhythms only by reading them. In performance, the gulf was widened by the fact that an orchestra typically delays an entrance after a conductor cues it—and even the orchestra's briefest lag was noticeable when Wayne's band up front had a quicker attack.

In 1999, Wayne received another commission, this one from the Detroit Symphony Orchestra. He started writing a piece called "Syzygy"— the next-to-last S-word in the dictionary (*szechuan* is the last). *Syzygy* is the straight-line configuration of three celestial bodies, as when the sun, moon, and earth are aligned during a solar or lunar eclipse. Characteristically, Wayne wrote this celestial title while on a steady diet of mental junk food. "Wayne's music is truly about life in the most general way possible," Carolina said. "That whole piece, 'Syzygy,' he literally wrote it while watching television the whole time." And Wayne wasn't watching Carl Sagan's educational public television programs on astronomy, she said. "It was *Jerry Springer* or whatever crap happened to be on TV. He said he watches everything to see what is directing people's minds." Around this time, Carolina's teenage daughter Mariana went to Europe and had an epiphany about CNN's control of information in America. Together, Mariana and Carolina sermonized Wayne on the evils of TV, especially too much of it. Wayne said *they* should watch *more*. "When your wisdom is developed," he explained, "anything and everything is a ways and means to creating something valuable." With an advanced worldview, you could spin straw into gold, white noise into harmony, and apparently even transform the offerings of *Jerry Springer* into music of the spheres.

Wayne premiered "Syzygy" as well as another new composition, "Capricorn II," on January 2, 2000, at a concert with the Detroit Symphony Orchestra called the Millennium Jazz Celebration. Again, Robert Sadin presided as conductor and musical director, with Wayne leading a quartet up front and center. This performance was more unified than the symphonic work at Lincoln Center of two years before. The music used the full colors of the orchestra to better advantage, and Wayne's solos took off from more distinct intervals at the music's core. With this success, Wayne's booking agent, Scott Southard, widely promoted his availability for symphonic work. Wayne performed orchestral showcases that year with the ninety-piece Portal Orchestra of Portugal and with student musicians at the University of Southern California. John Patitucci played acoustic bass at these performances, though he was highly regarded as an electric bassist with Chick Corea's group and had played that instrument off and on in Wayne's pickup groups since 1987. "The USC show was superior," John observed, because "rhythmically the orchestra was more centered with us, with the quartet, rather than staid and set in their ways as a group." It also helped that Wayne had a little more rehearsal time at USC because he didn't have to pay the student musicians as he did professional musicians.

For most of these performances, the quartet fronting the symphony included Terri Lyne on drums, John on bass, and Jim Beard on piano. At the Monterey Jazz Festival in September 2000, Wayne brought in some new players. Along with John, Danilo Perez was on piano and Brian Blade was on drums. There was something about Danilo's abstract handling of chords and Brian's eruptive drumming that made Wayne play with more abandon and feeling himself, so that the improvisation was stronger, better balanced with the composed music that the orchestra played. Wayne thought back to the musical experiment he'd tried in 1969 on *Super Nova*: "People have been asking me to do an acoustic tour forever, and maybe these are the guys who could make it happen—they don't need me to say

'Once upon a time' with my horn before they know what to do." He took John, Danilo, and Brian into the studio to record a couple tunes for his next album.

While Wayne busied himself with symphonic performances, Carolina spent a lot of time working at the Florida Nature and Culture Center, a $20 million Buddhist retreat center north of Miami. The FNCC buildings and dorms are located on 125 acres of restored wetlands, a haven for native live-oak trees and Sabal palms and migrating birds like cranes—an idyllic setting for the international conferences that Soka Gikkai International hosts there regularly. In 2000, Carolina made five trips from California to work as a translator at these events. Their friends Loren and Fernando Oliveira lived nearby, in the booming town of Weston, and the Shorters considered investing in property there.

Those plans changed when they went to spend Christmas 2000 with Carolina's cousin in Aventura, Florida, just north of Miami. She lived on the fourth floor of a new condo, an imposing salmon-colored high-rise with turquoise trim, spectacularly perched between a bay and the ocean. The new condo was still mostly unoccupied. That night, Carolina's nieces discovered that the empty apartments were unlocked. They led Wayne and Carolina into a spacious penthouse. Wayne had a flashlight, but turned it off when he went into the apartment, which was lit by a huge moon . . . the space seemed to hover between the water and the sky. "This feels like a spaceship in here, like the mothership itself," Wayne said. "I'm gonna write some hip shit in this place." It had been decided. Wayne woke Carolina up at six the next morning, Christmas Day, asking her to call a real estate broker. Within a couple months they sold their home in Los Angeles, and in March 2001 moved into a condo on the twenty-seventh floor in the "mothership" building in Aventura. This was no retirement move. Ponce de León couldn't have been more excited to land on Florida's shores. As Wayne pointed out, Aventura was another name for adventure.

18

Prometheus Unbound

As WAYNE WAS MOVING to Miami, rumors were flying around the jazz world. "You heard about Wayne?" Like Herbie, Miles, Duke, or Bird, Wayne has one-name-only status among fans. "Wayne is going on tour with an *all-acoustic* quartet, and I heard he's playing older stuff." Fans were most wound up about the fact that Wayne was working with three younger musicians, all of them near the top of the field: drummer Brian Blade, bassist John Patitucci, and pianist Danilo Perez, the players who'd comprised Wayne's fronting quartet for the symphonic appearance at the Monterey Festival the previous fall. *Village Voice* critic Gary Giddins made joking reference to the frenzied anticipation of Wayne's appearance in New York: "Boomer heroes—notably Dewey Redman, Wayne Shorter,

Keith Jarrett, Jack DeJohnette, Chick Corea, Wayne Shorter, Michael Brecker, and did I mention Wayne Shorter?—accounted for most of the expectations and red meat at JVC 2001."

The group had its premiere in June at the Spoleto Festival in Charleston, South Carolina. The musicians had only two rehearsals before the show, one of which was actually the sound check—Wayne was paying them to practice in performance, as Miles had. At the sound check, the musicians were euphoric and giddy. Wayne was visibly happy, flippant, and puckish. He kept demonstrating basketball star Allen Iverson's handshake; the NBA Finals were on, and his beloved Lakers were taking on Iverson's Philadelphia 76ers. But when it came to the music, he was as oracular and remotely commanding as a gentle Prospero. As they rehearsed "Water Babies," his bandmates wanted to know how he planned to establish the tune's regular rhythm after a loose rubato intro. Wayne said, "Let's not set it. We'd rather go for elusiveness than clarification." His instructions to the group were as spare as his own playing, almost like a Zen master delivering koans. As Danilo Perez said: "I was playing for Wayne, and he said, 'Put more water in those chords.' There was a specific part he said he wanted me to put the water on. And I went to my room and I thought about it. I couldn't sleep, you know. I was thinking about water. When I came back, I broke out some watery chords, and he said, 'But the water has to be clean.' Right there I knew this was going to be an adventure."

Danilo was impressionable and game, and he took Wayne's instruction to heart, as did the other musicians. For the younger players it was a chance to learn from the elder statesman. A dream gig. But Wayne had no interest in being the group's guardian or hero. "Remember when Lois Lane was falling from the building, and Superman swooped down and grabbed her?" Wayne asked. "He said, 'I've got you.' And she said, 'Who's got *you*?' That's what I like to play music with, something like that." Wayne wanted to move beyond the traditional roles of leader and sidemen in the quartet—he refused to be the preacher on the pulpit with the other musicians over in the Amen Corner. He wanted full cooperative control of the music's form and mood.

During the rehearsal of "JuJu," Wayne said: "Let's do it multi-rhythmic all the way. The more contrapuntal stuff we use, the more it will sound like an octet." Brian understood this instruction. He was arguably the first original voice on the drums since Tony Williams. The Louisiana-born son of a preacher, Brian was bespectacled and soft-spoken, with his lanky long arms and legs making his small kit look like a Mickey Mouse drum set. Brian swooped into the tune and made his drums its conquering hero. Danilo looked a little bewildered at first, rifling through his sheet music to find the tune—but he adeptly brought a Brazilian bossa feel to the rhythm at a key point; he had covered a whole cross-section of New and Old World rhythms on his own *Motherland* recording. John Patitucci stood there like the deacon of the congregation, faithfully directing the action with his bass. After the rehearsal, John explained Wayne's reworking of "JuJu" this way: "Wayne always thinks compositionally. We play the tune in a straight rhythm that is African-oriented, sometimes in swinging time, and also very slowly, with almost a Brazilian feel. With all these options to choose from, Wayne keeps his rhythms swirling and pliable, and anything but predictable."

The musicians were all decades younger than Wayne and had grown up studying his music, both as composers and players. The music they played with Wayne validated their years of practice, given that they came up in the eighties and nineties, when the limber, adventurous model of the sixties Miles Quintet became more and more relevant to jazz. After the rehearsal, Wayne compared the new group to Miles's quintet. "With Miles we never thoroughly rehearsed anything, and no one judged one another," Wayne said. "We were busy having a good time, and Miles wanted to have a group like that, where his responsibility was to create, and he didn't have to be psychologist. Miles wanted to be entertained himself. He'd been playing longer than any of us, been on many stages. Everyone has to feel they're being entertained by each other. It was happiness at work onstage."

Now, at age sixty-eight, with his own younger players, Wayne was happily primed for a late-career renaissance. He'd always had a sympathetic musician or two in his bands, but now he had a whole group of like-minded artists.

It helped that they were playing in the entirely acoustic setting that Wayne had denied his listeners for so many years. And it didn't hurt that they played some of his well-known tunes from his sixties Blue Note recordings—those records had gained in stature over time. But Wayne challenged the critical consensus that his structural and melodic innovations largely occurred during his Blue Note and Miles years. Early on in the tour, he eschewed some of his more familiar early works like "Footprints" and "Nefertiti" for later compositions like "Atlantis" and "Aung San Suu Kyi." (This was especially exciting for the younger players. Wayne never published sheet music for his later work, so they were finally seeing authentic charts for music they'd labored to transcribe in school.) And Wayne tampered with the sound of even his catchiest melodies. At the first gig, in Charleston, his arrangements were so radically different that the music reviewer for *The Post and Courier,* a local newspaper, found them melodically unrecognizable.

Two shows down the road, the Wayne Shorter Quartet played Carnegie Hall, where the jazz cognoscenti were out in full force, nervously buzzing about the group's debut. With improvised music, you know it can be great, but are afraid it won't be. That makes the music good for the soul, but bad for the nerves. And people always have especially high expectations for Wayne. When a jazz legend like Ornette Coleman performs, he may have a good or bad night, but it isn't taken as a reflection on his character, as it is with Wayne. Wayne's shows are a barometer of the state of jazz, even the health of humanity itself. He is perhaps the only living jazz musician who's been touched by so many great jazz icons—Prez, Bud, Bird, Blakey, Miles—and still has the Promethean power to transform music today.

So when Wayne took the stage before this music-industry tribunal, he seemed a little intimidated and showed more hesitancy than he had in Charleston. Also, Wayne had mostly played soprano saxophone in recent years. When Wayne picked up the tenor, Danilo joked that he could "see dust coming out of Wayne's horn," like it had been up on the shelf for too long. Wayne's tone on the horn was still uneven, and he darted in and out of tunes teasingly, practicing his improvisational motto that no good thing bears repeating. Listeners expected him to start small and finish big, but instead he gave them his stream of consciousness, jumping around from character to scene to setting in the cinematic frames of his mind. The band's approach to music recalled Miroslav Vitous's comment that Wayne can wait longer than any other musician—the band played around a melody for five or six minutes before actually arriving at the primary melody.

A couple days later, Ben Ratliff's *New York Times* review was favorable, noting that the younger musicians were "scarily committed to the opportunity of making a perfect band for Mr. Shorter, almost ready to die for it." In *The Village Voice,* tastemaker critic Gary Giddins called it a "spellbinding hour, brimming with feeling and pleasurable apprehension" and added that "they re-created the kind of suspense that made the second Miles Davis Quintet a revelation—not merely backing the soloist, but collaborating with him on each measure. The result was a true quartet music, driven by spontaneity, impulse, and a shared commitment to the whole." By its next show, the Wayne Shorter Quartet was *the* touring phenomenon for jazz critics and fans, even attracting an elusive younger audience with its visceral performances. Wayne never stopped to worry about critical response to the music. He had the band he'd been waiting to lead for thirty years, and was content to let the group settle into a groove as a collective, onstage and off. Over the next year, it did.

Footprints Live: Nonstop Home

A key element in Wayne's group was its snappy dialogue. Dialogue is pretty much required of jazz musicians on the road—one of the only things Miles didn't like about Coltrane was that he was "stingy" in conversation. With Wayne's band, the talk was nonstop. Everyone participated in endless joking and philosophizing, including Wayne's trusty tour manager and recording engineer Rob Griffin. If Danilo opined, "I think Wayne's melodies stay with you forever, like a cologne," Rob was there to crack, "What kind of cologne do *you* use?" This conversation passed the time, but it was more than that. Through dialogue, the guys in the band negotiated the territory between speculation and pragmatism and the space between matters high and low, just as they did on the bandstand.

One day, traveling in a van from the Los Angeles airport to a show at UCLA, Wayne started riffing on the politics in his resident state of Florida. "They know that if you can change Florida, you can change the country," he said. "Florida is a fulcrum. It was the last state to be desegregated. Now nobody speaks English there. Hey, we fixed them!"

Brian laughed. He was often the first one to laugh at a joke, a contribution in its own right.

Danilo jumped in with his own story about cultural politics in Florida: "One time I was at a Concord Records release thing in Miami. [Trumpeter] Arturo Sandoval is on the stage talking up the musical contributions of Cuba. [Pianist] Hilton Ruiz—a Puerto Rican guy, right?—mumbles to himself, 'That shit ain't right. Puerto Ricans been here so many years, too.' So Hilton whispers into his mike during Arturo's speech—a barely discernible undercurrent—'Puerto Rico number one, Puerto Rico number one, Puerto Rico number one.' Everybody heard Hilton before Arturo did, so you *know* how embarrassed he was, man."

The whole band was breaking up with laughter. "They just went off and started screaming at each other!" Danilo concluded.

"Yeah, there's lots of innovation going on in Puerto Rico, Panama, and Venezuela," John affirmed, drawing out the theme of Danilo's story. "But Cuba takes credit for it all." Danilo appreciated John's acknowledgment— he'd just been appointed the cultural ambassador of his native Panama.

"Let's just make the music of one big country tonight," Wayne said. Agreement all around.

Wayne returned to the theme of governmental politics. "My mother used to say when I was growing up, 'Watch them dirty Republicans! They all have that gleam in their eye.'"

"Be advised, be advised," Brian said, mimicking a Southern preacher.

"But you got to keep your eye on all of them, no matter what party they're with," Wayne went on. "They want to stop stem-cell research. Don't want to let Christopher Reeve get on with his recovery. He's moving his hand anyway. He directs his finger to move and it moves. We've got to play some stem-cell research music."

The puzzling concept of stem-cell research music shut down the conversation for a couple minutes. Stepping onto more concrete ground, Brian and John discussed the years John had lived in Los Angeles. Danilo remained silent, apparently still hung up on stem-cell research music. Meanwhile, Wayne noticed that the van's driver was gunning it down the highway, weaving her way through traffic. "Are you Sagittarian?" he asked her. She was. "Dig it!" he said, lightening the mood; then he added, "I saw the bow and arrow with her darting around."

"Did you hear him? 'Dig it!'" Danilo repeated playfully, in awe of Wayne's astrological marksmanship.

The band carried its darting, changeable dialogue onto the bandstand. In the Weather Report days, Wayne and Joe Zawinul were close enough that Wayne could convey his opinion on a playback with a single glance. This quartet could intuit Wayne's intentions in the same way. When he pulled out "Beauty and the Beast" at the next sound check/rehearsal, he had a desired mood in mind for the piece's intro. He hunched his head down into his shoulders and crept across the stage to demonstrate a stealthy approach to the tune. Everyone laughed. "You want it kind of *sneaky*," John said. Accordingly, the group sidled up to the tune, expertly building and deconstructing the music around Wayne, as they had in the conversation back in the van. Listeners often "get" jazz for the first time when they realize the musicians are talking to one another through the music. With this band, there was a lot of conversation to "get."

As they continued to develop Wayne's music, it became more essential that all the players were also composers. Wayne brought in "Over Shadow Hill Way," a composition that he performed with his electric groups and recorded on *Joy Ryder*. Wayne said, "Okay, I want it opened up, made fresh again." The music on the page was thoroughly crafted, but that was just a starting point, not an end in itself. Familiar with the piece's overall structure, the musicians took the basic form of the rhythm in the intro and used it as a springboard for improvisation. Sometimes the group stayed on that form for a long time, just a few notes and a couple chords, but played lots of variations on top of it. Over the course of their tours, Wayne even started superimposing another tune over that form. The group immediately leaped to another page of Wayne's compositional history with him. Together, the musicians began to improvise not just on a single tune, but on Wayne's entire body of work—and that required broad compositional understanding from all of them.

One time backstage, Rob Griffin told a friend about his recording technique for the band's shows. "It puts the listener in the center of the band," Rob said. "It lessens the sense of the room." Wayne turned the comment on its head: "It lessens the room of the sense," he joked, pointedly. Wayne wanted the group's music to transcend any setting, venue, or situation. On one European tour, the band's equipment was lost in transit—not once, not twice, but three times. Wayne had to play rented or borrowed horns on these occasions. Though he could rightfully cancel his performances due to the lost instruments, he wanted to overcome the obstacle. He said, "Let's make a victory out of this," and gave focused performances regardless of the circumstances.

The group was inevitably affected by setting, and mostly in a good way. In the fall of 2002, after several visceral, fast-moving, peak-and-valley performances in the densely populated cities of the West Coast, the band played a late-October show in the quiet, big-sky country of Albuquerque, New Mexico. The stage backdrop was a screen of shifting images: a desert sunset, then some red desert arches, then turquoise stones. This scenery elicited a sensitive, painterly set from the group. Even the typically impulsive

Brian delicately daubed his way through the show with lots of brushstrokes. Reviewers tended to pigeonhole Danilo as the group's Latin rhythmic catalyst. He belied that role on this night with lots of classical minimalist repetition. The music reached a point where style was completely irrelevant—the audience was just waiting to hear how the music would fill up the canvas. The band's encore was "JuJu," as always. It was freer and sparser than ever, almost spooky, like a Halloween soundtrack. John played ghostly bowed strokes on bass, and Danilo foiled that by plucking strings inside the piano, while Wayne whistled into the microphone. They picked the tune clean, down to its bare bones, and then played up certain aspects of its skeletal structure, so that music projected from the desert landscape backdrop like a sun-bleached skull in a Georgia O'Keeffe painting.

The importance of setting was also evident when the group released a live recording in May 2002. *Footprints Live!* included tracks recorded in France and Spain, where audiences' wild enthusiasm inspired some especially hot-blooded performances. "In Europe, they can screen out the soundalikes, the wannabes," Wayne said. "And that's been definitely in operation in Japan, too. In Europe they know what originality is. They know when it walks like one, talks like one, and everything like that. When it doesn't walk and talk like one, it's recognized by them."

For Wayne, the recording was the sound of victory. "Only one word came to my mind when I was hearing it," he said. "The act of winning, of overcoming something. Celebrate. You see that in some writings all over the world, in sacred books: 'We celebrate with song and dance!' 'cause somebody won something, or somebody found out that *hey, it's not bad.*" Wayne himself was widely celebrated, receiving recognition after recognition for his musical accomplishments. *The New York Times* called Wayne the greatest living composer of jazz, and most critics agreed. In March 2002, Wayne received the Thelonious Monk Institute's Founders Award in Washington, D.C., which was presented by General Richard B. Myers, chairman of the Joint Chiefs of Staff. That same week, Wayne received the New School University's Beacon in Jazz Award. In Europe he earned not only Musician of the Year but also Artist of the Year awards. Backstage in

San Francisco, saxophonist Branford Marsalis humbly greeted Wayne with a genuflection. Wayne started laughing, but Branford didn't.

Alegría

In March 2003, Wayne released *Alegría,* his first studio recording since *High Life. Alegría* was also his first all-acoustic studio recording as a leader since 1967. Produced by Robert Sadin, it used a rich and broad palette of orchestral colors, including percussion, brass, woodwinds, and strings, and its repertoire drew upon musical inspirations spanning the past millennium. There was one new tune, "Sacajawea," a burning boogaloo named after the American Indian girl who guided Lewis and Clark across America, but mostly Wayne reexamined older material. For instance, "12th Century Carol" was a piece of sheet music that he stole from his college choir class. He tucked the music away "in a piano bench," he said metaphorically, where it remained for four decades until he rediscovered it in the late nineties. On *Alegría,* Wayne opened up the a cappella carol with some instrumental groove-based variations, like he'd reimagined the song while gazing up in a medieval church with its roof blown off.

From the same time-capsule piano bench, Wayne exhumed "Vendiendo Alegría," a 1930s flamenco tune popularized by Spanish singer Antonio Molina and Orquesta Montillo. Miles gave the music to Wayne back in the sixties, suggesting he "do something with it." "As I started investigating the tune," Wayne said, "I was struck by how simplistic the melody was, and I wanted to celebrate it with an arrangement that would have it grow." Wayne applied some of Miles's lessons in the tune's re-arrangement. "When Miles would change things in existing compositions, mostly he would take out notes notes notes notes to let all the jazz ditties out. Miles would make space for them. Space has its own groove and swing."

Wayne pointed out that the word *space* can have multiple associations, and connected its interplanetary meaning to his defining vision for *Ale-*

gría: "If you get into an aircraft and go a certain distance from the earth and turn on a sound device, you'd hear all different cultures and sounds going on at the same time. That's something like what I'm trying to do on *Alegría*; there is presence yet not intrusion, consonance yet not complete unity. And you've got to keep it all grooving, that's another challenge right there." On some previous records, Wayne's solos were necessarily focused on problem-solving, on reconciling musical elements, and his compositions keyed in on an obsession to reach for something higher. On *Alegría,* he settled in to a comfortable perspective on the acoustic jazz definition that he'd helped define, and was free to concentrate on expression in his playing. In Wayne's breathtaking tenor solo on "Orbits," he employed a single repeated note for a stretch, but spun a sardonic yarn with its rhythmic variation and gutbucket tone. Pianist Thelonious Monk could use a single note to similar effect. Throughout Wayne's career, people had periodically compared him to Monk: "I think the logic of Wayne's compositions, the identity of his melodies and harmonies are well integrated, like Monk's," said Wynton Marsalis, for example. On *Alegría,* Wayne finally achieved an integration of his full musical vision as a composer—the "Let's make the whole world!" notion he'd had as a kid playing with clay—with the play-your-heart-out feeling of his solos on 1960s tunes such as "Infant Eyes" and the wry humor of his Messengers masquerades.

There was still space for Wayne to grow. He originally recorded "Angola" back in 1965 on *The Soothsayer.* On *Alegría,* he revisited it with slightly askew harmonies. It was classic Wayne: In his playing he pushed the tune's melody to the outer reaches of its harmony; in the composition, he courted dissonance with the master plan of a classical European composer. Wayne liked to tell a story about Hector Berlioz, to illustrate how the shifting character of the composer affected his music: "There was this time he was following his girlfriend, and he had a gun. He was waiting to see if she had a rendezvous with someone. He was determined to shoot her. But then, walking through a corridor, he saw another girl fluttering her eyelashes. He took his gun, threw it out the window, and started following her! His symphonies sound like somebody whose thoughts are coming from that kind of place." In a similar way, Wayne packed a lot of drama into "Angola" with some strident brass and complex counterpoint. But "Angola" wasn't a symphony-length composition, it was a five-minute jazz tune, so the drama was overwhelming. Wayne needed a little more room to spread out and create his own *Symphonie Fantastique*.

Mostly, though, everything came together beautifully on the record. On his version of the Heitor Villa-Lobos composition "Bachianas Brasileiras No. 5," a plucked cello chorus and layered Brazilian rhythms combined into a luxurious Baroque. Wayne's practice sessions with Coltrane on string exercises paid off in his saxophone solo, the tone of which showed an uncanny empathy for the cellos' delicate strength; like his work with Milton Nascimento, the Brazilian piece brought out Wayne's romantic side. With its Songs of Innocence informed by Wayne's own Song of Experience, *Alegría* was a moving masterpiece. After Ana Maria died, Wayne made a determination to honor her existence by trying to become the happiest man alive. That came through on *Alegría*, which means "joy" in Spanish, and "joyful fun" in Portuguese.

Alegría is what Wayne embodies today. And all those years of struggling with the sadness of having a brain-damaged daughter? With the loss of his wife? With his own demons? With inconsistent bands and compromised creativity? "I was out in the garden of my mind, tending to the begonias and petunias," he says in retrospect, depicting the times of drought and plague as cultivation for the happily productive period that he's in now.

Wayne's "dominant tendency" in his earlier years was to "not speak up," he says. "For something to be a dominant tendency is to never turn that condition over and see the actual benefit that is there. I could have been blindsided, and not be the happy-go-lucky guy I am now. I could be living a life of regret and resentment, and not be fun to be around. All these good things would fall by the wayside. Not that I'm the heavyweight champion of speaking up now, or anything." Wayne cooled out and became contented after he discovered that the authentic way for him to "speak up" was by helping people through his own example. He became happy when he found an entire group of musicians sophisticated enough to do that with him onstage. "What you're doing onstage, if you're in this higher condition and you're performing, something transcends the music and reaches to the inside of someone else," he says. "And it's deeper and longer than a hit song. It's infinite. It triggers a well of wisdom. It could also be the theater or a good book—someone gets it, they leave, and they do their thing. Then something comes out of their mouth they didn't intend to say, or things start happening to them. A lot of people just call it luck . . ."

What Is Music For?

Wayne often questions the purpose of music. "When I do interviews, they say music, music, music, music, music . . . and I say no, no, no, no. Music is second, the human being is first. What is music *for*? What is anything *for*?" This can be a puzzling question, considering that it comes from a living legend. Wayne wasn't just on the scene. He *made* the scene. His compositions made a quiet but powerful contribution to at least four distinct eras in jazz, not to mention the impact of his playing on the pop world, in Brazilian music, etc., etc. As he defined the sound of various genres, he produced one of jazz's great oeuvres, crowding out the likes of Ellington and Coltrane for space in the fake book, a collection of standards that is required study for most jazz students. It's a rare night when one of his tunes is not called in a club somewhere. He has been an influence on generations of saxophone players. So if Wayne Shorter doesn't know what music is for, then what good is music at all?

And that is precisely Wayne's point. He wants his music to do some good. Wayne's humanitarian drive as an artist is a product of his Buddhist practice with the Soka Gakkai International, or SGI. Wayne is a founding member of a group called the International Committee of Artists for Peace, or ICAP, a group established by SGI in 2002. In April of that year, ICAP presented Carlos Santana with its first Humanity in the Arts Peace Award, in recognition for his work with his Milagro Foundation. SGI president Daisaku Ikeda issued this statement on the occasion: "The spirit of art and the spirit of peace are naturally bound together. Artists are the standard bearers for the creation of peace. I am convinced that art, as an expression of life itself, constitutes the highest form of value creation." Recognizing peacemaking as a creative endeavor, SGI puts artists in a position to promote cultural harmony.

Dialogue is very important to Wayne's Buddhist practice. President Ikeda conducts as many as seventy dialogues a year with artists, philosophers, and world leaders, who have included Mikhail Gorbachev, John Major, Margaret Thatcher, and François Mitterrand—and also, controversially, Manuel Noriega and Fidel Castro. Wayne has said that writing music is like writing a letter, and that through music he maintains a dialogue with listeners. When Wayne is on break from touring with his band, he often travels on behalf of ICAP. In May 2002, Wayne attended the Sixteenth Soka Gakkai Headquarters Leaders Meeting in Hachioji, Japan. He represented SGI-USA in a multimedia performance with musicians Herbie Hancock, flutist Nestor Torres, and guitarist Larry Coryell, and flamenco dancers Pascual Olivera and Angela del Moral. For an audience of five thousand, the group performed jazz arrangements of Ikeda's original compositions "Morigasaki" and "Mother," as well as Wayne's "Footprints." Later that year, Wayne went to Hawaii for the Aloha Peace Concert, a commemorative event held on the first anniversary of the September 11 attacks, symbolically staged near the Arizona Memorial at Pearl Harbor. Wayne returns from these events with a new sense of mission, like a kid who wants to be an astronaut coming home from space camp.

At these gatherings, in public panels with other artists, Wayne promotes the philosophy of Buddhism and discusses creativity. He performs for very receptive audiences of jazz neophytes who respond only to the spirit of his music. He wouldn't trade the heartfelt ovation he receives at one of these Buddhist performances for forty bravura concerts at Carnegie Hall. In March 2003, Wayne won his seventh and eighth Grammy Awards: Best Jazz Instrumental Album for *Alegría,* and Best Instrumental Composition for "Sacajawea." This recognition didn't mean nearly as much as the congratulatory message he received afterward from President Ikeda, who praised Wayne as "venerable Bodhisattva Wonderful Sound."

Wayne's work with ICAP has strengthened his resolve to serve as a cultural ambassador. More than ever, he is the "citizen of the world" he started to become with the Jazz Messengers back in the sixties. For Wayne, this work restores cultural relevance to jazz, the meaning it used to have back when it was the music of "social revolution." At these events he also gets to exercise the investigative twenty-year-old in him who got an A in his college philosophy class. But these are not just "wise man" ego trips. Wayne especially likes to visit the SGI center near his home in Florida, because he's not "Wayne Shorter the Jazz God" there. He's "Carolina's husband." His wife spends at least seventy-five percent of her time helping others, so he has a lot to live up to.

The Duty of Duty-Free Music

"Did you find enough sandpaper?" Wayne asked, as I was finishing the book. "Are you still looking for a conflict in my story? 'Cause if you are, I think it's art versus commerce."

Has Wayne resolved the artist's age-old struggle with commerce? I don't think so. Big-name rock stars sometimes ask him to play on their records for considerable financial reward. Like any jazz musician, Wayne could use the money, but he usually declines, partly because he's not sure where these rock stars are coming from. He's suspicious they will use him as a "legitimizing jazz beard" and fearful that the public will think he's "riding on the pop coattails." It's true that you can never be certain of someone's intentions, just as you can never control the reception of your work. But I do think it's entirely possible that someone may want him to play on a record just for the sheer life of his sound.

I'm also not sure we've heard all the weird and wonderful beauty of the music in Wayne's mind. I'm not talking about his refusal to play the expected fireworks in his solos. I'd rather hear him cycle through the more subtle scenes of the northern lights, the Milky Way, solar and lunar eclipses, and twilight, and that's what he gives us onstage. What we still haven't heard is a faithful recording or performance of Wayne's symphonic compositions. He'd need a resident orchestra of classically trained, jazz-schooled child prodigies to bring his compositions to life. He's now writing a forty-five-minute piece for opera singer Renée Fleming at her request, and maybe that will be the performance that finally satisfies. But I doubt it. With Wayne, it's like Duke Ellington said, the best song is always the next one. That's the duty of making "duty-free music," as he calls it.

Sonny Rollins, the only other living tenor saxophonist who may be more influential than Wayne, empathizes. "I've always been a musician who has considered myself a work in progress," Sonny says. "I've never been a guy who's gotten to 'my place,' so that I'm proven, tested. Integrity for me means trying to find something in my music. Of course physically I can't play the same way I played in 1946, so I couldn't do that anyways. But I wouldn't want to, 'cause I'm trying to improve my skills to find my own lost chord. Wayne's always had a lot of integrity about his music, so I assume Wayne does what he does musically because he's always hearing something on the horizon that he's not doing yet at the time."

Dramatis Personae

After serving as one of the principal architects of jazz for more than forty years, Wayne has developed a lofty goal for his music. "At this point I'm looking to express eternity in composition," he says. "I'm striving to open up those people who aren't used to thinking in those terms." It's a Buddhist thing. But in his practice he also seeks enlightenment through earthly desires, and that keeps him real. Backstage before a 2002 show, Wayne performed his daily ritual chant, reciting the Lotus Sutra and "Nam-myoho-renge-kyo" with deep deliberation. When Danilo thought Wayne was safely immersed in the chanting, he tiptoed into the front of his bandleader's dressing room and rummaged around for the wine supply. Wayne always has the good stuff. Sensing the intrusion, Wayne finished his chanting. He slipped like mercury into the other room, grabbed the bottle of wine from Danilo, and knocked back a quick "shot" of merlot. He punched the wall a couple times—in tribute to Miles's love for boxing, he said—and then walked out onstage doing a James Cagney impression.

Onstage and off, Wayne wants every note to count, to push the story ahead. "Miles used to bring up Humphrey Bogart in those mystery movies he played in," Wayne said. "Miles would say, 'You see the way Humphrey threw that punch?,' and I said, 'Yeah,' and he said, 'Play that.'"

"Well, I like to make music like that," he continued. "Musical motion pictures without movies. And life has become my own motion picture. That's *some thing*." That's a jazz musician's ultimate act of improvisation.

In Wayne's favorite movie, *The Red Shoes,* the ballerina protagonist, Vicky, couldn't make the choice between her husband and dancing, between life and art. Her solution was to throw herself in front of a train; she danced herself to death. I asked Wayne how *The Red Shoes* might have ended differently. He imagined a modern corrective to Vicky's romantic fatalism, a dancing Buddha character who seemed a little like himself. "The thing with Vicky was that she was a junkie for those red shoes," he said. "When she was hit by the train, she passed away, but even in passing away, according to the principle of eternal karma, she's still locked into the curse of the red shoes, still dancing in death, and can't stop. So maybe here comes another dancer in modern times, tap dancing, and he has his own junkie problems. But he finds a way to overcome his stuff and change poison into medicine, so he can rescue her from the curse. Vicky forfeited her life for art, but this guy saves her when his life becomes bigger than art."

Flagships

Wayne's earliest memory is of leaving the Ironbound confines of his Newark, New Jersey, neighborhood to visit a lake, and trying to imagine where the water and sky finally met on the horizon. Seventy years later, I called him at home in Miami one day. He cheerfully reported that he was "standing out on the balcony watching ships slip off the edge of the ocean."

Some of those ships are loaded cargo boats heading to ports in the Caribbean or South America. Others are cruise ships filled with passengers on their way to the Mediterranean. Wayne has been to those places and more, favoring the world's stages with many roles. He was an agitator with Art Blakey in Algeria; a knight with Miles Davis in Chicago; a bullfighter with Carlos Santana in Madrid; and a sprightly sage at Buddhist concerts in Japan. But that's all just information, or "disinformation," as Wayne says, to have a little fun convoluting the point.

The essential thing is that he never stopped wondering about where the water met the sky, and always sought that mysterious meeting—most famously, through music. And now, Wayne Shorter thrills with the knowledge that the water and the sky finally meet up where everything else does. In eternity. Which is to say, in himself: "The one thing that's immutable and has no beginning or end is *us*. When we're hip with this, we can afford to die."

Unless cited below or attributed to other sources in the text, all quotations in this book are from my original interviews. Between 2003 and 2004, I conducted more than seventy-five interviews with various sources, and had at least that many discussions with Wayne Shorter himself. My musical analysis is based on study of Wayne's original scores whenever possible. Discussion of live performances in Wayne's early career is based on viewings of bootleg videos. I periodically accompanied the Wayne Shorter Quartet on tour from 2001 to 2004.

1. WATER BABIES

"My father liked country and western . . . Martin Block": *Jazz Journal International,* May 1996.

"Film scores—what we called 'soundtracks' or 'background' . . . curious about sound": Interview with Bob Blumenthal for *The Classic Blue Note Recordings,* June 2002.

"Some people think . . . you can't see it": Charles Kingsley, *The Water Babies* (New York: Dodd, Mead and Co., 1916), p. 77.

"Newark was a hell of a place . . . just daily survival": David Breskin, *Musician,* July 1981, p. 56.

2. BOP FIEND: "AS WEIRD AS WAYNE"

"place where few whites . . . whatever that meant": Philip Roth, *American Pastoral* (New York: Vintage Books, 1997), pp. 49–50.

"Wayne was precocious . . . sheer technical infallibility": Amiri Baraka, "Introducing Wayne Shorter," *Jazz Review, Inc.,* 1959.

3. THE NEWARK FLASH

"When I was in music class . . . in my mind . . .": David Breskin, *Musician,* July 1981, p. 56.

"She said, 'This may be incorrect . . . Every time": David Breskin, *Musician,* July 1981, p. 56.

"'Bing and Bob' were the police . . . right side of the audience": Whitney Balliett, *American Musicians II* (New York: Oxford University Press, 1986), p. 271.

"Ringleaders in a cult of progressive jazz . . . across their polytonal orbit": *Playboy,* May 1956, p. 9.

"When we went to New York City . . . what's he doin' in there?'": Iain Ballamy, "Mysterious Traveller," *Jazz UK,* May/June 2003, p. 11.

"We were playing . . . a hell of a night!": Mel Martin, *The Saxophone Journal,* vol. 16, no. 4 (January/February 1992).

"[Joe and I] met on the corner of Birdland . . . huggin' goin' on": Brian Glasser, *In a Silent Way* (London: Sanctuary, 2001), pp. 252–53.

"The playing is characterized . . . usually makes it": Amiri Baraka, "Introducing Wayne Shorter," *Black Music* (New York: Apollo, 1970).

4. HARD DRINKING, HARD BOP WITH THE JAZZ MESSENGERS

"The kind of timing I learned with Art . . . being remembered by everyone." Tim Logan, "Wayne Doubletake," *Down Beat,* June 20, 1974, p. 16.

"It is the self-perception . . .": Al Calloway, "An Introduction to Soul," *Smiling Through the Apocalypse: Esquire's History of the Sixties* (New York: McCall Publishing, 1970), p. 712.

5. THE ELDERS

"The reason we read more deeply . . . electrifying intensity": Gary Giddins, *Visions of Jazz* (New York: Oxford University Press, 1998), p. 324.

"I wrote 'Sakeena's Vision' . . . about Art's wife": Conrad Silvert, *Down Beat,* July 14, 1977, p. 58.

"Wayne was the only person . . . the only one": Miles Davis with Quincy Troupe, *Miles: The Autobiography* (New York: Touchstone, 1989), p. 273.

6. CHILDREN OF THE NIGHT

"I argued with them . . . to come up with a better idea." *Down Beat,* June 21, 1962, p. 43.

"I never saw anything like it . . . never a word": John Litweiler, *Down Beat,* March 25, 1976, p. 16.

"In those bands . . . like Fats Navarro": Tim Logan, "Wayne Doubletake," *Down Beat,* June 20, 1974, p. 16.

"So Wayne was getting all these calls . . . it happened real soon": Miles Davis with Quincy Troupe, *Miles: The Autobiography* (New York: Touchstone, 1989), p. 270.

7. MILES SMILES

"Tony played . . . beginnings": Tim Logan, "Wayne Doubletake," *Down Beat,* June 20, 1974, pp. 16–17.

"It wasn't the bish-bash, sock'em dead routine . . . colors started really coming": Conrad Silvert, *Down Beat,* July 14, 1977, p. 58.

"Wayne would just write something . . . because Wayne is a real composer": Miles Davis with Quincy Troupe, *Miles: The Autobiography* (New York: Touchstone, 1989), pp. 275–76.

"Tony used to get upset with Wayne . . . Tony would just stop playing": Miles Davis with Quincy Troupe, *Miles: The Autobiography* (New York: Touchstone, 1989), p. 280.

"We were actually tampering with something called . . . own harmonic road or avenue within a certain eight measures": Eric Nemeyer, "An Interview with Wayne Shorter," *Jazz Improv,* vol. 2, no. 3, 2001, p. 75.

"Wayne has always been someone . . . see the music I played go": Miles Davis with Quincy Troupe, *Miles: The Autobiography* (New York: Touchstone, 1989), p. 273.

8. SANCTUARY

"What do you do with your hands . . . do with yours?" Gregory Tate and Craig Street, "Shorter Stories," *B Culture,* vol. 1, no. 1, p. 8.

"A lot of the songs I wrote . . . things in my childhood": Scott Yanow, "The Wayne Shorter Interview," *Down Beat,* April 1986, p. 57.

"When I first met Wayne . . . Destiny": David Breskin, *Musician,* July 1981, p. 62.

"To me, the soprano saxophone is like the dolphin . . . shooting higher than the waves": Jürg Solothurnmann, *Jazz Forum,* vol. 112, no. 3, 1998, p. 35.

9. MUSIC FOR FILMS THAT WOULD NEVER BE MADE

"I just looked at the horn . . . a lot of Latin stuff": Tim Logan, "Wayne Double-take," *Down Beat,* June 20, 1974, p. 17.

"seeming desire to renounce the notion of the improvising musician . . . I wish he wouldn't": Larry Kart, *Down Beat,* 1974.

"They wouldn't say yes . . . to build that club up": Kristian Brodacki, "The Original Batman," *Jazz Forum,* January 1992, p. 25.

"*I Sing the Body Electric* is a beautiful, near-perfect LP . . .": Bob Palmer, *Rolling Stone,* no. 112.

10. WE WERE ALWAYS HERE

"Now I'm going to say it . . . one of the greatest concerts I've ever heard." Bob Protzman, "Caught in the Act: Weather Report," *Down Beat,* May 24, 1973, p. 29.

"With a group like Weather Report . . . wanting it to stay, knowing it won't": Jim Szantzor, "Caught in the Act: Weather Report," *Down Beat,* October 26, 1972, p. 31.

"As I hear it . . . which includes everybody in the group." Tim Logan, "Wayne Doubletake," *Down Beat,* June 20, 1974, p. 17.

"These albums showcase the steady growth of Wayne Shorter . . .": Marv Hohman, *Moto Grosso Feio/Mysterious Traveller* review, *Down Beat,* November 7, 1974.

11. NATIVE DANCERS AND FAIRY-TALE FRIENDS

"I got a letter from a surgeon . . . citizen in the world." Jim Macnie, "Uncommon Differences," *Musician,* September 1988, p. 103.

12. ELEGANT PEOPLE IN HEAVY WEATHER

"Wayne always told me . . . drinking filled up that hole": David Breskin, *Musician,* July 1981, p. 62.

"It takes a human revolution . . . external catastrophes": David Breskin, *Musician,* July 1981, pp. 58–59.

"I was struggling . . . I'd wonder": David Breskin, *Musician,* July 1981, p. 58.

"Shorter, who played ferocious tenor sax . . . 'In five years I'll be fifty! Fifty!'": Bob Blumenthal, "The 8 Year Weather Report," *Rolling Stone,* no. 282 (December 28, 1978–January 11, 1979), pp. 60–68.

13. WILD FLOWERS

"There was a group of mixed-marriage couples . . . also a chanter": Tina Turner, *I, Tina* (New York: Avon, 1986), p. 172.

"Right across the street . . . to get little Tina!": Tina Turner, *I, Tina* (New York: Avon, 1986), p. 196.

"They don't even have a name for her stuff anymore": Jim Macnie, "Uncommon Differences," *Musician,* September 1988, p. 103.

14. JOY RYDER

"story line . . . in close truth the legend of Atlantis," "tactical function," "I thought this was a discotheque when I walked in!": Gene Kalbacher, *Upbeat: WBGO Program Guide,* January 1986, p. 18.

"It is not the sort of album one should listen to . . . an album to learn from and live with": Robert Palmer, "Jazz Artist Makes His Main Move," *The New York Times,* November 3, 1985.

"That means, to me . . . on vacation—quite a long vacation": Adam Sweeting, "After the Storm," *The Guardian,* September 26, 2002.

15. "GET YOUR CAPE OUT OF THE CLEANER'S AND FLY, SUPERMAN!"

"Wouldn't it be interesting to explore the *uncommonness* of people?" Jim Macnie, "Uncommon Differences," *Musician,* September 1988, p. 100.

16. HIGH LIFE

"Miles had lost so much weight . . . going back to a baby": Kristian Brodacki, "The Original Batman," *Jazz Forum,* January 1992, p. 28.

"To sum up Miles . . . against the vampire!": Kristian Brodacki, "The Original Batman," *Jazz Forum,* January 1992, p. 26.

"In some places, there's an intention . . . when a certain character appears": Josef Woodard, "The Artful Dodger's Return," *JazzTimes,* November 1995, p. 32.

"may be the most important living jazz musician . . . dump the rest": Peter Watrous, *The New York Times,* October 15, 1995.

17. SUPER NOVA

"It's not true . . . The opposite was happening": Kyle Smith, *People,* July 28, 1997.

"That's my premise . . . it's not finished": Interview with Ed Bradley for "Speak No Evil: The Music of Wayne Shorter," *Jazz from Lincoln Center* radio program, 1998.

"Wayne's compositions are living organisms . . . as he evolves": Interview with Ed Bradley for "Speak No Evil: The Music of Wayne Shorter," *Jazz from Lincoln Center* radio program, 1998.

18. PROMETHEUS UNBOUND

Many interview quotes from this chapter have previously appeared in my articles and reports for *The New York Times,* National Public Radio, and later in promotional materials for Verve Records.

Michelle Mercer, "He's a Jazz Riddle Wrapped in Self-Made Mystery," *The New York Times,* June 24, 2001.

Michelle Mercer, "Wayne Shorter," NPR's *All Things Considered,* June 25, 2002.

Michelle Mercer, "Music Review: Wayne Shorter's *Alegría,*" NPR's *All Things Considered,* May 6, 2003.

"Boomer heroes—notably Dewey Redman, Wayne Shorter . . . accounted for most of the expectations and red meat at JVC 2001": Gary Giddins, "Minnie the Moocher's Revenge," *The Village Voice,* July 11–17, 2001.

"scarily committed to the opportunity . . . almost ready to die for it": Ben Ratliff, "At 67, Inspiring a Quest for Perfection," *The New York Times,* June 30, 2001.

"spellbinding hour, brimming with feeling . . . a shared commitment to the whole": Gary Giddins, "Minnie the Moocher's Revenge," *The Village Voice,* July 11–17, 2001.

Bibliography

The following is a selection of sources drawn upon for this work. Artic.es were too numerous to mention.

Balliett, Whitney. *Collected Works: A Journal of Jazz 1954–2000.* New York: St. Martin's Press, 2000.

Bianchi, Curt. *Weather Report: The Annotated Discography,* website, 2001. *www.binkie.net/wrdisc*

Causton, Richard. *The Buddha in Daily Life: An Introduction to the Buddhism of Nichiren Daishonin.* London: Rider, 1995.

Coolman, Todd. *The Miles Davis Quintet of the Mid-1960s: Synthesis of Improvisation and Compositional Elements.* Doctoral dissertation, New York University, 1997.

Davis, Miles, with Quincy Troupe. *Miles: The Autobiography.* New York: Touchstone, 1989.

Dyer, Geoff. *But Beautiful: A Book About Jazz.* New York: North Point Press, 1996.

Giddins, Gary. *Visions of Jazz.* New York: Oxford University Press, 1998.

Glasser, Brian. *In a Silent Way.* London: Sanctuary Publishing Limited, 2001.

Hajdu, David. *Lush Life: A Biography of Billy Strayhorn.* New York: Farrar, Straus and Giroux, 1996.

Hayes, Harold, ed. *Smiling Through the Apocalypse: Esquire's History of the Sixties.* New York: McCall Publishing, 1970.

Hochswender, Woody, Greg Martin, and Ted Morino. *The Buddha in Your Mirror.* Santa Monica, CA: Middleway, 2001.

Institute of Jazz Studies at Rutgers, Newark, New Jersey. Wayne Shorter, Joe Zawinul, Miles Davis, Herbie Hancock folders, including promotional materials and flyers.

Jost, Ekkehard. *Free Jazz.* New York: Da Capo Press, 1994.

Kirchner, Bill. *The Oxford Companion to Jazz.* New York: Oxford University Press, 2001.

Milkowski, Bill. *Jaco: The Extraordinary and Tragic Life of Jaco Pastorius, "The World's Greatest Bass Player."* San Francisco: Miller Freeman Books, 1995.

Macero Collection, Teo Macero Collection, Music Division, The New York Public Library for the Performing Arts, Astor, Lenox and Tilden Foundations.

Morrison, Toni. *Jazz.* New York: Plume, 1992.

Nicholson, Stuart. *Jazz-Rock: A History.* New York: Schirmer Books, 1998.

Paudras, Francis. *Dance of the Infidels: A Portrait of Bud Powell.* New York: Da Capo Press, 1998.

Roth, Philip. *American Pastoral,* New York: Vintage, 1997.

Schwartz, Steve, and Michael Fitzgerald. *Chronology of Art Blakey and the Jazz Messengers,* website, 1996, *www.jazzdiscography.com/Artists/Blakey/chron.htm*

Szwed, John. *So What: The Life of Miles Davis.* New York: Simon & Schuster, 2002.

Turner, Tina, with Kurt Loder. *I, Tina: My Life Story.* Avon, 1986.

Weiss, Michael. *A Treasure Trove of Innovation: The Pen of Wayne Shorter—A Survey of the Past 20 Years.* International Association of Jazz Educators Clinic, January 24, 2004.

Pure Poetry: Compositions by Wayne Shorter

Compiled by Michelle Mercer and Bertrand Überall

This listing shows the first recording of each composition. In most cases, this is the master take, although in some cases an alternate version is used if it chronologically precedes the master take. Exact recording dates are shown when available, but in some cases only an approximate month or year is known. The title shown is the one under which the piece is best known, and is not necessarily the first one used. Alternate titles are given in parentheses. Unless otherwise indicated, Wayne Shorter is the leader of the session. Only authorized recordings are listed.

Recorded Compositions

TITLE	ALBUM TITLE	DATE
Adam's Apple	*Adam's Apple*	2/3/66
Adventures Aboard the Golden Mean	*Beyond the Sound Barrier*	11/02–4/04
Africaine	Art Blakey: *Africaine*	11/10/59
The Albatross	*Second Genesis*	10/11/60
The All Seeing Eye	*The All Seeing Eye*	10/15/65
Ana Maria	*Native Dancer*	1974

This composition has some similarity to "Moto Grosso Feio (Feio)."

Angola	*The Soothsayer*	3/4/65
Anthem	*Joy Ryder*	1988
Antigua	*Moto Grosso Feio*	4/3/70

Although it was not recorded until 1970, this composition (arranged by Gil Evans) was performed at the Berkeley Jazz Festival on 4/19/68 by the Miles Davis Quintet with the Gil Evans Orchestra (Down Beat, 6/13/68).

Armageddon	*Night Dreamer*	4/29/64
As Far as the Eye Can See	*Beyond the Sound Barrier*	11/02–4/04

This composition has some similarity to "Go."

Atlantis (Circe)	*V.S.O.P.: Five Stars*	7/29/79
At the Fair	*High Life*	1995
Aung San Suu Kyi	Wayne Shorter/ Herbie Hancock: *1+1*	1997

This composition was written in the mid-1950s, when Wayne was a student at New York University.

The Backsliders	Art Blakey: *Roots and Herbs*	5/27/61

TITLE	ALBUM TITLE	DATE
Backstage Sally	Art Blakey: *Buhaina's Delight*	11/28/61

Ballroom in the Sky   Santana/Shorter: 7/14/88
(Wayne II)   *Montreux 1988* (DVD)

This composition, copyrighted on 10/16/89, was played by the Carlos Santana/Wayne Shorter band on a 1988 tour. A DVD from this tour is scheduled for release in late 2006. This will be the first time this piece is issued. This composition is sometimes listed as "Wayne II."

B. Because   Unissued Blue Note session   10/13/70

This composition appears on an unreleased Blue Note recording session. It is most likely a collective improvisation by Wayne, McCoy Tyner, Miroslav Vitous, Alphonse Mouzon and Barbara Burton. No definitive titles were chosen for this session.

Beauty and the Beast   *Native Dancer*   1974

Beyond the Sound Barrier   *Beyond the Sound Barrier*   11/02–4/04

This composition has some similarity to "Go."

The Big Push   *The Soothsayer*   3/4/65

Black Diamond   *Introducing Wayne Shorter*   11/10/59

Black Light   Material: 1993
     Hallucination Engine

Bill Laswell is joint composer of this piece.

Black Nile   *Night Dreamer*   4/29/64

Black Swan   *High Life*   1995
(In Memory of Susan Portlynn Romeo)

Blackthorn Rose   Weather Report: 2–5/74
     Mysterious Traveller

Blues à la Carte   *Introducing Wayne Shorter*   11/9/59

This composition is incorrectly listed on some recordings as "Harry's Last Stand."

Brown Street   Weather Report: *8:30*   2–6/79

Joe Zawinul is joint composer of this piece.

TITLE	ALBUM TITLE	DATE
Callaway Went That-a-Way	*Wayning Moments*	11/2/61
Call Sheet Blues	Dexter Gordon: *The Other Side of 'Round Midnight*	8/20–23/85

Herbie Hancock, Ron Carter, and Billy Higgins are joint composers of this piece.

Calm	*Odyssey of Iska*	8/26/70
Capricorn	Miles Davis: *Water Babies*	6/13/67
Capricorn II	*Alegria*	2000–2002
Cathay	*Joy Ryder*	1988
Causeways	*Joy Ryder*	1988
Cee	Unissued Blue Note session	10/13/70

This composition appears on an unreleased Blue Note recording session. It is most likely a collective improvisation by Wayne, McCoy Tyner, Miroslav Vitous, Alphonse Mouzon, and Barbara Burton. No definitive titles were chosen for this session.

Chaos	*The All Seeing Eye*	10/15/65
Charcoal Blues	*Night Dreamer*	4/29/64
The Chess Players	Art Blakey: *The Big Beat*	3/6/60
Chief Crazy Horse	*Adam's Apple*	2/24/66
Children of the Night (From Eden to Nod)	Art Blakey: *Mosaic*	10/2/61

This composition was copyrighted under the title "From Eden to Nod."

Cigano	Weather Report: *Live and Unreleased*	11/27/75

This composition was not issued until the Weather Report CD Live And Unreleased *(2002), which consisted of previously unreleased live performances.*

Condition Red	*Phantom Navigator*	1986

TITLE	ALBUM TITLE	DATE
Contemplation	Art Blakey: *Buhaina's Delight*	11/28/61
The Creation	Unissued Blue Note session	10/13/70

This composition appears on an unreleased Blue Note recording session. It is most likely a collective improvisation by Wayne, McCoy Tyner, Miroslav Vitous, Alphonse Mouzon, and Barbara Burton. No definitive titles were chosen for this session.

Crianças	*Atlantis*	1985
Dance Cadaverous	*Speak No Evil*	12/24/64
Dara Factor Two	*Weather Report (1982)*	1982

Joe Zawinul, Jaco Pastorius, Peter Erskine, and Robert Thomas, Jr., are joint composers of this piece.

Daredevil	*Joy Ryder*	1988
Dead-End	*Wayning Moments*	11/2/61
Dear Sir	Lee Morgan: *The Procrastinator*	7/14/67
Dee	Unissued Blue Note session	10/13/70

This composition appears on an unreleased Blue Note recording session. It is most likely a collective improvisation by Wayne, McCoy Tyner, Miroslav Vitous, Alphonse Mouzon, and Barbara Burton. No definitive titles were chosen for this session.

Deluge	*Juju*	8/3/64
Devil's Island	*Wayning Moments*	11/6/61
Diana	*Native Dancer*	1974
Dolores	Miles Davis: *Miles Smiles*	10/24/66
Down in the Depths	*Introducing Wayne Shorter*	11/10/59
Edda (Spiritual Madness)	Lee Morgan: *The Rumproller*	4/21/65

Wayne does not appear on any recordings of this composition, including Lee Morgan's.

TITLE	ALBUM TITLE	DATE
Effe	Unissued Blue Note session	10/13/70

This composition appears on an unreleased Blue Note recording session. It is most likely a collective improvisation by Wayne, McCoy Tyner, Miroslav Vitous, Alphonse Mouzon, and Barbara Burton. No definitive titles were chosen for this session.

Elegant People	Weather Report: *Black Market*	12/75–1/76

This composition was written in the mid-1950s, when Wayne was a student at New York University.

The Elders	Weather Report: *Mr. Gone*	5/78
Endangered Species	*Atlantis*	1985

Joseph Vitarelli is joint composer of this piece.

E.S.P.	Miles Davis: *E.S.P.*	1/20/65

Miles Davis is incorrectly listed on some recordings as joint composer of this piece.

Etcetera	*Etcetera*	6/14/65
Eurydice	*Weather Report (1971)*	2/17/71
Eva	Art Blakey: *Ugetsu*	6/16/63

This composition was written for the Joseph Losey film Eva *but not used in the film. It was not issued until the CD release of the album* Ugetsu.

Face of the Deep	*The All Seeing Eye*	10/15/65
Face on the Barroom Floor	Weather Report: *Sportin' Life*	10–11/84
Fall	Miles Davis: *Nefertiti*	7/19/67
Fee Fi Fo Fum	*Speak No Evil*	12/24/64
Fire	Lee Morgan: *Expoobident*	10/14/60

Wayne does not appear on any recordings of this composition, including Lee Morgan's.

Flagships	*Phantom Navigator*	1986
Footprints	*Adam's Apple*	2/24/66

TITLE	ALBUM TITLE	DATE
Forbidden . . . PLAN IT!	*Phantom Navigator*	1986
Free for All (Free Fall)	Art Blakey: *Free for All*	2/10/64

This composition was copyrighted under the title "Free Fall."

Freezing Fire	Weather Report: *Tale Spinnin'*	1–2/75
El Gaucho	*Adam's Apple*	2/24/66

Irene (Teruko) Shorter is joint composer of this piece. This composition has some similarity to "Penelope."

Genesis	*The All Seeing Eye*	10/15/65
Giantis	Art Blakey: *Like Someone in Love*	8/14/60
Go	*Schizophrenia*	3/10/67

This composition has some similarity to "As Far as the Eye Can See" and "Beyond the Sound Barrier."

Gwagwa O De	Bahia Black: *Ritual Beating System*	1992

Herbie Hancock and the percussion group Olodum are joint composers of this piece.

Hammer Head	Art Blakey: *Free for All*	2/10/64
Harlequin	Weather Report: *Heavy Weather*	10/76
Harry's Last Stand	*Introducing Wayne Shorter*	11/9/59

This composition is incorrectly listed on some recordings as "Blues à la Carte."

High Life	*High Life*	1995
House of Jade	*Juju*	8/3/64

Irene Shorter is joint composer of this piece. Her contribution is also mentioned in the liner notes to the album Juju.

Indian Song	*Etcetera*	6/14/65

This composition has some similarity to "Shere Khan, the Tiger."

TITLE	ALBUM TITLE	DATE
Infant Eyes	*Speak No Evil*	12/24/64
Interlude	*Alegria*	2000–2002
Iris	Miles Davis: *E.S.P.*	1/22/65

Miles Davis is incorrectly listed on some recordings as joint composer of this piece.

Iska	*Moto Grosso Feio*	4/3/70
It's a Long Way Down	Art Blakey: *Indestructible*	4/15/64

Irene Shorter is joint composer of this piece.

Joelle	Art Blakey: *The Witch Doctor*	3/14/61
Joy	*Odyssey of Iska*	8/26/70
Joy Ryder	*Joy Ryder*	1988
Juju	*Juju*	8/3/64
Lady Day	*The Soothsayer*	3/4/65
The Last Silk Hat	*Atlantis*	1985
Lester Left Town	Art Blakey: *Africaine*	11/10/59
Limbo	Miles Davis: *Directions*	5/9/67
Look at the Birdie	Art Blakey: *Roots and Herbs*	2/18/61
Lost	*The Soothsayer*	3/4/65
Lusitanos	Weather Report: *Tale Spinnin'*	1–2/75
Mahjong	*Juju*	8/3/64
Mahogany Bird	*Phantom Navigator*	1986
Manhattan Lorelei	Wayne Shorter/ Herbie Hancock: *1+1*	1997

Herbie Hancock is joint composer of this piece.

TITLE	ALBUM TITLE	DATE
Manolete	Weather Report: *Sweetnighter*	2/3/73
Marie Antoinette	Freddie Hubbard: *Ready for Freddie*	8/21/61
Masqualero	Miles Davis: *Sorcerer*	5/17/67
Master Mind	Art Blakey: *Roots and Herbs*	2/18/61
Maya	*High Life*	1995
Meridianne, a Wood Sylph	Wayne Shorter/ Herbie Hancock: *1+1*	1997
Midnight in Carlotta's Hair	*High Life*	1995
Milky Way	*Weather Report (1971)*	2/22/71

Joe Zawinul is joint composer of this piece.

Miyako	*Schizophrenia*	3/10/67
Montezuma	*Moto Grosso Feio*	4/3/70
The Moors	Weather Report: *I Sing the Body Electric*	11/71
More Than Human	*Super Nova*	9/2/69
Moto Grosso Feio (Feio)	*Miles Davis: The Complete Bitches Brew Sessions*	1/23/70
Mr. Chairman (Grapevine)	*Second Genesis*	10/11/60

This composition was copyrighted under the title "Grapevine."

Mr. Jin	Art Blakey: *Indestructible*	5/15/64
Mysterious Traveller	Weather Report: *Mysterious Traveller*	2–5/74
Nefertiti	Miles Davis: *Nefertiti*	6/7/67

Miles Davis is incorrectly listed on some recordings as composer of this piece.

TITLE	ALBUM TITLE	DATE
Nellie Bly (Mama "G")	Wynton Kelly: *Kelly Great*	8/12/59

On an unofficial live recording of this piece by the Jazz Messengers, Art Blakey announces that a studio recording of it was made for Blue Note records, but there is no evidence to support this claim. This composition was also part of the repertoire of both the Maynard Ferguson Big Band and the Gerry Mulligan Concert Band, although neither group recorded it.

Night Dreamer (Night, Dreamer)	*Night Dreamer*	4/29/64
Noise in the Attic	Art Blakey: *Like Someone in Love*	8/7/60
Non-Stop Home (Non-Stop, Home!)	Weather Report: *Sweetnighter*	2/7/73
On the Eve of Departure	*Atlantis*	1985
On the Ginza	Art Blakey: *Ugetsu*	6/16/63
On the Milky Way Express (O Americano)	*High Life*	1995

This composition was copyrighted under the title "O Americano." The copyright deposit for "O Americano" also contains supplementary material.

One by One	Art Blakey: *Ugetsu*	6/16/63
Orbits	Miles Davis: *Miles Smiles*	10/24/66
Oriental Folk Song	*Night Dreamer*	4/29/64

This composition is based on a traditional song.

Over Shadow Hill Way	*Joy Ryder*	1988
Palladium	Weather Report: *Heavy Weather*	10/76
Pandora Awakened	*High Life*	1995
Paraphernalia	Miles Davis: *Miles in the Sky*	1/16/68
Pay As You Go	*Second Genesis*	10/11/60

TITLE	ALBUM TITLE	DATE
Peaches and Cream	Various Artists: *The Young Lions*	4/25/60

This composition is incorrectly listed on some recordings as "Scourn'."

Pearl on the Half-Shell	Weather Report: *Sportin' Life*	10–11/84
Penelope	*Etcetera*	6/14/65

This composition has some similarity to "El Gaucho."

Ping Pong	Art Blakey: *Pisces*	2/12/61
Pinocchio	Miles Davis: *Nefertiti*	7/19/67
Playground	*Schizophrenia*	3/10/67
Plaza Real	Weather Report: *Procession*	7–12/82
Port of Entry	Weather Report: *Night Passage*	8/80
Powder Keg	*Wayning Moments*	11/6/61
Predator	Weather Report: *Domino Theory*	1984
Prince of Darkness	Miles Davis: *Sorcerer*	5/24/67
Pug Nose	*Introducing Wayne Shorter*	11/10/59
Reincarnation Blues	Art Blakey: *Buhaina's Delight*	11/28/61
Remote Control	*Phantom Navigator*	1986
Rio	Lee Morgan: *The Procrastinator*	7/14/67

This composition was recorded by Joe Chambers on his album New World, *under the title "Wayne Shorter's Bossa Nova."*

Roots and Herbs	Art Blakey: *Roots and Herbs*	2/18/61
Running Brook	Lee Morgan: *Here's Lee Morgan*	2/3/60

Wayne does not appear on any recordings of this composition, including Lee Morgan's.

TITLE	ALBUM TITLE	DATE
Sacajawea	*Alegría*	2000–2002
Sakeena's Vision	Art Blakey: *The Big Beat*	3/6/60
Sanctuary	Miles Davis: *Circle in the Round*	2/15/68

Miles Davis is incorrectly listed on some recordings as joint composer of this piece.

Scarlet Woman	Weather Report: *Mysterious Traveller*	2–5/74

Joe Zawinul and Alphonso Johnson are joint composers of this piece.

Schizophrenia	*Schizophrenia*	3/10/67
Scourin' (Scourn')	Various Artists: *The Young Lions*	4/25/60

This composition is incorrectly listed on some recordings as "Peaches and Cream."

Second Genesis	*Second Genesis*	10/11/60
Seeds of Sin	Various Artists: *The Young Lions*	4/25/60
The Seven Powers	Bahia Black: *Ritual Beating System*	1992

Herbie Hancock and the percussion group Olodum are joint composers of this piece.

Shere Khan, the Tiger	Carlos Santana: *The Swing of Delight*	1979

This composition has some similarity to "Indian Song."

Sightseeing	Weather Report: *8:30*	1979
Sincerely, Diana	Art Blakey: *A Night in Tunisia*	8/7/60
Sleeping Dancer, Sleep On	Art Blakey: *Like Someone in Love*	8/7/60
Someplace Called "Where"	*Joy Ryder*	1988

The lyrics for this composition were written by Dianne Reeves and Richard A. Cummings.

TITLE	ALBUM TITLE	DATE
The Soothsayer	*The Soothsayer*	3/4/65
Speak No Evil	*Speak No Evil*	12/24/64
Storm	*Odyssey Of Iska*	8/26/70
The Summit	Art Blakey: *Meet You at the Jazz* *Corner of the World*	9/14/60
Super Nova	*Super Nova*	8/29/69
Surucucú	Weather Report: *I Sing the Body Electric*	2/13/72
Suspended Sentence	Lee Morgan: *Minor Strain*	6/60
Swamp Cabbage	Weather Report: *Domino Theory*	1984
Sweet 'n' Sour ("D" Waltz)	Art Blakey: *Caravan*	10/24/62

This composition was copyrighted under the title "'D' Waltz."

Sweet Pea (Swee-Pea)	Miles Davis: *Water Babies*	6/23/67
Sydney	Wynton Kelly: *Kelly Great*	8/12/59
Tears	*Weather Report (1971)*	2/16/71
Tell It Like It Is	Art Blakey: *The Freedom Rider*	5/27/61

This composition (performed by Craig Handy) was used as the theme song to the television series The Cosby Mysteries.

Tenderfoot	*Second Genesis*	10/11/60
Teru	*Adam's Apple*	2/24/66
This Is for Albert	Art Blakey: *Caravan*	10/23/62
Those Who Sit and Wait	Art Blakey: *The Witch Doctor*	3/14/61

TITLE	ALBUM TITLE	DATE
Three Clowns	Weather Report: *Black Market*	12/75–1/76
The Three Marias	*Atlantis*	1985
Tinker Bell	*Beyond the Sound Barrier*	11/02–4/04

This composition is a collective improvisation by Wayne, Danilo Perez, John Patitucci, and Brian Blade, and credited to all four.

Tom Thumb	Bobby Timmons: *The Soul Man*	1/20/66
El Toro	Art Blakey: *The Freedom Rider*	5/27/61
Toy Tune	*Etcetera*	6/14/65
The Traitor	Herbie Hancock: *Man-Child*	7/75

Herbie Hancock, Melvin Ragin, and Louis Johnson are joint composers of this piece.

Trapped	Lee Morgan: *The Gigolo*	6/25/65

Lee Morgan is incorrectly listed on some issues of the album The Gigolo *as composer of this piece.*

Twelve More Bars to Go	*Juju*	8/3/64
Two Faced	Miles Davis: *Water Babies*	11/11/68
Umbrellas	*Weather Report (1971)*	2/17/71

Joe Zawinul and Miroslav Vitous are joint composers of this piece.

United	Art Blakey: *Pisces*	2/12/61
Venus Di Mildew	Lee Morgan: *The Rumproller*	4/9/65

Wayne does not appear on any recordings of this composition, including Lee Morgan's.

Virgo	*Night Dreamer*	4/29/64
Virgo Rising	Various Artists: *The Manhattan Project*	12/16/89

This is probably the same composition as "Wayne I" from the 1988 Santana/Shorter tour.

TITLE	ALBUM TITLE	DATE
Visitor from Nowhere	Wayne Shorter/ Herbie Hancock: *1+1*	1997

Herbie Hancock is joint composer of this piece.

Visitor from Somewhere	Wayne Shorter/ Herbie Hancock: *1+1*	1997

Herbie Hancock is joint composer of this piece.

Vonetta	Miles Davis: *Sorcerer*	5/16/67
Water Babies	Miles Davis: *Water Babies*	6/7/67
The Well	Weather Report: *Procession*	7–12/82

Joe Zawinul is joint composer of this piece.

When It Was Now	*Weather Report (1982)*	1982
When You Dream	*Atlantis*	1985

The lyrics for this composition were written by Edgy Lee.

Who Goes There?	*Atlantis*	1985
Wildflower	*Speak No Evil*	12/24/64
Wind	*Odyssey of Iska*	8/26/70
Witch Hunt	*Speak No Evil*	12/24/64
Yamanja	*Phantom Navigator*	1986
Yes or No (Yes and No)	*Juju*	8/3/64

This composition was copyrighted under the title "Yes and No."

Zero Gravity	*Beyond the Sound Barrier*	11/02–4/04

This composition is a collective improvisation by Wayne, Danilo Perez, John Patitucci and Brian Blade, and credited to all four. It is a bonus track that appears only on the Japanese issue of the CD.

Unrecorded Compositions

When available, a copyright date or BMI registration number is shown. In some cases a performance date is also given. This is not necessarily the first performance of this piece, but one that can be documented by newspaper or magazine reviews or concert programs as well as Wayne's personal recollections.

TITLE	PERFORMANCE DATE	REGISTRATION
Andalusia		BMI #40946

Boneapart — Copyright 5/22/62
This composition was copyrighted in a booklet titled "Original Selections by Wayne Shorter," published by Ecaroh Music (Horace Silver's publishing company).

Burial for a Belle — Copyright 10/1/59
This composition was copyrighted in a booklet titled "Short Snorter," published by Ecaroh Music. Most of the pieces in this booklet were written before Wayne joined the army. This piece was rehearsed by the Maynard Ferguson Big Band but never performed by the group.

California California — BMI #169570

The "Creature" — Copyright 10/1/59
This composition was copyrighted in the booklet "Short Snorter."

Dramatis Personae — Lincoln Center 4/23/98
This composition was commissioned by Jazz at Lincoln Center and premiered on 4/23/98.

Iggely Wiggely — BMI #1853142

The Legend — UCLA 5/12/67
This composition was performed by the Miles Davis Quintet with an orchestra conducted by Gary McFarland at UCLA on 5/12/67.

Main Event — Copyright 8/15/67
The lyrics for this composition were written by Cherry Miles, an acquaintance who lived across the street from Wayne in New York City.

Mambo Moderato — Copyright 7/31/56
The copyright deposit states that the date of composition for this piece is 8/1/55.

TITLE	PERFORMANCE DATE	REGISTRATION

Mambo X

Mass '65 — Copyright 6/2/65

Although this piece was copyrighted in 1965, the copyright deposit states that it was composed in 1958. Wayne is currently revising this composition and may give it the new title "Miss Neena's Fantastic Journal."

Message from Sol — Copyright 10/1/59

This composition was copyrighted in the booklet "Short Snorter."

Midget Mambo — Copyright 7/31/56

The copyright deposit states that the date of composition for this piece is 8/26/55. It was performed at the Palladium in the mid-1950s.

No Minors Allowed — Copyright 10/1/59

This composition was copyrighted in the booklet "Short Snorter."

Occam's Razor — Detroit 1/2/00

This is more of a melodic motif than a composition and was first performed with an orchestra in Detroit on 1/2/2000. It has also been performed as an introduction to "Sanctuary" by the Wayne Shorter Quartet since 2001.

One More for Diz — Largo, MD 1/93 — BMI #1787943

This composition was performed in January 1993 by an all-star ensemble as part of the festivities for President Bill Clinton's first inauguration. The BMI registration states that Ron Carter, Al Grey, Herbie Hancock, Illinois Jacquet, Thelonious Monk, Jr., Clark Terry and Grover Washington, Jr., are joint composers of this piece.

Pawn — Copyright 10/1/59

This composition was copyrighted in the booklet "Short Snorter."

Prometheus Unbound — Walt Disney Concert Hall, LA 1/28/06

This composition has been performed a number of times in the last few years, particularly as part of the repertoire of the Wayne Shorter/Herbie Hancock/Dave Holland/Brian Blade Quartet during their 2004 tour. (A London concert was broadcast by the BBC.) It was also performed by the Wayne Shorter Quartet with the L.A. Philharmonic at Walt Disney Concert Hall in Los Angeles on 1/28/06. This piece is a reincarnation of "Capricorn II."

TITLE	PERFORMANCE DATE	REGISTRATION
See-Saw "C"		Copyright 5/22/62

This composition was copyrighted in the booklet "Original Selections by Wayne Shorter," published by Ecaroh Music (Horace Silver's publishing company).

The Singing Lesson

This is the title of an opera Wayne has been working on since the late 1950s. He may change the title.

Sticky Stuff   Copyright 10/15/64

Susurus (Melba)   Copyright 10/1/59

This composition was copyrighted in the booklet "Short Snorter."

Syzygy   Detroit 1/2/2000

This composition was performed with an orchestra in Detroit on 1/2/2000. This piece is still in progress.

Tartar   Copyright 10/1/59

This composition was copyrighted in the booklet "Short Snorter."

Terra Incognita   La Jolla, CA 8/18/06

This composition was commissioned by Imani Winds, a woodwind quintet, and will premiere in La Jolla, California, on 8/18/06.

The 13th Thorn   Copyright 10/1/59

This composition was copyrighted in the booklet "Short Snorter."

Twin Dragon   Copyright 3/16/81

This composition was written for Miles Davis, although Miles never performed it. Some sections of it were used in later compositions.

Universe   Copyright 8/22/69

The copyright deposit for this composition states that the score was composed, arranged, and orchestrated by Wayne, and the trumpet part was written for Miles Davis, although he never performed it. The instrumentation shown is as follows: C flute, alto flute, English horn, two French horns, two bassoons, tuba, trumpet (Miles), saxophone (Wayne), electric piano, marimba, tympani, Hawaiian guitar, mandolin, guitar, Fender bass, drums, and harp. This instrumentation is almost identical to that of the piece "Falling Water," credited to Miles Davis and Gil Evans and recorded by Miles (with Wayne and the Gil Evans Orchestra) on 2/16/68.

TITLE	PERFORMANCE DATE	REGISTRATION
La Vie et la Mort	NYU 1956	

Wayne wrote this composition while he was a student at New York University. It was originally written for two organs, but was performed instead as a solo piano piece by fellow student Mae Feuer. Wayne may revise this composition in the future.

Acknowledgments

My thanks to:

All the interviewees, especially those who are not directly quoted in the book but who so richly informed my perspective.

Dave Dunton, agent extraordinaire, for graceful diplomacy and steady encouragement.

Editor Sara Carder of Penguin, for patience and perspective. Ashley Shelby, also of Penguin, for shepherding this book into print. Katie Grinch, for getting it out into the world.

Ben Ratliff, for facilitating the assignment through which I first met Wayne.

Robin Tomchin, for the idea to write this book.

Tad Hershorn, Esther Smith, and Joe Peterson at the Institute of Jazz Studies, for research assistance, and especially institute director Dan Morgenstern, for the gift of his capacious memory.

Garrett Shelton, Theodora Kuslan, Regina Joskow, and J'ai St.-Laurent at Verve Records; Seth Rothstein at Sony; and Cem Kurosman at Blue Note, for swift delivery of recordings and other vital materials.

Mark Brady, Kate Garner, Michael Cuscuna, Peter Erskine, S. Uchiyama, Tom Terrell, Michael Weintrob, and Jan Persson, for photographs.

Bob Belden, Richard Seidel, and Michael Weiss, for research materials and illuminating discussions. Tom Carter and Eugene Holley, for careful readings of the manuscript. David Weiss, for introducing me to Wayne's complete body of work, for musical aid, and for strengthening my motivation with his skepticism. Hal Miller, for invaluable "imports," multiple readings of the manuscript, and most of all, for a passionate interest in all things Wayne.

Bob Boilen and Quinn O'Toole, for smart editing and production of National Public Radio stories in which some of this material previously appeared.

Scott Southard, for transforming his duties as Wayne's booking agent into a stewardship.

Milton Nascimento and Marilene Gondim, for arranging my trip to Tres Pontas and a visit with Milton's family. Maria Dolores, for her guidance through Tres Pontas and her intimate biography of Milton. Anthony, for driving me safely to and from Rio. John Krich, for wondering why Brazil dances.

Carlos Santana, for a unique appreciation of Wayne's gifts. Joe Zawinul, for repeated discussions of deepening value. Joni Mitchell, for poetic descriptions and luminous insights. Maria Lucien, for providing missing parts of the story. Herbie and Gigi Hancock, not just for giving interviews but for offering a detailed and loving portrait of Wayne.

Howard Mandel, for mentoring and frank criticism. David Hajdu, for counseling during a critical stage of the writing process. Joe Woodard, for decades of sympathetic coverage of Wayne. David Breskin, for the most lucid take on Wayne's complexity in print and for just getting it. Gary Giddins, for early encouragement and for raising the standards of music criticism.

Danny Nagashima, Patrick Duffy, Guy McCloskey, Joel Drazner, Greg Martin, and Kay Yoshikawa, for manuscript comments that deepened my understanding of Soka Gakkai Buddhist practice. Liz Myers, for materials on Buddhism. Ethan Gelbaum, for a gift of books from the SGI's New York Cultural Center. Barbara Walters, for hospitality at SGI meetings in Brooklyn. Loren Oliveira, for the tour of the Florida Nature and Culture Center, for good-humoredly entertaining my pesky questions about Buddhism, and for the *deliciosa moqueca de salmão*.

Rob Griffin, John Patitucci, Danilo Perez, and Brian Blade, for brotherly tolerance of me on tour.

Steve Cline, for my teenage introduction to jazz. Brian Coleman, for a wonderfully warped outlook on all things. Mitch Myers, for special encouragement when it mattered most and for pressing the hard questions. My sisters Carrie and Jenny, the Fair One, for twin-language conversations. My mom, for coming through with cookies in the end. Gretchen Parlato, whose singing showed me another way to hear Wayne. JSF, for his love of music. And thanks especially to my best friend, Mark Eshelman, for unconditional support, always.

Carolina Shorter, for generously opening her home to me and for sharing her profound understanding of Wayne. Nadia, for a bright presence around the Shorter house.

Bud Powell, Marlon Brando, Igor Stravinsky, Lester Young, Superman, the Green Lantern, and Charlie Parker, for inspiring Wayne's musicianship.

Most of all, I thank Wayne Shorter, for the movies, book recommendations, foresight, imagination, endless wordplay, and boundless compassion, all of which showed me a better way to live.

Index

FLAGSHIPS

Printed in the United States
by Baker & Taylor Publisher Services